THE LIGHT
IN HIGH PLACES

A Naturalist Looks at Wyoming Wilderness, Rocky
Mountain Bighorn Sheep, Cowboys,
and Other Rare Species

Joe Hutto

Skyhorse Publishing

Skyhorse Publishing books may be purchased in bulk at special discounts for sales promotion, corporate gifts, fund-raising, or educational purposes. Special editions can also be created to specifications. For details, contact the Special Sales Department, Skyhorse Publishing, 555 Eighth Avenue, Suite 903, New York, NY 10018 or info@skyhorsepublishing.com.

www.skyhorsepublishing.com

10 9 8 7 6 5 4 3 2 1

Library of Congress Cataloging-in-Publication Data

Hutto, Joe.
The light in high places : a naturalist looks at wyoming wilderness, rocky mountain bighorn sheep, cowboys, and other rare species / by Joe Hutto.
p. cm.
ISBN 978-1-60239-703-3 (alk. paper)
1. Bighorn sheep--Diseases. 2. Natural history--Wyoming. 3. Bighorn sheep--Effect of acid precipitation on. 4. Wyoming--Environmental conditions. I. Title.
QL737.U53H88 2009
508.787'2--dc22
2009022946

Printed in the United States of America

CONTENTS

PREFACE

A vast area of Wyoming exists as an environmental enigma. Rarely in the history of our voracious human diasporas across the face of the planet has wilderness survived long after "modern man" made his appearance upon the land. It is a strange irony that although humankind has been gnawing at the heels of Wyoming's wilderness for untold millennia, a great expanse of this country still displays all of the characteristics of a truly wild place. The coexistence of wilderness and human culture in healthy balance has become a paradox on earth. That this area of the Rocky Mountains persists in a wild condition may be attributed to the sheer overwhelming physical obstacle of this country: remote, inaccessible, a granite fortification guarding and preserving an authentic natural landscape. At last, however, even these most remote extremes are beginning to feel the inevitable effects of human saturation of the earth. Wyoming's rugged culture, both wild and human, is now being worn to a fragile state. The inevitable consequences of our global culture and technologies are now even leaking into these secluded and pristine lands with dire consequences.

From the most inaccessible alpine peaks to the high sage brush deserts, rare breeds of wild things are disappearing. Ancient ways of living are imperiled—romantic ideals and statuesque silhouettes are fading from view. I have come to these mountains to learn why the elusive Rocky Mountain bighorn sheep are disappearing. What I learn has as much to do with their decline as to that of other vanishing species, including the working back-country cowboy. Silently, without fanfare of apparent lament, without a sigh or whisper from the crowd—it appears that the final sun may be setting on some of our most revered creatures and some of America's most sacred icons.

In wilderness there exists an old and familiar voice that, given an opportunity, still echoes down the canyons and off the granite walls and has always called to those who might be inclined to listen. It still has the power to resonate in the hardest human heart, challenging us with the inescapable question: Is the world composed of just so many "natural resources," or is the world, in fact, a sacred entity? And as humans, do we have the integrity and intelligence to know the difference?

I have come to this high place to observe rare creatures, to learn from the ancient wisdom that resides here, and to simply pay attention. Humanity and wilderness appear to be in opposition—in contradiction—but in the most vital and elemental sense, we may discover that we are in fact, in the end, inseparable.

Part 1

1

GRAVITY BECOMES AN ISSUE

The study of Rocky Mountain bighorn sheep in the high country of Wyoming requires that the researcher travel light and stay long. Simply coming to work can be by far the most difficult aspect of your job. It seems impossible that a person could live alone for months in a small backpacking tent with a "footprint" the size of a footprint, but with time, life can become surprisingly comfortable. In fact, after a few weeks of acclimation, life alone far above the tree line can feel, at last, curiously perfect. A 12,200-foot mountain dictates that your life must be honed and pared down—where wants are reduced to near irrelevance and needs are redefined by reality. The human creature is a marvel of adaptive possibilities, and after a while, with a little habituation and perhaps a small measure of resignation, you may eventually make the surprising observation that you have never been so comfortable in your body or so at home in your surroundings.

For over a decade now, the wild bighorn sheep in the Wind River Mountains of Wyoming have been in a disturbing population decline. Rocky Mountain bighorn sheep, like all living things, are defined by the particular ecology they live in, and they have chosen to live in one of the most exotic but inhospitable habitats in the world. They are, of course, only one small part of an intricately constructed fabric woven through time from the warp and weave of high mountains, great glaciers, obscure alpine vegetation, peculiar soils, and dramatic weather. It is my job here, as a member of the Whiskey Mountain Bighorn Sheep Study, to help determine how and why the fabric of this extraordinary ecology is becoming tattered, and perhaps determine how or if it can be mended.

The Whiskey Mountain Bighorn Sheep Study exists by way of endowments from the University of Wyoming, the Wyoming Game and Fish Department, the Foundation for North American Wild Sheep, and other governmental and private entities that have offered support for the study over the years. It is a modest endowment, however, and a handful of dedicated researchers have been employed not only to monitor the bighorn sheep living throughout an entire wilderness but also to make observations on atmospheric conditions that can cause radical changes in soil chemistry that may contribute to anomalies in alpine plant development.

Sitting on a convenient overlook just below my campsite on this remote mountain, with six bighorn sheep casually grazing a few meters behind me, my legs dangle precariously some two thousand feet above a glacial chasm exposed below. My innate fear of heights seems to have mysteriously waned or probably just worn out, and so I somehow sit quite comfortably. I estimate that if an unfortunate creature fell or jumped from this rocky prominence, it might strike the mountain once on the way down. Across a great abyss, enormous white hanging glaciers, some a half mile wide, sag and drape across the dark, contrasting rocky face of the mountain in gleaming defiance of all the laws of physics. White water slips and cascades down below each glacier, eventually coming to rest in a remote and inaccessible blue-black lake waiting below. A rare momentary pause in the wind reveals miles of vascular rushing waters making a low breathy sound—a ceaseless sigh—a continuous gentle moan that softly wells up from below. Coupled with the persistent voice of the wind, this is the timeless mechanical sound of a great canyon simultaneously being created and destroyed—the busy murmurings of a great work in progress.

An enormous glacier once embraced the complete perimeter of this mountain, grinding, plowing, and reducing the surrounding granite to a gorge over a mile wide and nearly one-half mile deep, thus the name Middle Mountain. For many tens of thousands of years the glacier labored, and before receding, it scoured, ground, and polished the floor below, leaving glacial lakes, ponds, and potholes, collectively referred to as tarn. Gouged from high on the Continental Divide, great smooth granite boulders litter the valley land, transported like small pebbles—glacial erratics—delivered effortlessly as the opportunistic freight of a massive slow-moving icy train. The till, dozed up before the advancing glacier, still stands below as terminal moraine. Successive but less-extensive advances and recessions have left other similar moraines that serve now as natural dams and dykes creating a series of deep lakes, slowing the progress of the water below. First Trail

Lake, then Ring Lake farther downstream, Torrey Lake, and finally Lake Julia have all been constructed from the orderly assortment of mountain parts: boulders, cobbles, pebbles, gravel, sand, granite meal, and flour.

Gazing across the canyon to the broad expanse of this outwash a vertical mile below, I can see Torrey Creek as it wanders from these mountains and joins forces with the Wind River—a green ribbon meandering a few miles out. Just beyond, the rugged Washakie range and the rolling Owl Creek Mountains sprawl to the north, while farther to the east, the Bighorn Mountains rise as a pale irregular blue form on the far horizon—a distance of perhaps two hundred miles. In a single glance I oversee the entire Wind River Basin and a great portion of northern Wyoming.

Lying due north, the Absaroka volcanic pile is geologically distinct and appeared in a series of catastrophic geothermal events. Enormous belches of steaming pyroclastic material originating from the Yellowstone caldera slopped across northern Wyoming. Dramatic disfiguring erosion sculpted this solidified volcanic soup, resulting in the exposure of several thousand vertical feet of stratified volcanic tuff, or tuffacious rock—conglomerates of concreted steam, gravel, and ash—hardening into a mountain range fifty miles across. Natural mechanical forces clawing down through the relatively soft but durable strata have gradually formed one of the most distinctive and spectacular mountain formations in the world. The Absarokas constitute much of the eastern portion of the greater Yellowstone ecosystem where they intersect the northern extremes of the Wind River Mountains, forming an ancient pass.

There are but two passes providing thoroughfare across the Continental Divide in this area of the Rocky Mountains. Over one hundred miles to the south is South Pass, of Oregon Trail fame. This celebrated pass traverses the rolling southern slopes of the Wind River Mountains, also called the Winds, as they join the Great Divide Basin and the solitary Red Desert stretching another one hundred miles to the south. Above the Winds to the north and winding up through the Absarokas is Togwatee Pass. At a maximum elevation of 9,544 feet above sea level, this pass was named by early white explorers for a well-known Sheep Eater medicine man and chief. Sheep Eaters are known to be a distinct but obscure band of Shoshonean-language people who lived exclusively within the extremes of the northern Rocky Mountain high country. Their way of life and subsistence was almost entirely dependent on the Rocky Mountain bighorn sheep and the rich diversity this ecology provides. Long before Togwatee Pass was probably used by early white explorers such as John Colter from the Lewis and Clarke expedition and later by many French and American trappers, it was an established trail providing passage to and from the Yellowstone country to the west, and across these mountains to the rolling plains of the great Wind River Basin to the east. For hundreds and perhaps thousands of years, this has been the country of the Flathead, the Blackfoot, the Nez Percé, the Crow, and of course the various diverse groups of Shoshone—Bannock, Lemhi, Sheep Eater, and Eastern Shoshone.

Frontier trail. *Copyright © Cathy Keene*

Upon my arrival in Wyoming in the 1970s, I visited an old government-owned lodge near the summit of Togwatee Pass built during the Depression in the 1930s. It was constructed of local massive spruce and fir logs and was situated on a half-mile-wide glacial lake. Surrounded by lush green alpine meadows, patches of ancient forests, and encircled by the eerie towering pinnacles of the Absarokas, this is some of the wildest country in north America, where grizzlies are still abundant and moose may be seen browsing on the waist-high willows surrounding the lake. Not on the tourist trail, even the lodge concession was operated by what appeared to be itinerant wanderers, as were the few visitors, all of whom I noticed had Wyoming vehicle tags. It was technically spring, but mid-May is still wintry in this high country. Only a few people wandered about—a couple of cowboys with a dozen replacement heifers in an old stock truck taking a lunch and beer break, along with three spring bear hunters and one or two disappointed trout fishermen. We seemed to all be seeking refuge from the biting cold and the overwhelming grandeur—in the bar. The firelight flickered through the dim room and danced across massive log beams. The few patrons seemed to murmur quietly—an atmosphere more like a cloistered library than a rowdy Wyoming bar. My friend Sid and I sat at the bar silently staring at our drinks and alternately studying the strange objects and artifacts that invariably wind up in backcountry watering holes—the ragged and poorly crafted remains of animal heads and parts, branding irons, bear traps, a collection of old spurs, a 1945 Wyoming license plate, rusty and bent—all sacred Wyoming *relicarios*.

We eventually gained the eye of the only other person sitting at the bar. He smiled politely and nodded hello. Wearing strange and well-maintained boots, a brown wool tweed jacket, and a trim wool felt hat, he was obviously not from Wyoming. He appeared to be in his midseventies, was small of stature, wiry, square-jawed, and well preserved. Sid, being affable and outgoing, has never met a stranger and soon cultivated a lively discourse with this dapper gentleman. With a distinct European accent and our encouragement, he began giving us a short synopsis of his life and his reason for being in this unlikely place. He spoke as if he were appreciative of the gift that had been his birthright. He had been born in Austria shortly after the turn of the century into privilege, wealth, and nobility. He did not mention the specifics, and we politely did not inquire. He described a life spent in the pursuit of his every whim, which largely involved the adventures of education, travel, and the discovery of new lands and new peoples on every continent on the earth. While he and his late wife were exploring Yellowstone Park and the Rocky Mountain West just prior to World War II, he had by accident discovered this place—Brooks Lake. With some apparent reverence in his voice, he explained that in a lifetime of travel, he was convinced that this was possibly the most beautiful place on earth, and he had needed to return at least one more time before his life was ended. We finished our drinks, shook hands, and thanked him for sharing his story. With good-lucks all around, we left with a new perspective on our good fortune. Though my travels were much less extensive, the old man had no trouble convincing me of what had been a strong suspicion about this place.

Sitting on this smooth granite rock a few hundred feet below my tent, I overlook the Tetons and Yellowstone Park that all lie west of the Absarokas and rise toothlike on the horizon forty miles away. The so-called Yellowstone hot spot has been continually covering Wyoming with volcanic ash for millions of years. The ash is in fact microscopic shards of glass, often compacting into what is known by geologists as bentonite, and when mixed with soils and moisture, gumbo to the rest of us. It is slippery, like liquefied ball bearings, and adheres to all it contacts like wet plaster. There may be no limit to how much of it will eventually adhere to a boot, and a vehicle tire is limited in circumference only by the depth of the wheel wells. In 1978 Mount Saint Helens erupted, sending a billowing cloud thousands of feet into the air, transporting as much as four inches of similar atmospherically born ash. Wyoming has places where a single deposition, representing a single geothermal event, may be sixty feet deep. Fortunately, bentonite is quickly transported by rain and snow runoff, so valley lands remain mired but mountains have been washed clean.

To my west, the flat plain of Jackson Hole is represented as a vague but perceptible vacancy between the distant Tetons and the nearby Gros Ventre range that intersects these—the mighty Wind River Mountains where Middle Mountain rises anonymously among a multitude of other peaks. The Winds, the highest mountain range in Wyoming, have been called the backbone of the Rocky Mountains, with peaks approaching fourteen thousand feet. These mountains average about fifty miles wide and run roughly one hundred and twenty miles from northwest to southeast. They are regarded as perhaps the largest uninterrupted stretch of wild lands in the lower forty-eight states.

Hundreds of active major glaciers and thousands of lesser glaciers still cling to the many jagged cirques and the vertical upper reaches of the summits. Nearby Dinwoody Glacier is said to be the largest active glacier in the continental United States. Thousands of pristine alpine and subalpine lakes abound in such profusion throughout the range that many have no names. No road or jeep trail has ever scarred the heart of this mountain range, and no privately owned land threatens its wild integrity. The Wind

River Mountains are comprised of national forest, designated wilderness, Bureau of Land Management, and Wyoming state land. Together with the contiguous Greater Yellowstone ecosystem and the Red Desert to the south, these lands constitute by far the largest expanse of undeveloped wild lands in the lower forty-eight and certainly one of the great surviving natural wonders in North America.

Every mountain is extraordinary geologically and environmentally, and each in some way seems to possess a certain identity or personality. But among the many mountains in this range exceeding twelve thousand feet, perhaps Middle Mountain does not by itself express the ultimate drama and grandeur that other mountains evoke in our visual sensibilities. Middle Mountain, however, has managed to situate itself dead center among some of the most dramatic and awesome geography on the North American continent.

From twenty miles out in the basin, Middle Mountain appears rugged but, deceptively, seems to lack the vertical granite faces that characterize some of the surrounding peaks. From this distance, the area above the timberline appears rough, gravel covered, and distinctly inhospitable. On closer examination, this rough gravel is eventually revealed to be enormous granite boulders the size of houses and locomotives. And as distance always hides the scale and complexity of a mountain terrain, Middle Mountain's gently rolling summit becomes steeper and somewhat labyrinthine in reality. Upon first being shown Middle Mountain from far out in the basin, my initial response was a jovial and ironic, "You mean I'm going to be living on the top of that rough monster?" My colleague John, with a big grin born of an intimate experience replied, "Yep, that rough monster."

Middle Mountain is approached from the east and northeast along the Torrey Creek drainage, which joins the Wind River just east of the small community of Dubois, Wyoming—population 550 or so. Dubois lies on the road to Togwatee Pass and to the Yellowstone country and is home to the Whiskey Basin National Bighorn Sheep Interpretive Center. Following this same road back to the east and south seventy miles, you pass through the Wind River Indian Reservation and arrive eventually in the larger community of Lander, Wyoming, with a population hovering in the range of six thousand.

The gravel road following Torrey Creek leaves the Wind River with dramatic red and purple sandstone badlands behind and wanders upstream six or seven miles. With the Whiskey Mountain bighorn sheep winter range on the right and a string of deepwater glacial lakes on the left, it eventually rounds the steep southeast-facing cliffs of Whiskey Mountain known as Torrey Rim. You then look west into the divisions of two great canyons separated by the mountain in the middle—Middle Mountain—looming several miles beyond the termination of the road. Here, a national forest/ wilderness area trailhead begins with foot or horse trails leading up both drainages: Whiskey Basin to the right; Arrow Mountain, Torrey Creek, and Bomber Canyon to the left. Middle Mountain is steep and daunting and so no designated trail exists. From the trailhead you are tormented by an alluring glimpse up into so much alpine splendor—vertical black granite walls, sparkling white glaciers—haunting beauty but also the intimidation of haunting inaccessibility.

The trip up Middle Mountain is not so much a hike as an evolutionary process. The creature that arrives at the summit at sunset is not the same one that left the trailhead at first light. Excitement and anticipation resulting from weeks or months of preparation turn to skepticism as the mountain you could almost touch from the trailhead appears no closer after two hours of vigorous hiking up Torrey Creek. Skepticism turns to awe as the magnitude of the canyons and mountains become more apparent. After leaving the trail and wading across a rushing whitewater Torrey Creek, awe is finally replaced by tedium and heartbreak as the first two-mile leg of Middle Mountain's lower slopes are negotiated. The hiker is soon reduced to scrambling ever more vertically upward until, finally, handholds on trees and rocks become intermittently necessary. Gravity becomes an issue. The paperback novel you packed the night before now becomes a superfluous liability. Priorities are reordered. Then optimism returns along another two miles of a more gradual assent along a timbered ridge. At some point as the day passes, you become aware of the increasing irreversibility of the venture—turning back is no longer an option. An unfamiliar vulnerability sets in. You will either continue climbing miles more up the mountain to the summit or spend the night in the subalpine forests with the grizzlies. A new motivation now comes into conflict with your body's desire to rest. You discover and begin to exploit new and untapped internal resources

that drive you to new heights. Then, after traversing upward across deep
forested creeks and ravines, the subalpine zone is left behind, and you
find yourself, at last, above the tree line. Open space clears your head, but
then your mind begins searching hopelessly for some reference to the
horizontal. How did this mountain become so immense? How in only one
day could you climb this high? Yet another two miles of steep assent with
noticeably less oxygen assures you that all your capacities and capabilities
have been surpassed and left somewhere on the trail below. Only a will
born now of desperation and a fifty-pound pack remains. Just when you
can take no more, you must traverse, "posthole" style, straight up a series of
steep glacial snow fields. But then, lifting your heavy head you realize that
the summit of Middle Mountain is only a short mile or so above. Instantly,
a new exhilaration begins to infuse shaking leg muscles with confidence.
After finally rounding over the strangely gentle summit, you are filled
past overflowing with the incomprehensible 360-degree vastness that is
the panorama surrounding Middle Mountain. You are rescued by a vision
of eternity.

I gaze around this unpeopled and rocky wilderness and wonder how
I have found myself in such circumstances. One could never through
conscious intent contrive such a life. But it may have something to
do with the possibilities that dreaming will allow. I am reminded of a
recommendation or perhaps even a warning Henry David Thoreau left for
us to ponder: "If one advances confidently in the direction of his dreams,
and endeavors to live the life which he has imagined, he will meet with a
success unexpected in common hours." Of course this also dovetails nicely
with the old adage about being careful what you wish for.

From this solitary position, the horizon is vast and filled, not with
landscape merely but teems with experience and activity. I stare at untold
millions of years of geology, but unlike the ancient human monuments of
antiquity, this is not a vision of the failed aspirations of the past but rather a
master work that nears completion in every present moment and is forever
receiving the next finishing touch.

This mountain appears to be a place where time and space are reconciled—where time fails to slip into the past but rather heaps forever upon
itself, making the present moment evermore infused and enriched with
a suspended state of perpetuity. This remote Wyoming landscape vibrates

with life, an active geology, a thriving ecology, and a rich human history that also seems to be persistent and will not fully recede into irrelevance and obscurity.

As transitory humans, we cannot see time but can only feel the vagueness of its passing. What to us is a billion years, or even ten thousand?—an increment so small as to be barely measurable geologically. Here, we are reminded that the individual human experience is fleeting, like this thistledown, floating aimlessly by, transported up the mountain by the winds of chance. Such a revelation can be a paralyzing vexation to the spirit, or liberating—a magnificent humiliation.

As I gaze across the rivers, basins, and deserts, up the canyons and through the mountains of Wyoming, I see that somehow my own history has become inextricably entwined with my surroundings. Exposure to this country many years ago proved to be infectious. Perhaps there was an inevitable vulnerability or some congenital predisposition, but it seems I will never be rid of the Rocky Mountain West. But there is no one else to blame, for I willingly opened myself to the possibilities and let Wyoming happen to me. It has been a most benign affliction, however, and has at the least saved me from a life unlived.

Living alone in a wilderness for weeks and months with only the essentials that can be carried on your back, to some, would constitute the equivalent of a dreadful prison sentence at hard labor and in solitary confinement. But it is fortunate that we may all dream different dreams, for to me there seems to be neither confinement nor loneliness. As my eyes wander around Middle Mountain and a great expanse of Wyoming, I try to remember the many years and the peregrine path that carried me to this remarkable place. Without question, the path has been winding, uphill, and rocky, but occasionally the view is spectacular. So, well into a new millennium I now contemplate a great natural environment, infused with so much life and so much history. In some small way, I have allowed myself to become, if not a part of this continuum, then at least one of the many pilgrims who have also passed this way. But I am a gentle traveler and these words will be my wagon ruts—my name and date scratched into a rock.

2

BIGHORNS AND HIGH PLACES

Wyoming and the Wind River Mountains are home to one of the largest herds of wild mountain sheep in North America—the Whiskey Mountain herd. The Rocky Mountain bighorn sheep (*Ovis canadensis*) is considered by many to be among the most majestic wild mammals in the world, a creature that prefers only the highest and most remote alpine habitats. Because the bighorn has chosen a most exclusive environment to live in, it's no wonder that such an inclination should preclude the possibility of the species ever becoming overabundant. Predictably, the Rocky Mountain bighorn, if only by the definition of its ecology, is a rare animal. Wild sheep throughout the world are rare and in many cases threatened, endangered, or too often, extinct. Wild sheep are ecologically highly specialized, and specificity in any creature can be a dangerous adaptive strategy.

Sheep are caprids and closely related to goats but are genetically distinct from them. Caprids are ruminants and so share a relationship to bovids, which include cattle, sheep, goats, deer, and antelope. Ruminants typically have multiple stomach chambers making them capable of digesting rough plants, thus permitting access to forage nutrients normally denied other herbivores. Ruminants are classified more broadly among the order of artiodactyls, which are ungulates or hoofed mammals with an even number of toes.

It appears that sheep diverged from goats some time in the Pleistocene and developed in response to the continental glaciation occurring in the Northern Hemisphere. Sheep are thus described properly as a pereglacial species. Of the thirty-five or so forms of wild sheep that have survived into recent times, most have retreated into high mountains as glaciers have receded. Paradoxically, sheep are considered to be an adaptable and successful group evolutionarily, in terms of numbers, geographical distribution, and a long period of existence as a clearly recognizable genus (Valerius Geist, *Mountain Sheep: A Study in Behavior and Evolution,* 1971). They may have originated in Eurasia but over thousands of years dispersed across Europe, through Asia and the Himalayas, into Siberia, and eventually, via ice age land bridges, into North America. North America has been inhabited by wild sheep from Alaska to northern Mexico, and east as far as the Dakotas. The so-called Dakota bighorn, or Audubon's bighorn, was eradicated in the 1800s, but DNA studies indicate that this sheep is genetically indistinguishable from the Rocky Mountain bighorn. Lewis and Clark described an abundance of wild sheep on the upper Missouri River in 1804.

Worldwide, it appears that all wild sheep (*Ovis*) when kept in captivity are capable of hybridization, and the resulting offspring, unlike many hybrids, are reproductively viable. As such, a strict species definition by genetic exclusivity would be inaccurate. The various forms of wild sheep have evolved certain reproductive barriers—through behavioral and environmental differences—and so, in the wild, close cousins rarely have the opportunity to muddy the gene pools.

Of the nine recognized varieties of wild sheep in North America, it is convenient to differentiate between three distinct species: the Stone's sheep; the Dall's sheep of western Canada and Alaska; and the bighorn sheep of southern Canada and a broad western portion of the lower forty-eight. The bighorn species may be subdivided into two major groups. Mountain sheep are represented by the California bighorn and the Rocky Mountain bighorn. The second race, the desert bighorn, is further subdivided into five or so differing forms. Each bighorn form is identified by certain defining physical characteristics, variations in habitat preference, and often by geographical isolation.

With adult rams occasionally pushing the three-hundred-pound mark, Rocky Mountain bighorn sheep are the largest and most robust of the North American wild sheep, retaining their status as a creature founded among other great "megafaunal" species of the late Pleistocene. This period was often characterized, not only by the development of robust body proportions—an obvious adaptation to the cold, using a thermal-mass strategy, but also the development of enormous horns, antlers, and tusks, possibly representing a significant modification or elaboration in behavior. Sharing the landscape with wild sheep were elk, moose, the great *Bison latifrons* and *Bison occidentalis*, and the Columbian mammoth, as well as formidable predators such as the dire wolf, the giant lion—*Felis atrox*—and the great saber-toothed cats—all displaying an evolutionary development in size and armament never before expressed in mammals of other time periods.

The Rocky Mountain bighorn sheep of the Wind River Mountains have been in a population decline for several years. The survival rates of lambs have been low, and so recruitment of adult ewes to compensate for these losses is waning as well. The reproductive life of an adult ewe can be seven or more years, so any yearly dropoff in lamb survival may affect the availability of adult lamb-bearing ewes for nearly a decade. A cascading ripple effect is created in the overall sheep population, and a few consecutive years of high lamb mortality can be catastrophic.

The Whiskey Mountain herd, although historically the largest herd in North America, has plummeted from a historic high of about 1,500 animals in the early 1990s to about 650 today. A 50 percent population decline in less than ten years could become a story of decimation or even extinction if the trend continued. When this trend was first recognized in the mid-1990s, the Whiskey Mountain Bighorn Sheep Study was established to investigate possible causes.

Biologist John Mionczynski has been employed intermittently by the Wyoming Game and Fish Department for over three decades and since 1998 has been spearheading the Whiskey Mountain bighorn sheep research. In the 1970s Mionczynski began studying wild sheep in the Wind River Mountains where he worked with noted scientists, such as Frank Craighead, and by 1975 was employed with Wyoming's pioneering grizzly bear study. In 1984 John was invited to participate as a botanical specialist with *National Geographic* magazine and the Missouri Botanical Garden in the first successful scientific exploration of the Omo River in Ethiopia. The expedition was fraught with life-threatening difficulties, and John still suffers some health consequences today. In more recent years he has participated in a dizzying array of documentary films by PBS, the History Channel, and even an in-depth documentary profile by CNN featuring John and his research titled "Man on the Mountain." He has been the subject of magazine articles and newspaper features and editorials—national and regional—too numerous to mention. Mionczynski even appeared with actor Robert Redford in a *National Geographic* article that explored and retraced the notorious Outlaw Trail that passed through nearby Atlantic City, Lander, and eventually northward one hundred miles to the Hole in the Wall near Thermopolis, Wyoming. John still focuses much of his attention on the bighorn sheep and the disturbing trend taking place in Wyoming's highest places.

Pat Hnilicka, a biologist employed with the Wyoming Game and Fish Department and the U.S. Fish and Wildlife Service, is based in Lander, and served as the administrative director of the study. Like John, he has a passion for the research and the gravity of a developing environmental crisis that they have been called upon to investigate.

John Mionczynski, 2008.

Lander, Wyoming, is a small, close-knit community, and after twenty-five years almost everyone is a familiar face. I had known John only peripherally for decades through a few mutual friends and a shared love of music. John is not only known as a highly respected scientist but also as a fine ragtime piano player. Occasionally on a Saturday night he will snowshoe down from his one-room log cabin to the old Mercantile Saloon (one of only two existing businesses) in the little historic mining community of Atlantic City (the sign reads, POPULATION: 25 OR SO). Atlantic refers to the eastern side of the Continental Divide that separates South Pass. There John will don his old derby hat and tickle the ivories until everyone in the bar is on their feet. Eventually he climbs back aboard his snowshoes, slogs a mile or two back above the 7,600-foot-elevation town, and disappears. Returning home late one moonlit night from "the Merc" John was flattened into the snow by a large moose before he could make it to the cabin. He recalls being breathless, face down in the snow, as the moose, in an unexpected gesture, pressed his big warm nose against John's back, leaving some unidentifiable discharge that quickly turned to ice.

Several years ago I ran into John for the first time in a long while at a Lander restaurant and bar and casually dropped a book on his table that involved my somewhat unique study of the wild turkey in Florida. I merely said, "You might get a kick out of this," and with little other conversation said good-bye. Several weeks later I was back in Florida when I got a call from John asking me how I fared at high altitudes and suggested that I might possess certain powers of observation that could be useful on his bighorn sheep study. The job would involve camping alone for months at a time on a remote mountaintop while following and closely observing bighorn sheep. Having always fared well at high elevations and with a particular curiosity about the nature of bighorn sheep, I thought the job sounded about perfect. And so, with little coercion on my part or his, I was invited to join the project. Immediately, I began making preparations for the upcoming field season.

Living and working at an elevation of twelve thousand feet for months at a time has certain demands. Equipment has to be no nonsense and uncompromisingly good. My latest forays into the wilderness employed large animals—pack mules and horses with packsaddle and panniers that transported my "possibles" and "accouterments" into the backcountry. As a result, my backpacking gear was decades old and reflected a disregard for weight and bulk. New technologies have revolutionized mountaineering paraphernalia, and so I began pouring over all the outdoor gear catalogs and obsessively thinking in terms of the diminutive—ounces not pounds, cubic inches not cubic feet. Pertex, Nalgene, Gore-Tex, titanium, merino wool, windproof, waterproof, and dehydrated became my mantras. Comfort is always measured against practicality and efficiency, utility is measured against necessity and human frailty. Can I carry it up the hill? Will it sustain me? Is it completely bulletproof? Will I be completely miserable without it? All these questions must be answered. It is one thing to be inconvenienced and uncomfortable for a few days camping in the backcountry but quite another to live that way for several months. I had to be able to sleep well, eat well, stay dry, and get warm under the direst of possible weather conditions. At twelve thousand feet you can expect with certainty a three-day blizzard with fifty-mile-per-hour sustained winds in July. Equipment failures are not merely inconvenient or uncomfortable but potentially deadly. Equipment prefixes such as "expedition" and "high performance," adorned the descriptions on my exponentially more expensive sales invoices. One day a box arrived in the mail from some snobby little catalog accompanied by a $104 sales invoice, and it felt as if there were absolutely nothing inside. At some point I caught myself debating between the purchase of two items—one costing $100 more and weighing two ounces less. Common sense intervened at the last moment and I opted for the stainless steel—not the titanium. Including food, I strive to keep my pack under forty pounds, but more often my load nears fifty. Still, by ordinary long-range backpacking standards, that's traveling with a modest load.

To sustain life with at least some measure of comfort for long periods, it is mind-boggling how many individual items must be included in a backpack. Things must be divided into general categories of necessity and priority. These include science gear, shelter, sleeping paraphernalia, cooking items, toiletries and hygiene products, a first-aid kit, tools and repair kits, photographic equipment and film, clothing, footwear, lighting, eyewear, notebooks, reading material, and of course food, fuel, and an occasional sip of twenty-year-old tawny port. Each category is further broken down into many constituent parts—often dozens of them—and under various circumstances every item is indispensable. Additionally, each general category must be somehow containerized in the form of ziplock bags, stuff sacks, Nalgene enclosures, and the like. Each enclosure may contain yet smaller enclosures permitting greater levels of organization and thus preventing utter chaos from wrecking your life. One objective is to include items that can serve multiple functions. For example, dental floss makes an excellent thread for emergency clothing or tent repair; ziplock bags can keep various things dry or clean, prevent food odors from attracting animals, and they weigh almost nothing. We use hundreds of them in the collection of fecal samples, forage samples, soil samples, shed fur, and the containment of foods. Duct tape can close a tear in a tent, close a severe wound, and bind splints on a broken tent pole or a broken leg.

The total list of individual items needed for a months-long stay above timberline is nightmarish. Before actual packing can occur, these items must first be spread out on a floor in orderly rows and neat piles, then checked and rechecked. It seems impossible that so much clutter, strewn from wall to wall, can eventually disappear into a medium-size backpack. This phase must be accomplished with the utmost care and attention to detail, otherwise the ceaseless agony of equipment insecurity will accompany you all the way up the mountain. Pound for pound, such doubts are probably the heaviest of all burdens. Once you establish a camp, it can take weeks before everything becomes organized and readily accessible. A few days of frustration are inevitable before you can finally put your hands on the thing you need at the time you need it.

The Whiskey Mountain Bighorn Sheep Study revolves around the paternally dedicated researcher John Mionczynski, who is known far and wide to possess extraordinary skills as a scientist and as a mountaineer. Even in Wyoming, where many people spend part of the year living and working in the backcountry, he is in a word, legendary. Few people have ever spent so much time in solitary wilderness environments, and after decades his understanding of the high country ecology is encyclopedic. Because of funding restrictions, other researchers and employees are involved intermittently and often for only days, weeks, or fortunately in my case, sometimes months. However, a loyal nucleus of personalities seem to be permanently attached to the study, if only by a shared devotion to the plight of bighorn sheep and perhaps even to John. John is frequently the administrator of the study's funds, and at his discretion he is often the last to get paid and often the one who must sacrifice his earnings to benefit the study. John's dedication to the bighorn sheep goes far beyond a job and represents a devotion that is more compelling than mere science.

Ironically, some of the personalities involved in the sheep study are other caprids that aid the project and in some sense have made themselves indispensable. Pack goats are employed by the study each year to initially install the base camp in the spring and to retrieve it in the fall. Experimental equipment, heavier expedition tents, and stores of food and fuel are packed miles into Wyoming high country on willing and sturdy backs. It has been suggested that John introduced the idea of the pack goat to people working in high country environments. John published the definitive book on the topic in 1992, *The Pack Goat*, and brought the logical idea of using an animal that is perfectly adapted for living and carrying loads into rough mountainous terrain.

The Alpine breed of goat is a robust and sturdy animal that loves to be in the high country and is congenitally devoted to the company of humans.

The neutered males, like oxen, become large and strong, reaching weights of two hundred and fifty to three hundred pounds. A big goat can carry a load of fifty pounds when distributed evenly on a wooden and leather packsaddle all day without showing signs of fatigue. Furthermore, when goats are properly raised, they follow faithfully like dogs—lead ropes are unnecessary. They are sedate and gentle, even affectionate, never aggressive toward people, and display problem-solving intelligence. The alpine vegetation is a perfect diet, so there is no need to pack supplemental food. Even with a load, they bound and hop from rock to rock with the agility of a cat; their hooves have no detrimental effect on the delicate alpine ecology, and the higher they go on a mountain, the happier they seem to become. Controversy does exist, however, concerning the possibility of introducing diseases peculiar to domestic animals into a wild population of sheep. Care must be taken to rigorously avoid any direct contact.

Horses by comparison do not do well in rock and cannot climb through boulder fields, talus, or scree. Their hooves are destructive to trails and vegetation, the higher they go in elevation the more nervous they become, they must be supplied with supplemental grain, they cannot carry proportionally as great a load, and every horse-packing trip always involves at least one inevitable rodeo.

John introduced goat packing in the Wind River Mountains and the Red Desert in the 1980s with the outfitting business known as Wind River Pack Goats. He pursued this enterprise for several years before selling it to Charlie Wilson. Charlie and Wind River Pack Goats are now often employed to assist the sheep study. Dave Keller is Charlie's intermittent employee and often leads the goats on their various excursions. Dave's home is in Colorado where he builds log cabins, serves as an elk hunting guide, and at five foot seven, has a history of working as a bar bouncer. Dave is in his late thirties, athletic, and filled with enthusiasm for any activity that will get him into the high country.

My first excursion up Middle Mountain in 2000 involved the preliminary installment of my base camp, just over and below the summit. It was the end of June and still wintry at this elevation, but we would deliver food, fuel, experimental gear, and tents in preparation for my permanent return in another ten days or so. Further, other new personnel needed an orientation trip so any of them could find their way back if called upon.

You don't just point to Middle Mountain on a map and say, "I'll see you up there somewhere a week from Thursday."

    After a 5:00 AM breakfast at the Highwayman truck stop in Lander, John, Dave, and I, along with two new college-age field assistants, Becky and Nate, leave Lander and eventually arrive with twelve pack goats at Middle Mountain trailhead around 8:00 AM. I start out gimpy with an injured back suffered the day before while loading equipment. After an hour or two of vigorous hiking, however, my injury seems to disappear. Even without the burden of backpacks, Middle Mountain is no easy assent, and by midafternoon the strain is beginning to show on all of us. The enthusiastic conversation and humor of the morning's climb has given way to a determined and concentrated silence, punctuated by the occasional murmurings of necessity. As we ascend to higher elevations, the rude grumblings of the human voice seem intrusive and even inappropriate. Dialogue is replaced by the more obvious forces that begin to weigh upon us—fatigue, altitude, hunger, and a respect born of the awesome scope and perspective of this place, which inspires a healthy measure of caution and perhaps even a little primal fear.

    Other than a brief midday food break, our only respite is to stop and collect a couple of mountain lion scats that we spot along the way. Both contain hair, of course, but neither appears to contain sheep hair. We examine a couple of rather large bear scats as well but do not collect samples. An interesting conversation ensues concerning the relative size of bear scat and at what point diameter alone can differentiate between black bear and grizzly. A conversation, I presume, that would be peculiar to wildlife biologists. John, our resident grizzly expert, is quick with the stats—in inches not centimeters. Once, I assumed that when people referred to a large male bear, the term was merely a gender-specific large boar bear. But after living and working for years in grizzly country, I now suspect the reference is one of magnitude, scale, wonder, and awe. The first time I saw an adult grizzly scat, many years ago, I was terrified by the spectacle and realized the term could refer to the awesome radius, circumference—the caliber even. And so I now know the more respectful and appropriate term to be *large-bore bear*.

    Leaving tree line behind is always transcendent in the truest sense. Although invigorating and liberating, like a voyage onto open seas, a certain sense of security gets left behind, replaced by vulnerability and exposure. A shifting and reordering of mind seems to occur—a bit primeval perhaps—as the primate steps from the obscurity and cover of the forest onto the great expanse of the short grass, or in this case, the alpine tundra. Certain advantages have been compromised—others are realized and assumed but perhaps in a dubious bargain. Time and space are now measured differently. Nature's grandeur as well as its dangers may be observed approaching slowly and from great distances. There are no trails above timberline except for the occasional ancient sheep trail marking the most conservative route along a narrow passage. Like a small boat at sea, you merely set a course using dead reckoning, and eventually you get to the destination. Like the minute hand on a watch that appears as if it were making no progress, after an hour or so you're consoled by the great distance that has somehow been spanned.

After leaving the embracing anonymity of the tree line below, we work our way up along a steep drainage and icy creek lined by a smattering of stunted transitional trees and vegetation originating from a series of glacial snowfields above. Our progress is slowed by fatigue and altitude while we posthole up through large unstable patches of ice and snow. We plod—one slow deliberate step disappearing into slush—one deep deliberate breath to compensate—yet one more deliberate step and then another deep breath—pneumatic monotony—cardiopulmonary periodicity. Glancing back, I notice even the goats have become resolute and somewhat mechanistic as they follow, each stepping only in the holes made by the preceding animal. Our steps become a calculated effort—aware that with each short stride the opposing leg must elevate the weight of the entire body another four, or at most six inches. After thousands of such repetitions the quadriceps begin to burn and tremble with each small incremental rise. Not only are you made aware of your weight, but more significantly you become aware of the irresistible and inexorable force of gravity that seeks to pull you downward. Weight, you now realize, is only the illusion created as the force of gravity draws upon your mass. You do not fall off a mountain, you are pulled—a significant revelation inspired by exposure to such high places. Without this mysterious force—gravity—we actually weigh nothing. It took humankind tens of thousands of years and the eventual insight of Isaac Newton to finally understand this simple but seemingly mystifying contradiction.

Some degree of oxygen deprivation always occurs at higher elevations. Hypoxia often overtakes a hiker, and the head begins to throb and the heart races. Weakness and confusion can occur, contributing to a more generalized malady known as altitude sickness. This can involve the accumulation of fluid or edema on the brain and in the lungs, and this all-too-common syndrome if ignored can result in coma and death. Ironically, the tortuous discomfort we feel when our breath is impaired, as when diving underwater, is caused not by starvation for oxygen but rather by a buildup and accumulation of carbon dioxide in the lungs. If we continue breathing normally and expelling CO_2, we won't feel the discomfort, even though the body may be deprived or even starved for sufficient oxygen. Unacclimated hikers must constantly remind themselves to breathe deeper and with greater frequency than what feels normal to make up for blood that lacks sufficient hemoglobin. After several days, the body gradually begins to compensate by producing a higher ratio of red blood cells, and after ten days or so you can start to become fully acclimated. Until this adaptation is complete, the mere act of rolling over in a sleeping bag can feel exhausting. The year before, a glaciologist working with John became deathly ill and suffered psychosis from edema on the brain and had to be evacuated from the mountain. Had his lungs not been pumped out on the way to the hospital, he would have certainly died.

With burning lungs, pounding heads, and shaking legs, we finally cross over the serpentine ridge of Middle Mountain's summit. Nate and I arrive ahead of the others by a couple of hundred yards. Both my arms rise uncontrollably above my head, as I am stunned into motionlessness by the impossible vision that stretches about me. Nate and I make eye contact and break out in big grins and laughter. Whatever agony has accompanied us to this place is now suddenly irrelevant. But, an ominous setting sun looms before us, partially obscured by foreboding clouds. Eerie shafts of filtered sunlight pierce a dark churning maelstrom and illuminate gleaming glacial ice across the vertical walled chasm that surrounds the mountain. The scene is biblical.

Nate and I wait as everyone gradually gathers on the summit to take a breath. A stiff forty-mile-per-hour wind counters our progress over and down the steep northwest slope of the mountain as we struggle to reach our campsite. We stumble and scurry over half a mile downward, and we still must unpack, pitch tents, and cook before darkness and bad weather overtake us. Dave Keller and the goats hurry ahead. We reach our campsite in a grassy draw above a great cliff face that is sheltered on one side by enormous loosely stacked granite boulders the size of school buses and dump trucks. Dave falls to his knees and vomits. We politely avert our eyes and walk past as Dave mutters something about blood sugar. Moments later he is pulling packsaddles off goats, feeling fine. We all help unload goats, freeing them of their burden, as we rummage around locating our individual equipment. Tents and tent flies begin flapping around wildly while we struggle in what is now a gale, popping shockcorded tent poles together and grabbing for stones to hammer tent stakes into the ground. Strange forms, like large button mushrooms, begin to take shape on the mountainside, and the clatter of wind-driven "popcorn" snow peppers our shelters and stings our faces. Darkness nears while the hasty pumping and hiss of white gas cookstoves are vaguely audible in the howling wind. This is a one-night "drop trip," so Dave and Nate chose to come without tents. They grab their gear, and with the goats, scramble like marmots into the inner recesses of the great pile of loosely stacked boulders. Soon I see the flashing and flickering of a cookstove glowing from some small sanctuary within the rock. Darkness falls fast as an ominous black storm moves in, and the rest of us, with little or no conversation, withdraw like startled hermit crabs into our respective shelters. The weather deteriorates rapidly. The wind increases, and soon we are in a full-blown whiteout blizzard with the added inconvenience of lightning and roaring thunder. *Welcome to Middle Mountain,* I say to myself, wondering about my new and untested equipment and the pounding it is now receiving. The wind howls and seems to blow from every direction at once, creating a deafening noise inside the tent—like a large plastic garbage bag held open outside the window of a speeding car. The shockcorded aluminum tent poles vibrate, bend, and shake violently as the storm slams the tent—first from one direction, then another. Snow is now being driven under the protective covering fly and begins to accumulate in a pile on the cloth screen forming the top of the tent. The snow, sifted by all the shaking, is like fine frozen flour showering down on me and my sleeping bag below. My Pertex-covered down bag is rated water resistant—not waterproof—and moisture is death to the ability of fine goose down to capture and preserve the body's warmth. I try to pop away the snow that is now sandwiched in the top of my tent with a tap of my hand, but the effort results in more snow showering into the tent. Pulling every waterproof item I own from my backpack, I attempt to cover my sleeping bag. It's not long before the temperature plummets, and the accumulating snow inside the tent is no longer melting—a dubious consolation. Fully clothed, I surrender and withdraw into the confines of my sleeping bag. But my $350 "expedition quality," "750 power down" sleeping bag now feels, to my horror, almost nonexistent—there is just nothing there—like lying in a large thin nylon sock. Soon, however, I feel a warmth radiating as the high loft down begins to work its magic. With the aid of my comfortable self-inflating camp mattress, I am enveloped in a secure and reassuring cocoon. Now if my tent doesn't fail, I think I'll survive the night. But of course at twelve thousand feet things can always get worse. A mere fifty-mile-per-hour wind can become one hundred. I experienced a catastrophic tent failure at these elevations twenty-five years ago in just such a storm and could have died of exposure. My brand new $35 tent was reduced to a green flag waving at the end of a single string in an unfortunate matter of minutes. Hard lesson learned: Never take a tacky tent above timberline.

The storm continues to intensify throughout the night. Lightning flashing, the strange reverberating crash of thunder, and winds gusting up to hurricane force make sleep, in spite of exhaustion, a cruel impossibility. I spend a long period in the night sitting and holding on to tent poles, back pressed against the tent wall, in an effort to prevent the whole structure from being crushed. I weigh the likelihood of a lightning strike against the prospect of a broken tent as I press my gloved hands against the aluminum rods. Eventually the winds subside to something I know is manageable for the tent, and I drift in and out of a restless sleep for a couple of hours, jerked awake now and then by a blast of wind shot out of Thor's cannon. Snow begins to accumulate in a sufficient quantity to prevent cold air and snow from blowing in around the base of the tent's protective fly. Icy snow is now packed tight between the top of the tent and the fly.

Day finally breaks, and I begin hearing the muffled ripping sound of sleeping bag and tent zippers. Winds are still gale force, gusting to stronger, so no one even attempts to light a camp stove. Without a word, everyone hastens to break camp, stow gear, saddle goats, and get off the top of this mountain before things become worse again. Dave and Nate have to climb back into the loose tangle of granite boulders to rouse and retrieve a couple of reluctant goats. I store my tent, staple food, extra fuel, and heavier gear that will sustain me for the months ahead within the inner recesses of the boulders and hope my supplies will still be there when I return alone in a week or so to begin the summer field season.

In less than an hour, we are trudging upward through a foot of fresh snow, back toward the summit of Middle Mountain. The footing is icy, steep, and obscured by deep snowfall, so we all slip and stumble as we cross fields of invisible cobbles and boulders. The goats struggle, even with empty panniers, and appear stressed from what must have been a long night for them as well. A couple of us are blown down by the occasional stronger blast of wind. I gaze back down into the canyon surrounding the mountain, and it is filled with churning angry storm clouds. Periodically, snow blows horizontally, and we're enveloped in a seething frozen fog of stinging granular snow. For the first time I appreciate the leather side shields on my glacier glasses. Two-thirds of the way to the top of the ridge, I turn to see the entire canyon back to our north infused with light by a break in the clouds, creating a great snowbow below us—the snowstorm equivalent of a rainbow. In spite of the urgency in our pace, I am filled with gratitude for the moment and the incredible opportunity this place will offer me for the next few months. Only now do I begin to grasp the power and magnitude of this mountain. Nate runs a quick recon over a ridge and observes nine rams and a group of ewes and lambs. The sheep are already moving up into their summer ranges, and I look forward with great anticipation to my return in ten days to begin my work. If good fortune permits, this remote wilderness mountain will be my home until the snows of October force me to lower elevations.

In an hour of steep ascent, we cross back over the summit and mercifully descend into the lee of the wind. Once we reach and enter the tree line below, Dave pulls a camp stove from a pannier and begins pumping. In a few minutes we are all drinking hot chocolate and munching on dried fruit and nuts, laughing and making light of the previous night. The goats all lie down in a perimeter around us. After a short rest, we descend gradually, first down the rugged alpine slopes into a forested subalpine winter wonderland with fresh bear and elk tracks all about, then out of the soft snow and into another season. We wander downward and eventually into the contradiction of a beautiful and brisk spring day in Wyoming. But, with the occasional glance back over my shoulder, I watch as the storm continues to rage on the mountain's summit for most of the remainder of the day.

It is June 16, 2000. I'll return to Middle Mountain to begin my study before the month's end.

3

A DARK FORCE

Many years ago, at a time when the world had proven itself to be without a doubt a place without integrity, Wyoming came into my life and offered up an alternative to the small, unreliable, and transient place I had come to know. As a mature young man with a determination to explore and expose life's possibilities, for better or worse, the world of humans had revealed itself to me, an anthropologist and a human being, as a source of irreconcilable disappointment. Wyoming in its vastness, its inaccessibility and grandeur—its inherent substance—seemed to offer up an alternative. This extraordinary country appeared to exist in spite of us, and not because civilization permitted but because human civilization and technology had proven impotent against an apparently irresistible force of nature. Wyoming appeared to be the stone wilderness, the granite wall, the great lithic anvil upon which the hammer of human industry had at last been crushed. This land provided the revelation that here things will remain unchanged and unaltered because of the mere overwhelming physical impossibility it imposed. We could gnaw at the fringes and margins with our cattle, chain saws, tractors, and rifles, but we have remained only a petty and humble force, scratching out the occasional raw place in the dirt or spilling the random gut pile here or there—only a small, temporary bloody spot in a vast snow-covered wilderness.

Wyoming was at last a place that offered reliability and proved to be a great consolation as an immutable land that would always be there, no matter what else changed in the world—a land unalterable. But now to our astonishment and bewilderment, Wyoming may be suffering, not from the bulldozer and the saw but from a dark shadow cast from Vulcan's great smoldering forge.

An obscure wave of sickness is quietly passing across the high and remote mountains of the Rocky Mountain West. The most obvious sign is the plummeting number of sheep. However, the Rocky Mountain bighorn sheep is just the large, high-profile, economically significant big-game species tourist and hunter alike all seek an exciting encounter with—a thrilling sighting to add to the list, a rare trophy head to hang on a wall. But the bighorn sheep is only the glamorous poster child that represents a grave, more systemic problem facing the entire Rocky Mountain high-country ecosystem.

One would logically expect any threat to a remote twelve-thousand-foot alpine habitat to come from below and gradually work its way upward to the more distant and inaccessible heights. Ironically, something mysterious is occurring that seems to affect the highest elevations most dramatically.

Several years ago, in 1999, John Mionczynski had the occasion to share his concerns about the unfolding plight of the bighorn sheep in Wyoming with John David Love. Dave Love was the renowned and beloved "grand old man" of Rocky Mountain geology whose life was chronicled so eloquently by writer John McPhee in his book *Rising from the Plains*. McPhee and Love created a literary vision of the big picture, of the complex geology of Wyoming, and likewise of a man's history and his contribution to our understanding of the world. Dave suggested to Mionczyski that he might consider the possibility of selenium poisoning affecting sheep in areas of the Wind River Mountains where he knew outcrops could possibly occur, suggesting that the Whiskey mountain area might be an area of natural high selenium exposure. Selenium (Se) is an elemental mineral that like many other essential minerals can be toxic when consumed and absorbed in large doses. Every organism requires minute quantities of otherwise toxic minerals to sustain proper body functions and good health, including iron, chromium, cadmium, zinc, copper, and even arsenic. Nutritional requirements for many of the essential trace minerals are so minute that they are measured in micrograms (millionths) not milligrams (thousandths). Still, deficiencies can and do occur and with dire consequences to good health. Selenium, although toxic in large quantities, is absolutely essential in all animals, particularly in the neuromuscular development of the very young. Dave Love had raised a red flag, and John immediately set about investigating the possible overabundance of selenium on the bighorn sheep range of the Whiskey Mountain herd. Ironically, after testing the alpine forage and soils in these areas, John and

Pat Hnilicka demonstrated that to the contrary selenium availability was almost zero in vegetation.

Mionczynski soon also learned of a phenomenon that domestic sheep ranchers had recognized for many years. Apparently, young lambs require relatively high doses of Se to avoid a condition known as selenium responsive disorder, and in its most extreme manifestation as white muscle disease. This syndrome is expressed as a form of nutritional muscular dystrophy, precipitated by a mother's milk or a diet deficient in proper levels of selenium. The body is so desperate for selenium that it will absorb or "resorb" calcium from the growing bones, actually mining the body for traces of Se that may have been deposited there. This calcium is mistakenly precipitated into the starving muscle tissue and in its most advanced stage a dissected muscle will literally appear white. As the deficiency progresses, the lamb becomes weak and crippled and also suffers impairments to the immune system, predisposing it to pneumonia and possibly lung worm infestation, and ultimately to an inability to elude predators. The bones become prematurely and irreversibly osteoporotic and unless corrected with supplemental selenium, the condition is progressive and eventually fatal. Lambs that recover suffer health consequences throughout their lives: weakened immune systems and poor dentition—contributing to an inability to chew and thus an inability to digest food properly, as well as predisposing them to pernicious periodontal infections. Indeed, every adult ewe skull that I have collected in the Whiskey mountain area has exhibited at least some evidence of this disease, with many showing signs of chronic disfiguring abscesses in the bone of maxilla and mandible. Interestingly, my anecdotal observation through collected crania seems to suggest that rams may somehow be less inclined to develop these infections. But some evidence suggests that the ram fetus will actually fare better than a female fetus in times of nutritional stress in the mother. The life span of any herbivore is usually dependent on the longevity of its dentition, and so when the teeth become dysfunctional from a lifetime of wear, the animal dies. Obviously, ewes that have experienced selenium deficiencies as lambs will tend toward early mortality, contributing fewer lambs to the herd. Further, it would follow that a less than healthy ewe will be prone to have a less than healthy lamb. The catastrophic domino effect that could result from selenium deficiencies in overall sheep populations is obvious. In addition to the disturbing trend occurring in bighorn sheep populations, other alpine species appear to be in decline as well. Researchers have observed declines in marmot numbers as well as significant reductions in pika populations. The sheep study has employed biologists with specific expertise in alpine species other than bighorn sheep to explain what changes are occurring that could adversely affect rodent and pika numbers.

Logically, one of the first experiments in substantiating the existence of a selenium problem was the development of supplemental mineral blocks with a high concentration of Se. As soon as the supplements were installed at stations throughout the sheep range in 1999, ewes were ravenously attracted to the blocks and would stay in the vicinity feeding for several days. Their lambs began showing noticeable improvements in their appearance and mobility. However, such supplements are considered an inappropriate way to manage a wild species over hundreds of square miles of wilderness, and worse, predators—particularly mountain lions—quickly caught on and began patrolling these sites. During the summer of 2000, I monitored a mineral lick site all summer at a location on the top of Middle Mountain that we call Pinnacle Pass. One or more lions had the curious habit of leaving scats around and even occasionally directly on top of the mineral block! I never approached the mineral block site without my pistol at the ready. We recognized that we would lose as many or perhaps more sheep to opportunistic predation than to selenium deficiencies and discontinued use of the mineral blocks, though some members of the public adopted the mineral blocks as a viable solution.

Remarkably, the Whiskey Mountain herd has somehow been aware of its own nutritional deficiencies. In desperation, ewes will often bravely abandon their lambs high on the mountain and migrate seven miles down and descend two thousand feet in elevation to natural mineral exposures known to exist in the valley below. These natural exposures are also known to contain concentrations of selenium. After two days below, and subjecting themselves and their lambs to the perils of predation, the ewes return and the lambs begin to show a marked improvement in appearance and mobility. But unfortunately, sometimes a ewe returns to the mountain only to find a missing lamb.

In order to investigate the cause of possible selenium deficiency, consistent baseline information on the environment must be recorded over consecutive years to document the various changes that are occurring in the northern Wind River Mountains. In particular, the weather as it relates to temperature and the nature of high country precipitation, that is, snowfall, rainfall, and glacial meltwater, is significant in order to record any change that may be expressed in the chemical composition of the tundra soils. Any changes in soil chemistry could have far-reaching effects on those species of alpine plants that are consumed by wild sheep. Forage must be sampled in many locations throughout the annual study period (from June through October) to determine the changes in availability of the various nutrients that could affect the health of the many herbivores living above timberline. Obviously, we must be watchful for the presence or absence of selenium and also for information concerning the changes in pH or the relative acidity of the tundra soils. Normal alpine soils are quite stable in their chemical composition and pH. These soils are often thin, the result of the reduction of granite through the weathering process and the gradual development and accumulation of organic plant humus that occurs over time. Granitic soils are compact, often dark and rich, but low in nitrogen because of lower relative temperatures and the tendency toward a slower exchange of organic matter and nutrients through decomposition. Alpine soil and the alpine tundra ecosystem exist within a narrow range of biochemical variables. Soil variability is contingent on the delicate web of interaction between an organic and inorganic chemistry, and the relationship this chemistry has to the subterranean micro fauna and flora—bacteria, nematodes, fungi, and so on. These forces interact in complex ways to facilitate the availability of nutrients the rich alpine tundra depends on. Any subtle change in hydrology, nutrient load, or pH can affect the balance among the sensitive but essential microorganisms in the soil. Alpine tundra plants exist within a narrow range of environmental parameters, and so plant populations will likely respond to the smallest incremental change in the overall soil ecology. The large herbivore populations will respond to the availability of the forage generally, but perhaps more importantly to the availability and abundance of the necessary nutrients they contain.

We began to suspect that the bighorn sheep were indeed the canary in the coal mine. The entire alpine ecology—from the most obscure fungus and nematode to the great, robust creatures—could be suffering from an insidious dark force.

4

MIDDLE MOUNTAIN

The return trip to Middle Mountain on June 26, 2000, flashed by like the blur of an intermittent dream—rocks, boulders, rushing waters, lush spruce and fir, occasional tangles of downed dead timber, the crashing of some large animal across the mountain just above me—all the sights, sounds, and smells of a perfect day in a high mountain wilderness. Late in the day, after finally descending from the top of the mountain, I soon spot John (who preceded me up the mountain by a day) down below, attending to some activity near his tent. Still 100 yards above camp we make eye contact as I approach, and we exchange a wave of hands and familiar smiles. We will be constructing the Forage Selenium Study plots—the brainchild of John and Pat Hnilika. John will also get me going with some orientation before he travels to his study area on adjacent Arrow Mountain to the south and east the day after tomorrow. Arrow Mountain is a visual stone's throw away—perhaps only five miles as the raven flies, but probably fifteen or twenty as the backpacker must meander. We exchange information on current sightings and events while I unload my backpack and briefly muddle around in the nearby boulders recovering my tent and other gear stowed ten days before.

Since then Middle Mountain has transformed into a different world from the harsh winter landscape we left. It's now a kinder, gentler world—green with a riot of flowers but no less awe inspiring in its sweeping vistas and physical magnitude. It is difficult to attend to the menial chores of pitching a tent and organizing gear with this overwhelming presence of the mountain bearing in all around—the ultimate case of trying to ignore the elephant in the room. Gravity, it appears, is no longer specific to any particular direction. Here the sky seems to pull as strongly as the earth. I fumble with all my little things—sheer synthetic fabrics, weightless aluminum tent poles, a cookstove that fits in the palm of my hand, a titanium cook pot the size of half a large orange—and all attended by this equally small person—all foreign and fragile. Over the years I have spent considerable time camping on or near the top of mountains in Colorado and Wyoming, but ordinarily a high alpine environment is defined by sweeping angles of descent. Occasionally a mountaineer can literally stand with one boot on the Pacific side of the Continental Divide and the other boot on the Atlantic. The visual effect is powerful and unnerving, as two halves of a continent appear to have slammed together directly beneath your feet. But a thirteen-thousand-foot mountain peak is disarming in that in most cases the climber has arrived at a place where a great mountain ceases to exist. The top of the greatest mountain can be a surprisingly small place. Middle Mountain is extraordinary in that its uppermost alpine reaches stretch for mile after mile, and so an otherwise overpowering experience is magnified in the extreme and can become confounding to even the most experienced mountaineer.

After a quick meal, John and I spend some time reviewing a few ideas and looking at our topographic maps. Although we have previously spent hours pouring over maps and discussing various research protocols and methodologies, the realities within the actual study area are no longer abstract or theoretical. My job will be to observe the sheep, monitor radio-collared ewes, collect fecal samples, man a weather station, and closely monitor the prime suspect in the case of the declining sheep population: precipitation.

By the end of the day, I'm exhausted from the climb and the altitude adjustment, and before darkness falls I crawl into my small shelter, grateful that my fatigue overwhelms my excitement and apprehensions.

The following day is spent measuring off various plots of land consisting of one square meter that will delineate similar stands of relatively level and well-developed representative alpine tundra. Several plots are merely marked with stakes at the corners and serve as control plots that will remain undisturbed and that represent the average alpine vegetation in terms of plant diversity and exposure to the elements. Other similar plots will be overwatered with each rainfall or snowfall event, using water collected in plastic tarps spread out in several nearby locations. When a measured rainfall occurs, some plots receive the equivalent of two times the amount of rainfall, sprinkled in carefully measured amounts from the tarps. Similarly, other plots are overwatered by a factor of three. And so, rain or snow that may have delivered one-half inch of precipitation to the uncovered control plots will result in the delivery of twice and three times that amount to others—one inch and one and a half inches respectively. Other plots have been covered with frames made of clear greenhouse material that exclude normal rain and snowfall. These are watered using pH-neutral distilled water that has been transported up the mountain at no small effort and expense. Some of these covered plots receive the same equivalent moisture as the rainfall on the control plots, and others are overwatered by a factor of two and three.

After John and I have measured off the plots, we erect the covers that Pat Hnilicka and I prefabricated two weeks before. All this material was delivered ten days ago on our initial trip up the mountain with the goats. By late afternoon the experimental plots are completed, and I install my weather station, consisting of a rain gauge and a good thermometer that automatically records high and low temperatures for each day. After John leaves tomorrow, I will construct the rainwater collection basins using natural depressions that will be covered by ten-by-ten-foot plastic tarps and weighted down with a solid perimeter of rocks. This water will be used in servicing the study plots. While shuffling around with the weather station gear, several bighorn ewes appear in the draw just above the tents. Without any apparent concern for our activities below, they browse through and out the draw on the outer side. I stand in awe as they seem to arrive with insufficient fanfare, and I am reminded that it is they who are the objects of so much interest, hard work, expense, and concern. A few minutes later a mule deer doe appears, miles from normal mule deer habitat, and dashes to a halt above us with mouth agape and gasping for air. Clearly she was being pursued up the mountain by some predator—probably a mountain lion at this elevation—so as she quickly bounds away, we prepare for a visit from a large and highly motivated cat. After several minutes we relax as no one appears. Without a word we continue with our chores in the draw, but the gasps of the mule deer speak loudly about the often narrow divide between expectation and possibility.

After our evening meal, we conduct a quick review of the use and functions of the radio collar receiving device, its antenna, and check the individual channel frequencies of twenty or so collared sheep. However,

John believes four may be dead with their collars still faintly transmitting. A channel signal that transmits persistently from the same location can mean a lost collar or more likely a dead animal. From a position several hundred meters above camp, we locate six signals but three are faint and may be ewes that are far away on nearby mountains. No rams have been collared in this study area. After finally agreeing that we are ready to get the field season under way we find some time to relax and share ideas. It is always a delight to visit with John, as his familiarity, comfort, and enthusiasm in this exotic realm is reassuring and probably a little contagious. John is a veritable walking anthology of backcountry stories and he possesses knowledge of the ecology that is extraordinary.

Later, we toast to good fortune and a productive field season with a warming taste of tawny port before retiring to our shelters. Pleasant weather, with morning lows in the midthirties and highs in the fifties, begins to deteriorate with forty-mile-per-hour winds and clouds. But compared to the storm of ten days earlier, this is nothing, and we each enjoy an uninterrupted night of sleep.

By midday John is packed and loaded to leave for Arrow Mountain, where he will monitor things for most of the summer while I continue to hold things down on Middle Mountain. After brief good-byes, I watch as he plods slowly up and over the top of the mountain. Every minute spent with John Mionczynski is a joy, and as he disappears over the far crest of the ridge, a feeling of loneliness seeps in for about fifteen seconds—but then almost instantly, a quiet sense of satisfaction washes over me. I won't see another human being for perhaps months. Something awakens in me to find that this is not loneliness, but in fact more like Christmas morning. Not because of John's absence, of course, but because at last I can begin my job and fulfill long-held expectations and objectives. Perhaps a little selfishly, I want to be undistracted and totally immersed in the lives of these remarkable animals and this imposing high alpine ecology. But then John probably understands this better than anyone I know. Alone, I begin to experience a different relationship to these surroundings. However unobtrusive the intent, two people always constitute a crowd in a natural environment. With three, wilderness becomes in large measure lost and unknowingly escapes in a radius around us like advancing ripples as we clumsily slosh through these still waters. And, of course, it is always our misfortune that, at best, the solitary human creature is still a party of one.

Thrashing around in my tent, I throw things into my small pack to begin making explorations and observations on the mountain—daypack, water bottle, food, binoculars, camera, notebook—all like trusted and reliable old friends. While still struggling to hoist my pack onto my shoulders, my legs impatiently stride up through firmly planted boulders that seem to block the most direct route up the mountain. Within seconds, a pounding heart and heaving chest are reminders that the elevation is still close to twelve thousand feet. Reducing my progress to something more steadfast and methodical, I begin scanning the slopes for sheep. Higher on the mountain and less than a mile from camp, they begin to appear— they simply materialize—scattered here and there among the many rocks and boulders that seem in some way to be parental. In color, texture, and contour, these creatures seem to have been born of the surrounding smooth, sculpted granite. Boulders even occasionally show the indisputable signs of lithic mitosis, as a million-year-old bulge in a rock promises an inevitable division—metamorphic metamorphosis—the replication of rock into ram. Ontogeny recapitulates geology—the probable phylogenetic predisposition of this particular species of granite—"gneiss." It is no wonder that these bighorn sheep are known specifically as Rocky Mountain.

Middle Mountain camp.

The "study" has arbitrarily divided Middle Mountain into several numerical areas to facilitate more accurate record keeping. This afternoon, I work less than a mile south of the campsite on the mountaintop's west-facing slope, just north of a rocky ridge that separates area 3 from area 4. The ridge provides a natural narrow passageway or corridor that John has designated as 3-4 Pass. Many bighorn sheep are drawn to this site as they traverse from one rich mountain pasture to another.

Ewes and lambs are relatively unconcerned with my presence on the mountain, as long as I don't display too much interest in their activities. The sheep, however, are immediately made uncomfortable by my obsessive gaze and will begin to watch me if I fail to avert my eyes to other things. It is possible to gradually work your way closer to a group, but only through shortening the distance by moving in indirect closing angles and never appearing as if you were moving toward them. By failing to show a specific interest, and by employing these simple techniques, an observer may gradually be accepted as just another benign browser on the landscape who may be minding his own business a mere fifty feet from a large number of sheep. Open terrain makes stealth impractical, and remaining concealed behind a rock will immediately raise concern among a group that had been comfortable with my proximity only minutes before. A prey species adapted to vast open terrain, wild sheep have evolved distance vision that is far superior to our own. In almost every case, when you've spotted a bighorn sheep one quarter of a mile away, you can be sure that you were already observed at twice that distance.

This afternoon I sit on a gently sloping expanse of soft green tundra overlooking the mountainside with ten ewes and two lambs calmly grazing a comfortable one hundred yards to the north. A light snowfall this morning subsided, surrendering the mountain to gentle breezes and warming sunshine. Months of planning and work are reconciled as I realize that the welfare of the Rocky Mountain bighorn sheep is the sole reason we have come to this place, and now at last all I need to do is my job.

The geology here is always, to say the least, conspicuous and projects a drama that although motionless to our eyes is nevertheless in full animation. To observe all of this directly is in some way disturbing—almost frightening, and so I find that it can only be comfortably experienced in small vignettes for fear of being somehow crushed by the power and weight of it all. Here, forces that we can never comprehend are still at work, but only visible like the photograph that has captured a great cataclysm in a single high-speed frame. These forces can only suggest to a fragile insubstantial creature an unimaginable but still imminent violence. But sitting calmly amid this most obvious conflagration, there is also an apparent contrasting gentleness that is equally pervasive. Amid this soft, fragile greenness, splashed with tinges of subtle color washing across the mountainside, an improbable but unmistakable kindness here is perhaps the underlying and even greater restraining force—perhaps the force that soothes a vicious sleeping giant into a perpetual slumber.

A pleasant hour passes as I familiarize myself with this group of ewes and lambs. Scribbling in a small field book, I observe the appearance and overall condition of each individual: Which ewes are caring for these lambs? How capacious are their udders? Do the other ewes show evidence of having nursed earlier in the spring but now are without lambs? Are the lambs bright and playful? Are their eyes clear and alert? Do they attempt to nurse? If so, how often and for what duration does the ewe allow nursing to continue? Does she reject her lamb's attempt to nurse? Which individuals display wounds, crippling injuries, or scars? Fecal samples are collected at the time of dropping but at the expense of forcing the sheep to move away. In particular, we want to observe the condition of the lambs: Do they have a persistent cough? Are their coats scruffy? Do their eyes appear weak or swollen? Are they lame or do they occasionally stagger? These are a few of the questions I will be asking for the next several months on Middle Mountain while John asks the same on Arrow. Watching the wonder surrounding me and noting how these creatures appear as a perfectly integrated component of the landscape, I ask myself how anyone might possess the capacity to gain any understanding of the complexities inherent in this apparently perfect place. The light at this elevation is extraordinary and seems to expose me as perhaps the only dull creature on the mountain. Like the adaptation to rare air, this extraordinary light will be a necessary part of my acclimatization.

As the sun nears the horizon I gather my notebook, camera, and a few items scattered around, hoist my pack, and carefully begin moving back to camp without raising a single head among the sheep. Shivering cool temperatures and gusting breezes have, without my realizing it, robbed me of warmth, but I seem to float weightless across the mountain as my feet sink into a deep spongy green carpet. In an instant, I sense that this mountain may not be cold, asleep, or indifferent, but may in fact be alive. In spite of evidence that seemed to suggest otherwise, my presence here feels safe—even welcome. This mountain may truly be formed from skin and flesh and bone with its soft and supple tundra integument, with strong muscular granitic soils and a skeletal armature articulated in solid stone. Without apparent indifference, it seems to welcome all those less-substantial beings who would choose to be here. Could it be that the mountain offers not the brutality of the sleeping giant that I imagined but rather refuge and consolation, as it shares some unfamiliar but nevertheless indisputable warmth? There is not only an unsuspected abundance here in this seemingly austere ecology, but also a subtle generosity. I have never felt so much at home.

Although controversial as a legitimate approach to good ethology—the observation and study of the life and behavior of any living thing under natural circumstances—I find it impossible to avoid falling in love with the particular individuals that are observed, and more troubling, I am then predisposed toward an obsessive affection for the species. My life appears to be a promiscuous series of such love affairs as I obsessively drift from one passionate association with a species to the next—and as with all affairs of the heart, and not uncommonly with any personal involvement with a wild creature, heartbreak is often bound up in the bargain. The overwhelming merits of this approach, I will argue to the death, far outweigh the possible blinding disadvantages of an observer personalizing and overobjectifying an organism in question. There could be a powerful and compelling argument that any student who somehow avoids an emotional entanglement with any species that is being closely observed is simply not paying attention. But I am without question hopelessly romantic when it comes to any living thing that will gaze back into my eyes and grant me the privilege of sharing space within its realm. It is clear that the graceful and gentle bighorn sheep scattered across this mountaintop have already begun to pull at my unapologetic heart.

Before becoming involved in the sheep study, it had been my good fortune to observe the Rocky Mountain bighorn sheep on occasion over the years, but most of my direct exposure had been at lower elevations when wild sheep descend to their wintering grounds. As a result, I had never spent time observing younger lambs. Many of the various alpine habitats I visited in the past had the misfortune of supporting no bighorn sheep populations at all. Rocky Mountain bighorn sheep, even in apparently perfect ecologies, are always an exception and never the rule. That it is common for an otherwise perfect alpine habitat to support no bighorn sheep population has long been a puzzle to Rocky Mountain ecologists and wildlife management agencies. And mysteriously, some bighorn sheep transplantations thrive like weeds in plowed ground, while others wither away after struggling to survive for many years.

On the wintering grounds of October and November, lambs are large, strong, and well developed, but now, after my first several days on Middle Mountain, I have had opportunities to watch small lambs for many hours. One of my first observations has been a consistent and disappointing lack of play behavior among groups of small lambs. The lambs of all sheep, both domestic and wild, are characterized by incessant play: jumping, frolicking, leaps and bounds on and off rocks, as well as chasing and head butting. The lambs of bighorn sheep should be as playful as the familiar domestic kitten. These lambs, I now recognize, spend little time at play and are often seen lying down while the ewes graze nearby. Occasional play jumps and head butting are often perfunctory and not only lack enthusiasm but often seem to lack the kind of finesse and agility that might be expected. Further, nearly all lambs exhibit a chronic and consistent cough, which is usually accompanied by repeated shakes of the head. Occasionally, I am alerted to the presence of nearby sheep by the sound of flapping ears and coughs. More disturbing are several lambs that not only exhibit these troubling behaviors but are small and poorly developed. Because of the synchronicity of bighorn sheep lambing, the disparities can't be attributable to differing ages, and further close anatomical observations indicate these differences are not because of sexual dimorphism, even though ram lambs eventually surpass ewe lambs in height and weight.

The lamb has always represented something gentle and appealing to the human conscience. The lamb of a wild bighorn sheep is arguably one of the most adorable creatures to ever walk the earth. To maintain an entirely clinical and scientifically detached perspective while observing a small wild lamb is probably impossible for any person who still possesses a beating human heart. And there can be few things more pathetic or heart wrenching than a sick and dying lamb. Perhaps it is my anthropomorphic and maternal projection, but I remain convinced that I can detect in the ewes with sick lambs a distinct air of resignation and despondence. Their maternal devotion is unwavering, but their demeanor seems to imply they are preparing for the cruelest of all disappointments

I am particularly concerned with collared ewe number Y-9 and have spent several days watching her and her lamb. This lamb is diminutive and underdeveloped by any comparison to other lambs. The coat of this lamb is peculiar and scruffy, lacking the smoother contours that other lambs display. Her fur stands out in erect patches—particularly around her head and neck. Her back is bowed slightly upward contributing to an odd gait, which is choppy and appears to place the weight of the lamb too far out on the tips of the hooves. Her eyes seem to lack focus and appear watery and bulging, giving her the appearance of having just awakened from a deep sleep. She coughs in spasms lasting up to a minute, and when shaking her head she occasionally loses her balance and staggers to stay upright. Her mother will wander quite far from the lamb while grazing, but the lamb lies sleeping, often with her nose on the ground. This lamb is slow to follow and Y-9 can be seen lagging behind the rest of a group as they meander about browsing. Now it is becoming clear why the sheep study exists. Clearly, almost all the lambs are displaying at least some symptoms of a general malaise. There can be little doubt—something is not right on Middle Mountain. (Only in subsequent years with better lamb survival did I come to fully realize that nearly all the lambs I observed that first summer were showing signs of disease. In fact, that first summer I probably never observed true healthy lamb behavior.)

5

THE LIGHT IN HIGH PLACES

Anyone sitting on this rocky prominence overlooking this high alpine ecology would agree that the world and all the immediate surrounding space has a peculiar, almost haunting, illumination. There is something about the light in high places—something extraordinary. An atmospheric clarity occurs at these elevations to be sure, but in time I'm struck by a certain clarity and stillness of mind that seems to follow. Often I'm distracted by various activities and chores that don't always directly involve the more important tasks of observing the bighorn sheep and the complexities of their experience. Many times my attention becomes focused on more trivial but necessary concerns like organizing equipment, preparing meals, and fumbling with journals, radio collar receivers, and the like. Sometimes, as I become distracted by such details, I'm suddenly reminded of my unlikely presence in this exotic and otherworldly environment, and my eyes lift. As I become aware of the surrounding light of the mountain, a stillness superimposes itself on the usual chatter resounding in my head. The transition is instantaneous and almost startling. There could even be some element of physiology in this response. Raising my eyes, it seems there is some transformation, almost like becoming a human version of the view camera—motionless—horizon in the center of my field of view, and eyes, as with the smallest of pinpoint apertures, focused from zero to infinity. Remaining in this state until fully and perfectly exposed, I wonder if in some obscure recess of the mind there exists a great archive where all these images are housed. Maybe it is not simply magnificent vistas and panoramic views that arrest our mind. Maybe it is the infusion of some less-familiar light—a subtle brilliance. The brain becomes the receiving emulsion, attempting to seize and trap the light as if capturing something essential.

Surely we all share an insatiable craving for light, and of course the role light plays in our psychological well-being is no secret. As our bodies prosper in proportion to the availability of clean, pure water, our spirit also must be nourished in proportion to the innocence and quality of the light that surrounds us. At twelve thousand feet, the light is pristine and unadulterated by impurities in the atmosphere or even by the dulling lens of water vapor. Here the light is unobstructed, unfiltered, less refracted, and in its most perfect earthly form. It penetrates the eye and at once illuminates our deepest recesses with its incandescence, calming the dull prattle of the ceaselessly imperfect mind. I periodically drink from this great wellspring like crystal waters. High mountain light must be the true nectar of the gods.

Long before the sun peaks over the eastern horizon, the mountain light becomes intense. The thin materials of a backpacking tent are translucent, and so the interior is quickly illuminated in a brilliance more suitable for laboratory dissections than sleep. Oversleeping, irrespective of any fatigue, is not an option. Inside the tent, clothes are applied in layers while lying in a roughly horizontal position, and each garment in succession feels as if it were pulled from a refrigerator's freezer compartment, except for those that were stuffed in a sack and used as a pillow. Hiking boots are stored just outside the tent wall under the fly and are often frozen quite hard, depending on how much moisture they absorbed the day before and how low the temperature plunged in the night. When at last the tent fly is unzipped, crisp mountain air begins relieving your face of the last vestiges of the night's accumulation of downy warmth. After locating a water bottle, or in colder times, scooping up a pot of fresh snow, a small gas backpacking stove—a trusty old WhisperLite—is pumped and started. Boiling eventually occurs in precisely measured amounts corresponding to one big mug of coffee and one small pot of oatmeal. Enough ground coffee for one cup is contained in a sealed foil "tea bag," and dry instant oatmeal is dolled out and mixed with a handful of dehydrated milk, a spoonful of sugar, dried butter buds, and a dash of salt—anything to make it more interesting. The boiling water goes first on the coffee bag in the mug, and the remaining water in the cook pot receives the dried oatmeal concoction. With persistent high winds, I can say with confidence that none of my meals has ever been prepared that did not include a thorough sprinkling of wind-born detritus from the mountaintop—typically organic but not always botanical, and no effort is ever made to retrieve it—like a mixture of local seasonings—*mountain medley* I call it. The always futile objective is to consume the coffee and oatmeal before they become stone cold—an unlikely accomplishment in stinging cold winds and with the thermal transparency of titanium cookware. Any residual oatmeal is painstakingly wiped up and eaten with half of a heavy industrial-strength whole wheat bagel. A small amount of water is placed in the pot; the water is instantly boiled and the pot is wiped out with a dry washrag. Writer George Wolfe once accompanied me on a cold windblown, three-day expedition to the top of Whiskey Mountain. Following a string of unfortunate events in a single dedicated effort to create a meal, he finally mistook his package of desiccant for seasoning, applied it to his dehydrated supper, and then observed: "A perfect end to a perfect meal."

The morning meal is a chore that when completed often fills the mountaineer, not with a sense of satisfaction but rather with the attitude of good riddance. After tending to morning hygiene including teeth brushing and the application of a bulletproof sunblock, the workday begins.

First, I grab a waterproof canvas tote bag and proceed to an area two hundred meters away and retrieve a gallon of glacial meltwater for camp needs. I also fill two small water bottles that will accompany me all day across the mountain. The meltwater discharge area is near the forage selenium study plots, so if any precipitation occurred in the previous twenty-four hours, I service the plots at this time using the nearby collection tarps and distilled water stored in plastic containers. Each morning I record twenty-four-hour data from my weather station that includes high and low temperatures and precipitation. If rain or snow has occurred, I test for pH values at this time, record the results, and also preserve a clean sample from each event for future laboratory reference. Next, I grab the radiotelemetry receiver, its collapsible antenna, and climb to a vantage point a quarter of a mile above the camp. Here, I click the receiver from one channel to the next and begin locating as many collared sheep as possible. The antenna is directional, and each channel corresponds to the transmitted signal of an individual sheep. The headphones respond with an intermittent beep from a particular collar, and as you turn in a radius, the signal becomes stronger as the antenna points in the precise direction of a sheep. The strength of the signal is an indication of the distance, and multiple signals from the same location can indicate the presence of a larger congregation of sheep. With practice it is possible to guess if a signal is close enough to reach in less than half a day—remembering of course that it will take at least another half a day to return. And each day I continue to record the approximate location of every signal in my log and make a determination on which direction to proceed to make observations for that day. Frequently, as in the case of Y-9, I will attempt to watch a particular lamb and ewe or some other collared individual on consecutive days. And of course this is especially important if I've been watching a ewe with a sick lamb—and there have been several. Often sheep will have remained near the same location overnight, but on occasion I must walk an additional two or three miles to make contact with a group observed just the evening before. By climbing to any vantage point I can glass the mountainside and locate sheep and rarely have to walk more than one-half mile before encountering at least a few. Frequently, twenty or thirty sheep may be observed within a one-mile radius of the campsite. And at least every few days I only have to sit in camp as sheep will casually graze in or around my campsite. Middle Mountain was chosen, after all, because it is the heart of the Whiskey Mountain bighorn sheep herd summer range.

My midday meal nearly always occurs far from camp and usually consists of a nutrition bar—one a day—as well as cheese sticks, peanuts, raw almonds, and a few peanut M&Ms for quick energy. In the past I would carry additives like Tang to make water more flavorful and interesting but after years you get where you just don't care. Besides, nothing tastes better than water that is being discharged directly from the good earth. Normally by midday I have located the particular sheep I set out to find and have begun making notes and taking the occasional photograph. After slowly rehabituating a group of ewes and lambs to my presence, I may spend hours making observations. Throughout the summer, I continue to assess the relative health of the lambs, monitoring nursing behavior, the capaciousness of the ewe's udder, and the frequency and duration of nursing. Fecal samples are collected at the time of dropping and are recorded according to the particular individual when possible, date and location, then sealed in small plastic storage bags. Three or four fecal samples may be collected on any given day, and all are stored in a lingering snowdrift near camp to prevent deterioration. Sheep fecals are odorless, tidy, hard little pellets

resembling dark brown faceted English peas that will dry out in seconds
in a mountain wind, requiring collections to be made immediately. Many
times, observations will take me miles from the campsite; a rough estimate
might be a ten-mile circumnavigation of the mountain on any given
day. Workdays are long—probably averaging fourteen hours—although I
rarely take note of the time, and a ten-mile hike is easily accomplished at
a leisurely pace. Often the distance I stray from camp is determined by the
prospect of bad weather and the likelihood of being overtaken by a storm.
Summer thunderstorms are a common occurrence but typically build up
in late afternoon, giving me most of the day to wander far and wide.
But afternoon thunderstorms up here can be ferocious and are not to be
trifled with.

As the sun nears the western horizon, I am usually wandering back
across the mountain, and by early evening supper is under way. Each night
I boil a cup and a half of water and pour the contents of one commercially
prepared dehydrated meal—either beef stew or chicken and rice—into
the hot churning liquid. There is no advantage to variety in these meals
as they all taste essentially the same—varying from unappetizing at first
to downright revolting over time, and again, after a while you just don't
care. Manufacturers must presume mountaineers all have some sensory
impairment, and so any concoction masked with enough garlic powder
and salt will pass for food. "Pour contents into boiling water, cover, let stand
two minutes, eat." These meals are notoriously inadequate for a fourteen-
hour workday at twelve thousand feet, so I typically reinforce the volume
with either dried mashed potato flakes or couscous and add vegetables
in the form of dehydrated peas and carrots that I have brought up the
mountain in bulk. It fills the empty space and I remind myself that I did not
come up here for the fine dining. Long before dark, supper is concluded
and all food-related gear is cleaned and stored. Food storage sacks are
always suspended from rock overhangs to prevent animals—particularly
rodents—from helping themselves to the groceries. Over the course of
the summer, white-footed mice and golden-mantled ground squirrels—
the worst of many possible offenders—will eat more than a bear, and if
given access will gnaw convenient holes in each container, rendering them
useless. Once, I momentarily dropped a bag of bagels on the ground in the
"kitchen" area while going to retrieve something from my tent. I became

distracted for not more than five minutes and then returned to begin my meal only to find a golden-mantled ground squirrel scampering away. Grabbing the package of eight bagels with telltale crumbs scattered all around, I examined the contents and found that each individual bagel had one thumb-size divot systematically excised—as if the arrogant little rodent wanted to first sample each one for comparative palatability to make certain these bagels all measured up to the quality to which he had become accustomed. Bearing no real resentment, I gradually consumed every squirrel-gnawed bagel within a week or so. However, during each subsequent meal the little beggar was there pleading with sad little beady eyes for one more of those divots. Apparently the bagels met his rigid standards after all.

Darkness is slow to come on the mountain, and following the evening meal I will have an hour or more to scour the immediate vicinity and make additional observations on the teeming activity. When weather permits, the rocky prominence below my campsite is often an irresistible lure as sunsets on a twelve-thousand-foot mountain refuse to be ignored. I consider it part of my responsibility to somehow bear witness to every mountain sunset and when possible record each in detail. There is something tragic about a day that is not concluded with witnessing a sunset. However, high mountain atmosphere has a peculiar inability to withhold and retain ambient warmth, and in mere seconds after the disappearance of the sun, the winds become strong, cold, and bitter, and the air begins to sting, becoming unpleasant if not unbearable—even though temperatures may be above freezing. After climbing back up to camp, I quickly crawl into my small shelter, leaving my boots at the door and then zip up the tent for the night. Clothes are removed in reverse order, layer by layer, down to long johns and stored for retrieval the following morning. My fleece sweater is stuffed into a pillow sack, and I withdraw into my down sleeping bag just as my nose begins to sting from the cold. Immediately, I strap a small LED headlamp to my forehead and I begin jotting down as much of my day as I can recall with special emphasis on unusual sightings and occurrences. First, additional entries are made in my official log as I expand on notes taken throughout the day. Following my log, I attempt to write in my personal journal where my more subjective notions receive free reign, and more abstract ideas are safely housed for future reference. Over the years I have learned that with a certain minimum amount of information recorded in journal form, an entire day can be recalled, even decades later, in complete and complex detail. Even though it is my intention to write for at least an hour every night, my journal often reads like the encrypted shorthand of a committee of raccoons. I try to record as much of my day as my metabolically exhausted body will allow before unconsciousness overtakes me. Occasionally, however, on full moon nights, I am compelled to wander the windswept mountaintop where the eerie lunar light sets the boulders in a pale blue glow and casts deep, dark shadows in which my primeval uncertainties prowl and await me. Invariably my romantic motivations are gradually overcome by the annoying sound of chattering teeth and an overall hypothermic response that would become, in thirty-mile-per-hour winds and without proper shelter, irreversible.

As true darkness falls upon the mountain, I sometimes retrieve a little plastic flask from the corner pocket of my tent and sit up in my sleeping bag. Ever so carefully unscrewing the small jigger-size metal cap from the flask, I pour myself a small shot of twenty-year-old port. Slowly I sip this little spot of liquid gold until it gradually disappears and infuses me with its gentle warmth that may be more imaginary than real. This meager ounce of pleasure takes on the proportions of the most outrageous indulgence in this otherwise Spartan environment, and invariably a smug feeling of satisfaction overtakes me, as if I had just finished a lobster and half a bottle of Pinot Noir. Nestling back into my warm down bag, sleep usually follows in minutes. In this way, all my days are characterized by a certain uniformity and routine, but on this remote wilderness mountain, every day is unique and astonishing. I marvel at the irony that my many needs have never been so perfectly and completely met.

For some, solitude may best be understood in terms of time spent in the absence of other human beings, and surely this condition is somehow requisite in the definition. Perhaps more significant, however, true solitude invites the opportunity for an intimate companionship to occur with our more fundamental and universal relations.

Obtaining a state of solitude is always an achievement or accomplishment that can take on the proportions of an arduous exercise for some, or it can be an affinity for others. Many become acquaintances with solitude only after lengthy and often apprehensive or even painful conditioning. How many people reach adulthood and find an opportunity to spend three full days and nights without any form of human interaction? Imagine—three days—no radio, no stereo, no television, no phone, no contact with another human being. And what about three days and nights without even a printed word? Most people after considerable thought would have to answer, "Nope, not once." Probably, few mature adults could recall even a single twenty-four-hour period in their entire lives. A dear and learned friend, a worldly and experienced woman with a PhD and years of training and practice in psychoanalysis, once inquired about my frequent forays into solitary environments. Her interrogation went something like: "What do you do with all your time out there? Do you take something to read?" I was struck dumb. Was the implication that the experience must be somewhat empty—that life without human interaction would be uninteresting or even boring?

And so it seems our question is, how would we react under conditions of such apparent social deprivation? Many would be surprised. In the sheep study we have found that the younger people, in particular, often have deep-seated romantic notions about being alone in the wilderness but find that the journey into solitude can quickly take on a state of loneliness that for many becomes intolerable or even pathological in the truest sense. We have had highly motivated and accomplished graduate students or undergraduate field assistants literally abandon their research assignments and responsibilities in a desperate need for human company. They discover that in reality they have never spent more than a few hours without the company of other humans, and that void quickly becomes not simply uncomfortable but unbearable. Some come to recognize loneliness as a psychological condition, like a fear of heights or a morbid fear of snakes, and simply work around the difficulty. Others are so traumatized and embarrassed that they are forced to alter the type of research they are willing to do and to modify their scientific careers.

In general, older people seem to have less difficulty with loneliness and begin discovering the advantages and joys of solitude. However, some find solitude the most satisfying of pleasures, and like so many experiences that bring ultimate delight, it can be intoxicating. It is true that in no small measure our standing in life helps define and inevitably instills in us all a sense of who we are—family, friends, education, jobs, accomplishments, and so on. But in a much larger sense, perhaps in a more important sense, we are defined more properly by our relationship to the ancient universe that surrounds us, billions of years of evolutionary development, and by this unimaginably complex, inherently mystical, and unbroken continuum that simultaneously connects and transports us through time and space. It appears that each of us by living in this singular moment is a completely unique entity, one extraordinary individual expression of that most phenomenal continuum. With absolutely no understanding of the process that propels us, or by what mysterious means we arrived in this moment, we are that dog with our faces hanging out a window of the speeding and unknowable vehicle of life—and, remarkably, neither terrified nor questioning but rather thrilled and exhilarated. We abandon the prospect of understanding for the consolation of simple wonder, and for our brief moment drink in the rushing winds of time. Perhaps it is only a natural metamorphosis—we eventually shed our various costumes, guises, and identities and recognize that we are simply that dog. On this mountain, on this solitary precipice, if anything significant remains of me, it is my dog of wonder. Solitude is just an open window, waiting.

6

RISKY BUSINESS

On more than one occasion, it has been suggested to me by well-meaning family members and friends that living and working in backcountry environments, and in particular at a high elevation above timberline, is indulging in risky behavior. There are dangers associated with living in wilderness to be sure, but in my estimation, the drive to and from the trailhead is the most dangerous aspect of my job. With a little knowledge of the skills necessary to survive in the backcountry, good gear, and a little common sense, life even above timberline can be comfortably safe if not altogether routine. Over the years, I have visited the heights of the Rocky Mountains many times and lived for seasons on the highest reaches of Middle Mountain and Whiskey Mountain. In the months spent living on these remote peaks, only on a few rare occasions have I felt in any real danger.

The large predators that inhabit these mountains are not habituated to the company of humans and behave altogether differently from ones that live near urban areas and national parks. Mountain lions are reactive and unpredictable but typically terrified by humans. I defy you to intentionally go out and get a good look at a lion. Large wild bears can be arrogant but in general abhor the company of humans. Even though it seems that bears and humans are somehow predisposed to come into conflict, bears are intelligent creatures and so it is possible, by exercising a little caution, respect, and reason, to also appeal to their better judgment and thereby reach some sort of an accord.

Lightning strikes at twelve thousand feet are capricious, and a powerful electrical storm above timberline is a frightening experience. John was struck by lightning once but was fortunate in not suffering any permanent injury; his companion, however, was not so lucky.

Thunderstorms at high elevations are often particularly intense, and the frequency and distribution of strikes are like a high-altitude aerial bombing. With strikes occurring everywhere, you just lie there at night, surrounded by the only metal objects on the mountain, and as the sky lights up with the repeated flash and boom of lightning, the silhouettes of your crossed tent poles over your head say to the heavens: X marks the spot. However, precautions can be taken to reduce the possibility of a direct strike to a statistical improbability. Being in the exact right place at the exact wrong time is of course unfortunate.

Most of the time it's possible for a reasonable person to feel safer and more comfortable alone at twelve thousand feet than on any city street or highway. I would rather have a grizzly in my camp than a drunk on my road.

With only a few exceptions have my visits to the high country been anything other than predictable, pleasant, and comfortably safe. However, on the rarest of occasions, things can become troublesome.

During the summer of 2001, I was monitoring the sheep and attending to the soil plots, when late one day while preparing my evening meal I merely walked from the tent back to my camp stove. Ten steps from the tent, I hit the ground in agony, as though a bullet had just passed through my leg. I broke out in a cold sweat and felt nauseated. The summit of Middle Mountain was a bad place to have a serious injury.

When your job, and in some sense your life, depends on making astute observations and knowing at all times what is occurring around you, living becomes a balancing act in the most real sense imaginable. You must constantly watch where you put your feet, but you must always reconcile this necessity with the equally important need to know exactly what is occurring in your immediate surroundings. I have always chosen to pay more attention to my surroundings than to the placement of my feet. The price I choose to pay is the occasional stumble over the odd rock or downed tree, and I probably average some sort of minor fall once or twice a day. When traversing safer ground, I depend on my feet to have eyes of their own while I focus most of my attention on more critical or interesting concerns in the area. But, of course, on truly dangerous footing, the architecture of the landscape holds my close attention. Still, I refuse to divide my attention between a loose rock and a disturbed bear.

As the immediate pain in my knee began to subside, I recalled a couple of recent falls that may have contributed or caused some mechanical damage in this knee. Perhaps I had actually overtrained in the weeks prior to my arrival on the mountain as I combined running, weight training, and yogalike stretching, alternately tightening and shortening muscle groups and then forcing them back with stretches. I had always considered my knees to be indestructible, but in this case I was certain that something was seriously out of whack. By nightfall, my knee was swollen like a grapefruit, and the majority of the normal range of motion was lost to the swelling.

With only aspirin to help me through the night, I awakened to a world that, like my knee, had grown exponentially more vast, inhospitable, and intimidating. I painfully hobbled around the mountain attempting to continue all my responsibilities. Limping around at a snail's pace, I found that it was still possible to make observations far across the mountain. Having never felt the need or learned the virtues of the familiar hikers trekking pole, I didn't have one. There were also, of course, no wooden sticks above the tree line that could be used as a partial crutch. The simple act of sitting down or standing up was tormenting. It is interesting how the smallest seed of vulnerability can grow and quickly take on enormous proportions. We are all fertile ground for the propagation of insecurities. Long days, like this researcher, slowly crept by, as I found independence and self-reliance to be increasingly fragile states of being. However, I was consoled by some vague plans for a rare resupply of food and fuel involving Nate's eventual return to the mountain before the end of the month.

After an interminable ten days with no one aware of my deteriorating condition, Nate appeared late one afternoon. He had brought some sort of cell phone device that would actually work at certain locations on the mountain. The next morning we managed to reach John Mionczynski in Lander and advised him of the situation. After discussing the dire nature of my injury, John said that we would have to medevac me off the mountain by helicopter. The idea seemed abhorrent in many ways. The thought of jeopardizing people's lives by trying to maneuver a helicopter at twelve thousand feet with no atmosphere, with high winds, and no flat place to land in a ten-mile radius—well, it seemed outrageous. I said I would call him back—I needed to think.

An hour later we reconnected with John, and I explained that helicopters would be too dangerous and too expensive for the poorly endowed sheep project. We had tried before the field season to get me insured by the sheep study through the state of Wyoming, but as a backcountry "biological subcontractor," (with an implied lack of good judgment) I was quickly deemed uninsurable. And further, there was something humiliating and pathetic about being rescued from my own study area—off my own mountain. So I explained that if Nate could be patient enough to stay with me, I would rather try to get off the mountain on my own, or at least be allowed the dignity to die trying. John agreed—helicopters are expensive—field men are a dime a dozen. The other alternative would be to remain on the mountain and keep doing my job as best I could. John pointed out that one person alone in a wilderness environment with a highly visible crippling disability would quickly attract the attention of large predators, making me an easy and perhaps irresistible target. I had also been worrying about that particular scenario, so we agreed I would attempt a descent the following morning.

By first light, Nate and I were slowly moving up and over the summit of Middle Mountain. In case the trip proved to be too much for one day, I started down the mountain with about thirty-five pounds in my pack—just enough gear to sustain me for one extra night if necessary. As we reached timberline, I found an accommodating stick and began hobbling down the mountain with the use of one good leg and an awkward wooden prop. The pain was not unbearable, but my progress was probably excruciating for poor Nate. With only one stumble that wrenched my bad knee and left me writhing in pain for a few minutes, we incrementally worked our way down and out of the mountains. We reached the wilderness area trailhead some seven miles below just after dark. There Nate and I parted in separate vehicles for the seventy-mile trip back to Lander. Now, of course, after hopping seven miles down a mountain on one leg, my good knee then felt like the other of two bad knees.

The following day found me with an orthopedic surgeon in Riverton examining the results of my MRI. He squinted at an opaque object in my knee capsule that he suspected of being a chip of bone from the condyle of my tibia and asked, "You haven't been walking on this have you?" I confessed that I had gone for a "little walk" yesterday, and he emphatically suggested, "That thing needs to come out immediately." Former orthopedic surgeon for the University of Nebraska football team, Dr. Wekker had seen a few bum knees. I was in the outpatient surgery unit of the Riverton hospital at

7:00 AM the next morning, and at my insistence, the doctor performed his first arthroscopic surgery using only local anesthesia. I had fun watching the procedure on the monitor, walked out of the hospital four hours after my arrival, and went to lunch with Kathy Pappas at a Mexican restaurant. The only unpleasantness involved watching the entire OR staff—in spite of gowns and masks—visibly wincing when the rather long anesthesia needle entered my knee capsule.

The "opaque object" turned out to be a less-serious but equally painful plica, common to habitual runners, as well as a torn medial meniscus, which needed a good trimming. To my surgeon's horror, I was on the Lander high school track in seven days running laps and climbing bleachers with only minimal pain, and returned alone to Middle Mountain in less than four weeks. I have never had a minute of pain from that knee in the years that have passed.

In the early summer of 2006, a field assistant had a close call. I was going to join John Mionczynski and Bruce Mincher, an environmental scientist from the Idaho National Engineering and Environmental Laboratory, on Middle Mountain. John and Bruce were observing sheep and monitoring changes in soil chemistry with the use of a portable REDOX (reduction-oxidation potential) meter. My project that summer involved collecting shed sheep hair for high-resolution spectrometry analysis in a lab at Florida State University. The intent was to determine the levels of mercury and other heavy metals that could be accumulating in bighorn sheep, resulting from the atmospheric pollution that was obviously bathing the mountain.

I was asked to guide a new field assistant, Brady Frude, who was going to join John on Middle Mountain. I met Brady in Lander the day before our trip up. We got acquainted over supper and discussed what he might expect during his experience with the bighorn sheep study and talked in general terms about living on any twelve-thousand-foot mountain. Brady was an enthusiastic, sturdy-looking twenty-seven-year-old army veteran who grew up in Laramie and was attending Casper College in Casper, Wyoming. It seemed that Brady's physical condition was certainly not an issue, and living in Laramie above seven thousand feet, his compatibility with high altitudes should be excellent. Additionally, having grown up in Wyoming, he had experience camping in the backcountry, making him a natural candidate for the job. However, it was clear that Brady would be packing excess weight in the form of some outdated camping gear, large binoculars, and other equipment not well suited for backpacking in the high country. After carefully organizing our gear that night, the scales showed us that I would be assaulting Middle Mountain with a cumbersome fifty pounds, but Brady, disturbingly, was closer to sixty. In passing I asked Brady if he had done any training for this job, and he replied no but considered himself to be in relatively good condition. Personally, I think it advisable for anyone doing this work at any age to train as if preparing for an Olympic event, but I felt confident that Brady's relative youth would help usher him up the hill.

The following morning, we met for an early 5:00 AM breakfast in Lander and then drove the seventy miles to the Torrey Creek trailhead. After carefully checking that nothing was being left behind, we began the gradual incline up the Fitzpatrick Wilderness Area trail, passing near the foot of Middle Mountain. We began our hike up Glacier Trail around 8:00 AM, so we could expect to reach the summit of the mountain before dark. A few miles later we left the trail and waded across Torrey Creek, where we took a short break before beginning the first leg of the climb. Up until this point, while getting metabolically adapted to the incline and altitude, we had spent much of our time breathing deeply with little energy left for conversation. But after crossing the creek and eating a snack, we had a lighthearted visit, sharing some casual thoughts and voicing our enthusiasm for the project.

Refreshed, we saddled back up and wandered up the creek in waist-high willows with brook trout darting all about and fresh moose sign everywhere, enjoying one of those outrageous and perfect postcard vistas that these mountains heap upon you. Eventually we reached a little ridge line on the north side of the creek that begins the climb. The first two-mile pitch up Middle Mountain is certainly not a technical climb and there are no real hazards, but it is relentlessly steep with unstable footing. Every step forward and upward comes with the inevitable price of some slippage backward on loose gravel. Consequently, intermittent handholds on large rocks and small trees are often necessary. The entire slope is rocky and heavily forested, and so any psychological advantage gained by the perspective of actual progress is lost in a monotony of downed timber and a winding path, as you seek any route that may replace the actual need to climb using all fours. However, occasionally you do find yourself employing your hands and knees and scrambling like a loaded mule—a pack animal that wonders how many actual miles have been surrendered by sliding backward. Thirty minutes into the climb, Brady was struggling, and so we stopped momentarily to catch our breath as he expressed a need to sit down. Although it is probably not always good to let your heart rate return to a resting state, we stopped for a few minutes and for a drink of water. Brady was hanging his head, closing his eyes, and continuing to breathe deeply with beads of perspiration all over his face. Middle Mountain is steep, and not wanting to make him self-conscious, I pretended not to notice. Dehydration is always a danger at high elevations, but we were careful to hydrate ourselves completely at breakfast in the early morning, on the drive to the trailhead, and again before leaving the vehicle—we were saturated—awash. Many people mistake the dry mouth that accompanies aerobic or strenuous physical exertion with actual thirst and then waste precious water when in fact they are already sufficiently hydrated. If you are stopping occasionally to urinate, any water you drink is probably being wasted.

After several minutes of rest Brady was back on his feet, and we began slowly and methodically working our way up the slope. But Brady soon began stopping frequently and grabbing handholds. I asked him if he was feeling all right and he complained of being weak and somewhat nauseated. Halfway up the first leg of the mountain it became clear that Brady had a problem, but he insisted that he would be fine if we continued to go slowly. Within a short time however, his pace became progressively slower as he grew pale and was beginning to perspire profusely in spite of cool temperatures and a light breeze. He soon started complaining of a "sore head." Becoming alarmed, I began questioning him about possible maladies—diabetes, migraines, hypoglycemia, or perhaps the possible onset of a cold or flu virus. But Brady claimed he was healthy as a horse. Food poisoning seemed unlikely since we had identical meals the night before and for breakfast.

At last we reached the bench or ledge above the first steep slope and took off our packs for a long and much needed break. Brady sat down, leaned against a tree and then slowly rolled over on his side with his eyes closed. Asking him what was going on, he only replied after several unanswered inquiries that he was feeling very sick. Although we were probably barely above ten thousand feet, he appeared to be exhibiting the classic symptoms of altitude sickness. Regretfully, we had passed that point on the mountain where returning to the trailhead before dark would be a possibility. Now, even more disturbing, Brady's perspiration had ceased and was being replaced by chills. As we untied a cumbersome and heavy rubberized rain jacket from his pack and bundled him up, Brady said, rather unconvincingly, that he did not want to go down and if he just had a little time he would be fine. Frequently, dehydration accompanies altitude sickness and can even be a contributor, and although it seemed unlikely at this point, I urged Brady to drink some water. As I handed Brady his water bottle, he slowly sat up and took intermittent sips for several minutes. Suddenly, he climbed over on his hands and knees and began the most violent vomiting I have ever witnessed. The heaving and retching lasted for several minutes and then he fell over on his side. While trying to inquire about his symptoms, I realized he had become unresponsive, and when he finally tried to speak, the words were confused and incoherent. Mission Control—we have a problem! We were miles in the backcountry, Brady outweighed me by perhaps twenty pounds, and I couldn't possibly leave him to go get help. The only communication device I had was a small line-of-sight walkie-talkie with new batteries, but we were still out of site and range of John and the Middle Mountain camp.

Gradually Brady became lucid again and appeared to feel a little better. The next two-mile leg of the hike was along a timbered bench with a relatively gentle incline toward the top of the mountain, and although I did not trust his judgment at this point, he insisted on pushing ahead. Slowly we shuffled along, and I only hoped we would soon come into range of John's receiver. After perhaps another one-half mile, Brady went down on all fours and fell over. Once again he became incoherent and would not respond to my questions. Brady was by my estimation deathly ill, and although I tried to appear calm and in control, mortal fear was starting to grip me. Remembering an old outfitter's hunting campsite on a creek farther up the ridge, I pulled Brady's backpack off and hoisted it up high in a tree where bears would at least have to make an effort to retrieve it. It was clear now that Brady may not be able to walk, let alone carry a pack.

I got him back on his feet eventually, and we headed in the direction of the old outfitter's camp, hoping at that point that radio communication would be possible. After several more stops, the sun had become disturbingly low in the sky. Another hour passed before we finally dropped down into the run of the creek where sheep and elk hunters had trimmed lower limbs and removed any downed timber, making an accommodating campsite amid big fir and ancient spruce and with clear flowing water nearby. We found a level spot just above the creek under spreading boughs of spruce and Brady fell in a heap. Again, worried about possible dehydration, I made him sit up and take some water. Almost instantly, as if he had just swallowed poison, Brady began the same vicious vomiting and heaving. Falling over on his side, he could only respond with unintelligible mumbling. Brady had the classic symptoms of edema—fluid buildup on the brain—or even stroke causing the headache, confusion, and extreme nausea. The possibilities were all frightening. I have been with deathly ill people and accident victims. I have had people die in my arms—but only once, in the case of a brain aneurysm, have I ever seen a human being become this ill this fast. I was also reminded of the glaciologist, who a few summers before, only narrowly escaped with his life after suffering acute symptoms of altitude sickness.

Frantic, I crossed the creek with my pitiful little transmitter and climbed up on a huge pile of granite boulders and tried to reach John, who was at least another two miles up the mountain. With obvious desperation in my tone, I called for someone to answer. Finally, a static sound and a choppy voice replied—not from John, but from Andrew Allgierer, another sheep study biologist working many miles away on Whiskey Mountain. After I described the possibly deadly situation, Andrew said he would try to reach John from his position. Miraculously, he reached Bruce Mincher instead, who in turn relayed the message to John, yet another mile away. We began an awkward four-way communication as John told Bruce that he would hike down toward the old outfitter campsite until he could contact me with his radio. In turn, Andrew, back on Whiskey Mountain, relayed the news to me and also gathered more information about Brady's condition to be relayed eventually back to John. I sat helplessly at Brady's side for an eternal twenty minutes until at last I heard the electronic squawk and John's choppy voice coming across my receiver. John has a high level of expertise in handling backcountry illnesses and injuries, having participated in many high country rescues and evacuations. As I described Brady's symptoms and his apparent dire state, John said he would hike straight down to us and we would probably have to perform an emergency evacuation—possibly a dangerous nighttime evacuation—stating that time could be of the essence.

The day was beginning to wane, and John was a beautiful sight to see as he maneuvered down through the steep tangle of timber and boulders to the creek where we were waiting. He could see the gravity of the situation that by now had become etched on my face as I considered the possibility of a fine young man dying—one who in some sense had become my sole responsibility. With a little encouragement we were finally able to get Brady sitting up, and he gradually began to talk coherently.

To our great relief, Brady seemed to become progressively more lucid, and as John quizzed him about his status he continued to improve. Astonishingly, Brady began feeling much stronger as the nausea and headache subsided. He then began to reassure us over and over again that he was not in need of evacuation and, further, he wanted to try and stay on the mountain. John, with some reluctance, acquiesced and sat with Brady while I hiked a mile back down the mountain to retrieve his backpack from the tree. As the sun began to set, John climbed back up the mountain to his base camp with the understanding that we would stay in radio communication monitoring Brady's condition.

I dug out both our tents, prepared a quick camp, and made a light dehydrated meal of spaghetti. To my surprise, Brady had an appetite and managed to hold down some hot tea and eventually a small helping of his warm meal.

The dense forest along the creek run was prime bear habitat, so I was careful to keep everything as clean as possible with all food preparation accomplished well downstream. My bear confidence was shaken, however, by a nearby bucket-size pile of fresh, black, blood-stained scat, filled with fir, bone, and probably the vegetative contents of something else's stomach. All of our food-related items went into one large twenty-pound bag. Since the small fanny pack attached to my backpack was contaminated with food odors, I heaved a nylon line over a dead spruce limb fifteen feet off the ground and hoisted the bag and the pack up tight against the limb. Following a final communication with John that convinced him that

Brady was out of trouble—even if not yet out of the woods—we made plans to communicate first thing in the morning. Brady instantly fell into a deep sleep as I lay quietly in my small tent pitched close to his. Exhausted but wound up tight, I lay for a time, alternately listening for the reassuring calm breathing in the tent next door and for the noisy hot breath of a visiting bear. Eventually, fatigue overcame anxiety, allowing me to drift away into something approximating a bearproof coma.

The comforting sound of Brady stirring around in his sleeping bag awakened me early, and without sitting up I asked, "How are you feeling?" He replied, with a distinct tone of wonder, that he seemed to be feeling "just fine" and thought he would be able to proceed up the mountain. Calling John to relay the good news, I told him we would begin the two-mile climb in an hour or so. Over hot oatmeal and coffee, we reminisced about the strange events of the previous day, and both of us admitted being somewhat mystified as to the cause. I cleaned things up after the meal and we began breaking camp—stuffing tents, pads, and sleeping bags. The weather, although cool, was invigorating and sunny, the wind was gentle, and things at last appeared to be returning to a condition of normalcy. Finally, I went to retrieve the rest of the food and fanny pack but soon realized that in my effort to secure everything in the tree, I had managed to entangle the bags on a snag, ten feet out on a slender dead limb. Flipping and shaking the line over and over again, I tried to dislodge the bundle, but to no avail. After several minutes, I realized that I was probably just making things worse and the cord was hopelessly tangled on the limb. I began jerking and tugging. Having no success, I started leaning on the line using my body weight, hoping that something would eventually give. Now out of ideas involving any measure of finesse, and recognizing that the thing must come down, I just pulled out the metaphorical bigger hammer, running the line under my rear end and began pulling down on the line with more and more of my weight. At last, I was literally sitting on the cord like a swing. Nothing gave way, so I applied all my strength and began jumping with all my weight, stretching the line and violently bending the dead limb up and down until the inevitable occurred—the resounding snap of dead wood like a rifle shot. With all my weight, magnified by a big jump and a snatch of the arms—I landed right on my butt with a perfectly placed rock striking my right ischial tuberosity (those ill-conceived pelvis bones in your butt that become sore after riding a horse). Almost simultaneously, the bundle hit the ground at a velocity approaching the speed of light— fanny pack first—*ka-wham!* The sound was unmistakable—my heart sank. Opening my fanny pack, my fears were made real as I saw my expensive 35 mm Leica camera crushed; it rattled in my hand like a box of rocks. Part of my objective on this trip was to get photographs of—well, never mind. I limped back up the creek favoring a sore butt, a metaphorically flattened wallet, and by then a critically wounded sense of well-being. It seemed as though a second day was already becoming overrun with misfortune. Trying not to stress Brady further by going on and on about my problems, we loaded on our packs and carefully began the steep ascent out of the creek bed and up the mountain. Almost immediately we entered the ragged environmental transition zone where the forest gives way to the alpine tundra. Brady said he felt a little weak but otherwise was doing well.

A mile up the mountain, we were well above the tree line and following a lively outwash of meltwater from the glacial snowfields above. At last, after two long days, the mighty summit of Middle Mountain had finally come into view. The snowfields are steep, and so without crampons we climbed onto the ice and began stomping our boots into the surface slush, postholing up the incline with me twenty feet in the lead. With thinning air and a steep angle of ascent, we slowly and deliberately trudged, being careful not to stress Brady further, but also wanting to avoid sliding a few hundred feet back down the ice. Additionally, I was certain that Brady was feeling a little intimidated and perhaps even a little vulnerable by the apparent vision of inhospitality above us as the magnitude of this twelve-thousand-foot mountain was being revealed.

Fifty feet from the top of the first snowfield, I heard a sharp crack and suddenly felt the world disappear from under my feet. A hole opened up beneath me, and for one instant I was falling five feet or fifty—I didn't know. Ice rushed past me in some confusing blur and instantly I crumpled up in the darkness on a smooth granite boulder the size of a Buick. The melting ice had carved out a cavern and I had fallen into the resulting crevasse. Only a small black hole remained on the surface where I was standing only a moment before. Delighted that I had not fallen to my death and apparently had not suffered any terrible injury, I was merely grateful that the granite boulder had been there to catch me so soon. I quickly scrambled up on my feet, stood up on the boulder, and as my head popped up out of the hole, I observed Brady with a look of unmitigated horror on his face. Faking a big grin to reassure Brady that he had not lost his guide through some deep bottomless fissure that may immediately swallow him as well, I unstrapped my pack, heaved it up on the ice, and began clawing my way out. After emerging from the ice I reassured Brady that I was fine, failing to mention that my leg was badly bruised with a fifty-pound pack complicating my landing on the rock. Now, with a sore knee and leg, not to mention the humiliating and costly butt injury suffered two hours earlier, we pressed on. In another hour we reached John's campsite near the summit. Brady was fine. I was a wreck.

That evening I gave Brady a quick orientation tour around the top of Middle Mountain, and by the following morning Brady was back to perfect health. His enthusiasm, competence, and energy quickly gained the admiration of John and me, and he eventually proved to be a valuable asset to the study. Mercifully, the rest of the summer on Middle Mountain went beautifully, with the possible exception of a storm that blew in excess of one hundred miles per hour and destroyed every tent on Middle Mountain, including a rather high-profile contraption purchased by the University of Wyoming to house the portable spectrophotometer and some other expensive experimental gear.

7

Ecology of a Mountain

It is mid-July of my first summer, and my routine is well established. Early morning chores consist of camp responsibilities like gathering water for the day, recording twenty-four-hour weather data, servicing the forage selenium plots if precipitation has occurred, and collecting and sampling any rain or snow for pH values and future laboratory reference. Usually by the time the sun is warming the highest pinnacles of Middle Mountain, I have already located and recorded collared sheep signals with the receiver and begun my daily trek from camp.

Today, my interest lies with Y-9 and her sick lamb, while radio collar signals indicate she is near the same location visited yesterday. Her lamb has worsened day by day, and it seems improbable that she could survive. After climbing to a rocky prominence south of 3-4 Pass, I spot ewe and lamb lying together less than a quarter mile from last night's location. Gradually working my way down the mountainside, I soon arrive a short fifty meters from the two. Neither is disturbed by my familiar presence, and Y-9 barely offers me a glance as I settle down to make observations. Two other adult ewes, plus a yearling and two lambs, graze just below and offer me familiar stares before continuing their foraging activities. As I observe this sick lamb's progression over the course of many days, it becomes obvious that Y-9 is also becoming increasingly stressed. Her lamb's disabling illness is weighing heavily and without doubt represents a disability for her as well. The lamb will no longer make the effort to follow closely, and in the past two days I have only observed three abbreviated periods of nursing. Y-9, although devoted, displays a despondency and resignation that seems to speak to some understanding of the inevitable outcome and makes her steadfast dedication at once admirable and heartbreaking. Field researchers have lost their jobs for attempting to intervene in otherwise natural but unpleasant circumstances of injury, entrapment, disease, or predation. But I must admit I would love to experiment with a small injection of pen-strep and B-12 on this little lamb that I have in some way come to know.

The other three ewes and lambs gradually browse over toward Y-9 and the sick lamb. Y-9 stands as they approach and all begin grazing. The two lambs, noticeably larger than the sick lamb, casually wander over and all sniff noses. As the two then lower their head and gently engage in some lighthearted head butting, one breaks away and eagerly jumps on a nearby rock to entice one of them into a little game of king on the mountain. Calling on some nearly irretrievable and forgotten vestige of joy and enthusiasm, the little lamb responds with a perky nod of the head and an almost unrecognizable effort to jump and engage in play. The gesture sends her toppling over onto her side and back, with all four feet kicking helplessly in the air. Her pitiful struggles to right herself eventually result in her front feet planted beneath but with her hind legs folded underneath in a pathetic sitting position. The two larger lambs stare with confused expressions over her convulsive efforts as she continues to regain some orientation. My heart sinks as this one fragile little life seems to take on enormous proportions in this otherwise most powerful and now coldly dispassionate ecology.

Early the next morning, immediately following chores in camp and without consulting the radio collar receiver, I climb up and over the mountain, heading directly for 3-4 Pass. Scrambling up on a rocky promontory, I begin glassing the vicinity for Y-9 and her lamb. After several more attempts to gain proper advantage and locate the pair, I begin moving southward toward ten or twelve sheep browsing another quarter mile away. On my way to the twelve, I glance down the mountainside and spot a lone sheep with a familiar yellow collar—Y-9. Hastily I meander through a forest of waist-high boulders and take up position seventy yards above the ewe. Acknowledging me with a brief glance, she resumes systematically pulling vegetation from the tundra earth. While she calmly grazes within a wide expanse of lush green mountain pasture, I glass the entire area, but no lamb is to be found. Periodically the ewe raises her head and stares motionless back across the mountain to the north—one minute . . . two minutes . . . three. Do the bighorn sheep grieve in their own way? Is mourning included in their complex repertoire of behaviors? The vacuum that surrounds this ewe is conspicuous, palpable even, as she lingers in a solitude that must reside somewhere between liberation and desperation. Surely, weeks of dread culminated in a brief and anticipated moment of horror as an opportunistic predator finally brought the lamb's suffering to an end. That such violence and terror can now be expressed in so much stillness is almost unnerving—such stolid bravery and resolve. Would I be walking on the eggshells of science to suggest that true grief may be observed in this bighorn sheep? Rather, would a cautious scientist carefully refer to *grieving behavior*—always of course allowing for the thoughtless expression of mere "stimulus and response." Is it my projection, or can her anguish be objectively observed? Although responsive in every way, clearly her experience is by no means thoughtless. We all experience the pangs of grief and so it can be shared. Y-9 eventually lies down overlooking the great expanse of the surrounding canyon, and I remain with her for most of the day.

Like some ancient lithic library, a magnificent metamorphic archive storing the collected wisdom of sixty million years, Middle Mountain's eloquent narrative is housed in volumes bound in stone and written by the hand of time. Raise a solid mass of stone eight thousand feet above the surrounding earth—up into the abrasive effects of sun, rain, snow, ice, lightning, wind, and the persistent gnawing of lichens—then stand back for several million years. See what you get as the constant forces of erosion and gravity ceaselessly pull at the chaotic aftermath of this punishing activity. But perhaps these relationships are not as adversarial as they first appear. They could be complementary or even harmonious, as if some cooperative agreement exists toward the fulfillment of a preordained and desirable outcome. There is nothing about this great mountain that appears arbitrary, capricious, or even in the strictest geological sense, erratic. Here, chaos and disorder are compounded into a paradox of perfection—of absolution from the punitive effects of the ages. Middle Mountain displays none of the characteristics of a work in progress but rather projects an appearance or sense of stability and finality. It would seem that for countless millennia, master stonecutters have been toiling to smooth and soften the contour of every stone, and every stone has been elegantly placed in its most balanced and stable position. The boulders of this mountain have no sharp points or jagged edges. There are no piles of the ragged geological tailings know as scree. Instead, each pinkish granite boulder has been somehow considered, arranged in its most perfect place, ground to completion, and, finally adorned with lichens abounding in the colors of a coral reef. Megaliths and pebbles alike are then set firm and secure in the lush carpets of rich soil and soft green alpine tundra. It is as if a thousand robed monks with gentle bare feet have manicured this mountain's gently rolling summit for untold eons.

Middle Mountain's summit is winding and rolling and stretches for miles from north to south, culminating in the prominence known as Torrey Peak at 12,181 feet. Its thick green alpine carpet is studded with cobbles, boulder fields, and orbicular boulders ranging in size from automobiles to houses. Scattered across the rolling summit of this mountain and varying in height from fifty feet to hundreds, enormous granite pinnacles rise by the dozens, suggesting the ramparts and towers of great castles. The result of frost wedging, these pinnacles are all fragmented vertically and appear to be the exposed remnants of the more solid heart of the mountain. Perfectly nested and contoured megaliths rise everywhere across the mountain's summit. These granite towers seem to have erupted through the soft matrix of the rich tundra but in reality are left standing, the result of gradual exhumation. During this exposure, large boulders have on rare occasions broken away and are now arranged in stable piles around the base of each pinnacle in apparent support of the more central tower. From a distance the pinnacles appear as well-organized stacks of free-standing irregular columnar boulders, but in actuality they are set tight in the spongy earthen mortar of ancient granite soil and firm tundra. Many of the larger pinnacles can be entered like enormous vertical winding ziggurats with unexpected soft green carpeted pathways snaking upward into the highest recesses of the towers. The large adult rams often seek out these isolated heights for the bounty of lush vegetation and probably for the strategic ability to see danger coming from any direction. An abundance of mountain lion scats suggests that the great cats seek out these remote areas as well—perhaps to prey on rams—but also to gain a wide overview of the mountain and, I suspect, to keep an eye on my peculiar wanderings. Sheep bones are common, scattered here and there throughout the rocks. Golden eagles, ravens, and prairie falcons may be seen on the uppermost rocky points, using them as opportunistic raptorial observatories.

I meander up through the pinnacles, through the narrow and confined passages and feel a primitive sense of uneasiness. It's often impossible to know what lies in wait a mere twenty feet ahead. The damp tundra sod and the ever present wind make passage up through the rocks silent. Ignoring the remote possibility of a deliberate ambush by a large predator, I worry that a blind and quiet approach could startle a big cat or even an adult ram into a defensive attack. On two occasions I have had adult rams make aggressive gestures toward me, including an aborted charge that John witnessed. Both events occurred on open ground, so the confined quarters of these granite towers create an eerie, almost preternatural, sense of expectation. An assistant working on the study two years ago, watched helplessly through binoculars as a mountain lion stalked John. With apparent obsession, the lion followed and briefly crouched only twenty feet away in some overhead rocks but then, thankfully, gave up the hunt and disappeared. If not for the ravings of his colleague later that day, John would never have known. These stones are inhabited. After being alone on this mountain for weeks and months, you gradually begin to recall the ancient sensibilities that allow us to feel the presence of the predatory eye upon our back. These stones have eyes.

For those who would perceive a twelve-thousand-foot treeless alpine environment as stark, barren, and lifeless, nothing could be farther from the truth. In fact, these rocks do have eyes—thousands of them. As I slowly wander across the heights of Middle Mountain, there is never a time when I am not observing and being observed by at least dozens if not hundreds of pairs of eyes. In a single glance, I can usually see several big yellow-bellied marmots (resembling woodchucks of the east), numerous golden-mantled ground squirrels, least chipmunks, and dozens of pikas. Pikas are small animals the size of guinea pigs with short round ears. They look like rodents but are in reality lagamorphs and therefore closely related to rabbits and hares. Ravens, golden eagles, ferruginous hawks, prairie falcons, and the occasional northern goshawk are frequently visible, as they keep a watchful eye on the numerous rodents and pikas. Dozens of bighorn sheep may be seen on any slope of the mountain, and they in turn attract the attention of mountain lions, coyotes, and lately even wolves. In recent years, wolves have expanded their range from the Yellowstone area to include the northern Wind River Mountains, and we see their tracks and make sightings with regularity now. Following a snowfall, it is common to see the tracks of elk and bears that have crossed over the top of the mountain in the night, and sometimes I see where bears have paused to roll over stones and boulders, browsing for insects and their larvae. The high mountains are clear of snow for only a precious few weeks, and so their inhabitants are constantly involved with the industries and chores of survival. It could be said that a frenzy of activity characterizes life here with the demands of feeding, reproduction, food gathering and storage, rearing young, and generally preparing for the rigors of a nine-month winter. To my constant delight and wonder, the animals that inhabit these isolated heights have never had prolonged exposure to humans and never developed the fear and suspicion that normally characterize the relationship of nearly all living things with human beings. I am regarded here as simply a curiosity to be examined briefly but then ignored. While sitting, chipmunks and white-footed mice will occasionally run across my feet or climb up on a knee as they scurry about on their various missions and explorations. The fat lumbering marmots I see most regularly around my campsite eventually become oblivious to my presence and will casually browse only a few meters away. Pikas win the most adorable creature award, and although perhaps the most industrious animal on the mountain, they seem to be the most interested in my business and appear to express some particular fascination with my comings and goings. They will often perch on a rock nearby, briefly stare straight on into my eyes, lift their heads revealing a somewhat comical little mouth that opens wide and admits a silly high-pitched nasal *waeeh*. Then they resume their more defining activity of collecting and drying grasses in peculiar little haystacks. Once dried, the haystacks are retrieved in great billowing mouthfuls and then stored in some rocky larder for winter food—a well-insulated and edible nest. In preparation for deep winter snows that bury the mountain for two-thirds of a year, almost every pika activity is accomplished at a gallop. Empathizing with their inevitable exhaustion, I occasionally indulge in a fantasy that my next major study might involve an eight-month-long winter sleeping in a cozy grass-lined rock cavity with a pika.

The most treasured and sought-after nesting material on the mountain is of course raw wool, which the sheep shed in large scruffy patches for much of the early part of the summer. The visible exterior of wild sheep is characterized by stiff hollow guard hair and is similar to that of deer and other cervids. Wild sheep appear sleek and well contoured without any of the wooly outward appearance of domestic sheep. However, these heavy, dense guard hairs have an underlying thick layer of fine wool that keeps wild sheep perfectly insulated from the most extreme weather. If I want to collect a fur sample for future laboratory analysis, I must patiently observe a sheep rubbing on a rock and then beeline to the spot to beat all the nest builders that are my eager competitors. I have had pikas snatch a piece of wool off the ground five feet away and run to a pile of nearby boulders, thumbing their nose at me.

When asked how anyone could endure such social deprivation for months at a time, I can only laugh and reply that I have honestly not had a lonely minute on Middle Mountain. The society here is rich and completely satisfying. When below, I miss the company of bighorn sheep and pikas, marmots, and ground squirrels—I miss the whispering voice of the alpine tundra.

The arctic tundra and the alpine tundra of the northern Rocky Mountains share many similarities. The Arctic Circle, at 66.5 degrees above the equator, is drawn as an arbitrary circumpolar latitude defined by a more or less permanent presence of winterlike weather, the absence of boreal forests, and the existence of certain endemic plant and animal communities that define the ecology. Arctic summers are brief, tundra soils usually experience only superficial thawing, and permafrost persists throughout the short growing season. Climatologically, this relative latitude should change over time, from north to south, with variations in the duration and intensity of the winters. Ten thousand years ago, the last and most extensive glacial period, known as the Wisconsin glaciation, was retreating from a terminal advance that had extended into the lower forty-eight states and well south into the mountainous high country of the west. The Rocky Mountain alpine tundra can be defined, at least in part, as the vestigial ecological remnants of the present-day arctic tundra that has now receded over a thousand miles to the north. Our mountain plant communities share many species with the contemporary flora of the Arctic. Just as many ice age mammals such as brown bears and marmots are circumpolar, many of the same tundra plant species can be found growing on every continent in the Northern Hemisphere. Because of time and distinct environmental differences however, some alpine species are unique and endemic only to certain localized high country habitats.

Thus, certain plants growing in the Rocky Mountains of North America may also be found growing luxuriantly on the high slopes of the European Alps or similarly on the slopes of the Himalayas of northern Asia. The small but beautiful alplily (*Lloydia serotina*), of the ubiquitous family liliaceae, is an example of a common circumpolar species.

Although at first encounter, plants of the alpine tundra may seem unfamiliar and botanically abstruse, the flowers themselves eventually expose these seemingly exotic plants as comprising the typical families of plants found in any other North American ecosystem. Composites, legumes, lilies, roses, asters, yarrow, clover, wild onions, and cinquefoil are but a few of the immediately recognizable groups. Grasses, sedges, and rushes are likewise abundant and diverse but are merely forms adapted from the most familiar groups—*Brome*, *Panicum*, *Carex*, and *Juncus* all abound in these treeless alpine habitats.

On the other hand, wide basins and dry plains often separate mountainous alpine ecologies, creating an island effect, causing the dispersal of plant species to be unlikely or impossible. It is common, therefore, for mountain ranges or even individual mountains to support species that are environmentally isolated and rare.

All tundra plants share a common and defining attribute—pure unobstructed exposure to some of the most extreme weather on the planet. A universal adaptive strategy characterizing all arctic and alpine flora is *get down and lay low*. A great diversity of plant species have apparently learned to cooperate by the intermingling of thick root systems and vegetative parts to form a more or less uninterrupted and mechanically indivisible turf, or sod. Many tundra plants have a distinctly mosslike appearance with characteristically large flowers without stems that grow directly on the plant's vegetative surface. Because of the short growing season, a synchronicity occurs in blooming, and for a few precious days or weeks the emerald green mountain tundra is awash in color.

Normally one would not identify plants as life forms that express themselves with sounds, but it seems that such a presumption may not be altogether accurate. It appears that every botanical community has, in some sense at least, a collective voice, which can be heard with a little attention from the listener, that may express a most definitive chorus. And each "song," it could be said, is peculiar to a particular environment. A tropical

Aspens.

palm hammock produces, with the slightest provocation, a continuous and lively percussive clatter, rattling, and popping in an exuberant and cheerful cacophony. An aspen grove, perhaps the largest single organism on the planet, may be heard from a mile across a deep canyon perpetually "quaking" even in the most gentle of breezes. The subtle movement of the atmosphere through a solitary southern long leaf pine forest produces a gentle, persistent, almost heavenly sigh. The frequency and timbre of these floral voices are the result of a specific partnership that a community of plants shares with the air surrounding it and the unique interactive relationship that has evolved. It could be said that every plant is a creature of the air, and like birds they have responded evolutionarily to its affects. Plants have evolved to protect themselves from the potentially destructive forces of the wind and to exploit these same forces for reproduction and dispersal. A developmental awareness of the mechanical properties of moving air is expressed in the physiology and morphology of every plant. Drop almost any leaf and observe its peculiar and deliberate aerodynamic properties. Not surprisingly, plants of the alpine tundra have also developed, and may be identified in part, by their mechanical interaction with the ceaseless winds of the high mountains. The fine mosslike leaves of alpine plants have an almost gentle interaction with this otherwise powerful force and offer up no resistance or impediment to its will. Thus their voices are expressed as a soothing whispering hiss, a perpetual high frequency vibration, devoid of any visible movement or sway, except for the occasional nodding of a flower.

Though it may seem contradictory, there are trees growing above timberline. Scattered here and there in protected or slightly shielded locations, spruce, fir, white bark pine, or limber pine may be found trying to make a stand. Like ancient bonsai, dwarfed and gnarly little trees struggle for decades or perhaps even centuries in an ecology that is ironically defined in part by their absence. The phenomenon is referred to collectively as krummholz, and the term is applied to any species of conifer that will choose to survive in an otherwise treeless alpine environment. Most krummholz on Middle Mountain rarely grow beyond eighteen inches high but are often twisted and bent flat against the ground, spending the vast majority of the year beneath the crushing weight of mountain snows. Krummholz are opportunistic and live tenuous lives as solitary individuals or as small clusters of two or three, causing many alpine ecologists to regard them as an *indicator species*, lending insight into the health of the overall alpine ecology.

There are no active glaciers on Middle Mountain with the possible exception of the glacial-like snowfields on the eastern approach to the summit. These two snowfields of only a few acres each have been experiencing a gradual net loss in volume for the past several years because of drought and relatively warmer temperatures and are now beginning to reveal their more ancient heart. Exposed in the remaining ice of their lower layers are the telltale bluish green remnants of a true glacier. The snows of Middle Mountain gradually melt away throughout the summer, but below the tundra surface resides a reservoir of abundant water bound up as permafrost. During normal years, this frozen ground gradually thaws near the surface for much of the summer creating flowing rivulets of crystal clear water. Even on the mountain's highest promontories pure water is often found flowing freely throughout most of the summer months. The alpine tundra is thus provided with a constant subirrigation from the continuous thaw, keeping the vegetation soft, spongy, and lush.

This summer John and I work many miles apart on separate mountains that would involve two long, hard days of hiking if one of us wanted to join the other. Cell phones are of little use in this part of Wyoming, but small handheld walkie-talkies will operate with some predictability on a strictly line-of-sight basis. For safety reasons we each try to climb within eyesight of our respective mountains and touch base at 8:00 AM, noon, and 5:00 PM each day. Even if vocal communication is impossible, the squawk or call signal lets the other know at least he is alive. However, because of unfortunate logistics, we still occasionally go days or even weeks without a communication. The only time we try to communicate at night is when one of us crawls out of a tent and needs to report an aurora. People who have never observed a full-blown aurora borealis event often think it involves some vague fluctuations of dim-colored cloudlike areas in the northern sky. In reality, of all the truly awesome and wondrous phenomena that the natural world occasionally offers up—volcanoes, comets, eclipses, meteor showers, and so on and so forth—nothing has the power to overwhelm the normal human senses like the indisputable drop-dead magic of the aurora. The scientific astronomical explanation of the aurora may be entirely reasonable but proves to the primitive human brain, in the face of the actual ensuing event, to be woefully inadequate or outright insulting. The explanation involves first, enormous solar explosions separating elemental atomic particles that are blasted at unimaginable speeds—millions of miles per hour—like cosmic buckshot, at the unsuspecting earth and its humble inhabitants. Then, the speeding incoming particles are divided, north and south, by the earth's polar magnetism as they begin slamming into the distant ionosphere. Physicists and astronomers, in complete agreement, then cavalierly describe the effects of this violent collision. At altitudes of one hundred miles or more, a subatomic melee ensues as the incoming particles slam into the atmosphere and become disturbed and excited. Ionization begins to occur and the various elements start to fluoresce. Each element offers up a different signature electromagnetic vibration in the form of individual color frequencies. Oxygen ionizes blue, hydrogen ionizes red, helium yellow, methane green, or whatever. These explanations, by the way, if meant to be comforting to the bewildered human mind, prove to be useless, obtuse, and without consolation. A first encounter with a powerful aurora borealis can be disturbing to anyone expecting to be merely delighted, amused, or entertained. Luminescent curtains of vivid electric cosmic colors shimmer, wave, and flow. Concentric waves of colored light may flash from the North Pole and radiate out across the entire visible sky at unimaginable speeds, disappearing over the horizon to the south. The magnitude and brilliance of the overall phenomenon is impossible to record on film—indeed impossible to record upon the human sense of possibility. A major aurora can be life altering, and the suggestion that some biblical-scale cosmic cataclysm may have just begun is almost inescapable. The skies above Middle Mountain can offer an occasional display of irrefutable magic that is, even to the most objective mind, fearsome.

The edge of the sea, the top of a great mountain, or a starlit sky—places that in our eyes are permanent or at least persistent on a human time scale— seem to somehow bring our normal perspectives, if only momentarily, to a halt. We are the toolmakers, the thinkers, the ones who employ abstract thought, conforming and shaping the natural world to better suit our needs and desires; for we are the ones who craft the world into what we perceive as possibility. For better or worse, it is simply what we do as an organism. But at times the natural world can mercifully overwhelm our imperial sense of authority over nature, and like some great cosmic hammer, stop us dead in our tracks. In a time when so much of the world is worn and trod upon, this mountain is, if only by virtue of its overwhelming inconvenience, intact. I often measure the quality of my life by how many places my feet land where no human foot has gone before. It is impossible to discern of course, except by statistical probability, but I know that I regularly place my feet on a small piece of this earth where no other human foot has gone before. For me, it is the clearest definition of sacred ground, and so by the example of the creatures around me, I tread softly.

Is something sacred because we arbitrarily choose to consider it so, or might the sacred exist independent of any other consideration? Most of us choose to defer to theologians and philosophers to answer these difficult questions. Although it is interesting and even useful to contemplate the viewpoints of others and those great thinkers who have gone before, there is probably no greater human blunder than to let another's interpretations define our own experience of reality.

There is a timeless beauty and perfection here that is beyond my abilities to describe, and although these mountains are blessed with inaccessibility and obscurity, there is almost, impossibly, something amiss. In spite of hundreds, even thousands, of miles separating this ecology from the grinding consumption and wastes occurring across the globe, something ill has found its way to this most pristine heart of a continent. The Rocky Mountain high country of Wyoming is an ecosystem in peril. Our job here as researchers and scientists is to observe directly and be attentive to the mysterious symptoms that are becoming apparent in this remote ecology. It is obvious that the old tools and strategies—the dissecting microscope, the binocular, the radio collar and receiver—typically used by wildlife biologists are no longer adequate to uncover the problems that are being suggested, and so new models and new research paradigms must be devised. It seems we must now organize and bring together many divergent scientific minds in a multidisciplinary approach including glaciologists, geologists, meteorologists, botanists and wildlife biologists, soil scientists, and chemists. We must look at the extremely large things and the most diminutive, as well as the creatures that balance so precariously somewhere in the middle.

Since the days of Aldo Leopold, we have understood that no species exists in a vacuum but rather survives only as a member of a complex but integrated biological community. To fully understand the implications of this simple-sounding model will now require us to observe the minute world as seen through the atomic mass spectrometer, as well as through the macro perspective we get from satellites in space. An obscure riddle, with far-reaching and possibly devastating consequences, must be solved. Time is not our ally, and there are forces that would even impede our efforts to empirically tease the objective truth from the land—political and economic forces that would prefer to ignore, or worse, keep hidden certain sinister realities. Now we must bring to bear all our resources— intellectual, scientific, monetary, and philosophic, and yes even political— for surely simply doing the right thing has not entirely gone beyond the purview or scope of good politics. It is time to employ common sense, good science, and perhaps even some informed intuition to uncover the causes and mechanisms that are adversely affecting this rare ground and the voiceless inhabitants who live here.

Our culture creates the paradoxical illusion that the human species is somehow separated from the natural world, but it is only a clever and complex illusion—we are ultimately as bound to the mud as the toad. Sadly, many fail to grasp this most obvious perspective. Now it is time for us to make a dedicated effort to correct some of the damage we have wrought upon the land, not merely because these are our "natural resources"—a preposterously arrogant concept—or because as a species it serves our best interest in the most important ways imaginable, but perhaps more significantly because the world is an inherently sacred place, more important than the raw material that feeds the mill of human society. This planet is our sole progenitor. The earth is, of absolute necessity, more important than the people who live on it.

8

Skeletons in Our Closets

Consider that no one living can begin to visualize the expanse and depth of the eastern virgin forests that defined so much of this nation's early history. Likewise, the southern coastal wilderness, dotted with Native American communities, was a vision to early Spanish and European explorers that is today impossible to even imagine. Scarcely a remnant of the Great Plains habitat survives to prod our imagination as it stretched for thousands of square miles—a rolling ocean of grass—supporting millions of great beasts and the nomadic horse cultures with which the Indians of the American West are so strongly identified.

In contrast, gaze across any vista in Wyoming and know that some native hunter shared your same vantage point and an identical vision five thousand years earlier. You are joined by a companionship of perspective—at once startling, sobering, and for many, inspirational. This landscape permits us to make this fascinating connection to the past in every glance. The abstraction that normally characterizes our orientation to all the time that has gone before is absolved. As when walking on the stones of an ancient European castle, suddenly you know without doubt that, dejected and heartbroken, Anne Boleyn climbed these same granite stairs, and Henry's wretched and dreadful voice echoed through this same great hall. Similarly, the echoes of footsteps, voices, tramping hooves, and gunshots still reverberate from the granite walls and limestone canyons of Wyoming. For those who might listen, these persistent voices, though often faint, sometimes still cry out. There are places where history never fades but rather becomes a haunting that will not rest, will not be extinguished, and will not through irrelevance abate. As though wading through the fallen leaves of autumn, the ancient and deciduous vestiges of ten thousand summers are scattered about everywhere—the base of a paleo hunter's projectile point, a piece of polished greenstone shattered on the leg bone of a mighty bison, a gun flint, a buffalo hunter's spent cartridge tarnished and bent, or a sun-baked lens cap from a camera. Here, the past is mysteriously compressed into a single loosely integrated stratum. It is impossible to consider the ecology of Wyoming without seeing and feeling the living antiquity that pervades all your senses and surrounds you everywhere. And after all, in some sense, didn't the projectile point and the lens cap strike the ground almost simultaneously? Have we not all lived only in this present moment—the now? And so, is there any suggestion that either hunter's motivation could be more important, was either's quest more noble, was either's spirit more significant or more fragile? Setting aside all our troublesome but superfluous differences, it would appear that human history *is* but a single loosely integrated stratum. The cool, arid climate of the Wyoming high country will not allow the biological decomposition of the past, and geologically, it will not permit the past, for better or worse, to be buried.

Coming into this land many years ago, I immediately recognized that its rich and almost mythological history was still somehow alive. Like a loosely woven but durable fabric, this history I had heard so much of still enshrouded the present—perhaps torn and ragged but uninterrupted as it rolls eternally from the invisible loom of time. When we recall the history of the eastern United States we are confronted with a four-hundred-year abstraction that the human mind cannot easily negotiate. When we remember the dramatic history of the West, it is the generation of our grandparents whose lives were still richly entwined with those familiar legacies of glory, hardship, and horror. The native people of Wyoming, Indians and whites alike, are still richly steeped in this legacy. They seem to scarcely notice that they perpetuate the advantages and the scars of their unceasing historical continuum.

Everywhere you turn, there seems to be a historically significant family name, and as often, a face—the sons and daughters of historical peoples, places, personalities—direct living connections to events that transformed cultures and lives: the diverse Shoshones, with Sacagawea and the great Chief Washakie of the Shoshones; the Arapahos—great warriors of the plains; mountain men and trappers; miners; wagon scouts; notorious outlaws; famous lawmen; cavalry soldiers and Indian scouts who participated at the Battle of the Little Bighorn; people living who knew Butch Cassidy; people alive today who were born in tepees! These sons and daughters are to this day still cast on this same vast stage of a drama we all know. The wagon ruts remain, the buildings and cabins still stand, the uninterrupted human continuum is perpetuated in these faces as an uncanny reflection of a not so distant past—still reaping all that has been sown—a harvest of cattle, gold, timber, and tears—so many profits, so many losses. Seemingly indifferent to this extraordinary legacy, they appear to go about their lives in a most ordinary way—family ties, hard work, friends, and community. In spite of the necessity and perhaps even an unspoken effort to leave the lingering past behind—silently reconciling differences and exploring forgiveness— it is still possible to detect a lingering endowment, a faint repeating echo of earlier days. They are endowed with a past that perpetuates traditions of unimaginable courage and an iron will forged from blood and sweat. Here, the dust has not yet fully settled and the smoke has not entirely blown away. And in some, the ancient fire of unresolved injustice, residing now deep within the marrow of their bones, still smolders.

I came into Wyoming because I was drawn to the dynamic wildlife and geology—the wilderness and independence that I longed for and had not found in other environments. In addition to all this of course there was more, much more. I found myself in this rich wilderness ecology that was, at least in part, defined by these persistent cultures. To my delight and wonder, the Wyoming that I had stumbled onto in 1978 seemed to be all about cowboys and Indians, miners, trappers, loggers, and outfitters— people who made their living in large part from the land in the tradition of their forebears. To my surprise, the Wyoming wilderness was still providing people with a life, and most startling, without sacrificing the characteristics that define a landscape as truly wild. The culture was defined by cattle, horses, and elk meat, lodgepole pine house logs, fire wood, corrals and fences, pack strings, canvas-wall tents, and people who still actually needed a horse to get around. It seemed as though this was a place where people might still be living for the best reasons—living deliberately, living an authentic human life. This appeared to be a place that invited a resourceful person to try to make a life, and an ecology that might even dare a certain kind of person to make a home.

Many years later I find myself retreating into the most remote extremes of a land that is in general identified and defined by its remoteness. In an otherwise modern world that appears to abhor inaccessibility, I withdraw into these unpeopled islands of wilderness that still somehow seem to be accompanied by the prevailing winds of the past. It seems ironic, but it is almost impossible to discuss or understand the last ten thousand years of Wyoming ecology without including our own species. Even on the top of this remote mountain in this wild place, the palpable reality of Wyoming's rich history surrounds you everywhere, and even the Whiskey Mountain Bighorn Sheep Study is also inescapably and ironically woven into that history in the most stunning ways.

Early elk camp. *Copyright © Cathy Keene*

Gary Keene, an environmental scientist and intermittent employee of the sheep study, lives on the Wind River Indian Reservation where he and wife Cathy own a trading post called Ancient Ways just outside the town and reservation headquarters of Fort Washakie. Cathy is an "enrolled" Shoshone and a lifelong resident; Gary is white and has been married to Cathy for over twenty years. They have a beautiful young daughter, Kali. Ancient Ways buys and sells the rich bounty the Wyoming wilderness produces and the phenomenal arts and crafts that the Shoshones, Arapaho, and various other Indian people create from these revered and sacred artifacts of the earth. Hides, horns, antlers, bone, feathers, quills, claws, teeth, and furs are bought and sold as they are collected, and in return, all manner of functional, traditional, and sacred objects are skillfully crafted and returned for sale or trade.

Each year Gary hauls between five thousand and eight thousand pounds of freshly shed elk, moose, and deer antlers to the annual sale in Jackson, Wyoming. The antler of a bull elk is undoubtedly one of the most beautiful and intriguing forms in nature, and I have surely walked a thousand mountain miles in search of them, although my unfortunate predisposition is to keep all I find.

Gary's wife, Cathy, is, in a historical sense, well connected. She is the great-great-granddaughter of Edmore LeClair, and the LeClair name is still a familiar one on the reservation today. "Edmo" was raised in a Montana Flathead Indian village in the early 1800s, the son of an Iroquois woman and a well-known French physician turned fur trader and trapper named Mischelle LeClair. It is said that Mischelle removed the Blackfoot arrow from Shoshone Chief Washakie's face that created the scar visible in all his later photographs. Edmo's mother died, and Mischelle remarried a Shoshone-Bannock woman who spoke Flathead and Shoshone. In Edmo's youth, the family migrated out of Montana and took up residence at Fort Bridger in Wyoming, living among the eastern Shoshones and the colorful mountain men and trappers who were living and working in the area. Here young Edmo became acquainted with and developed lifelong relationships with the people of the eastern Shoshones including Sacagawea and her sons, Basil and Baptiste, as the four of them were often called upon to serve as translators. Edmo was present at the signing of the treaty of 1862, which formally designated the territory east of the Wind River Mountains as forever belonging to the Shoshones—the Wind River Indian Reservation. Many years later, an aging Edmo LeClair distinctly recalled the formalities and remembered Sacagawea standing and addressing the assembly. Edmo chose to live the rest of his life among the Shoshones in the Wind River Valley. Here he met and married Phyllisette Enos, daughter of John Enos, first cousin of Chief Washakie and the chief's best friend and confidant.

Shortly after marrying, Edmo LeClair joined in the war against the Sioux and Cheyenne and was employed as a multilingual scout for the U.S. Army and the Second Cavalry, speaking French, Spanish, Iroquois, English, Sioux, Flathead, Shoshone, and was a graceful, facile practitioner of Indian sign language.

Edmo lived a long life and had friends in high places. His granddaughter (Cathy's great aunt), named Mary Boyde, happened to be the common-law

Mary Boyde, third from right. *Copyright © Cathy Keene*

wife of another famous character in the history of the West, Robert Leroy Parker, also known as George "Butch" Cassidy. Butch and many of his "wild bunch" of business associates frequently passed through the Lander and reservation country as they traversed from Utah, South Pass, Lander, across the Wind River basin, up toward Thermopolis, and eventually to their sanctuary known as the Hole in the Wall. As a young man Butch Cassidy moved to the Lander area sometime in the late 1880s after a few years as a working cowboy, which included a hitch with the great Swan Land and Cattle Company, by far the largest outfit in Wyoming. Mary was the daughter of a Shoshone woman named Minnie LeClair, the daughter of Phyllisette and Edmo LeClair. Years later, in recalling her relationship with the young Butch Cassidy, Mary described herself as his common-law wife, and although their contact was intermittent, they maintained a relationship with letters and sporadic visits throughout Butch's outlaw years and even until his death in 1937.

Edmore LeClair was legendary even in his own time. After Butch finally gave up his outlaw ways, Edmo led a detachment of the U.S. Cavalry straight to the Hole in the Wall, where over twenty notorious outlaws were arrested and brought to justice, effectively ending an era. Edmo was noted not only as a great scout and tracker but also as a skilled hunter. His great-granddaughter, Cathy Keene, now carries on this legacy and has

Edmore LeClair. *Copyright © Cathy Keene*

become somewhat of a legend herself. Unlike many tribes, the Shoshones were endowed with a large part of their ancestral tribal lands. Nearly one hundred miles from north to south, running down the Continental Divide of the Wind River Mountains, up to the Owl Creek Mountains in the north and stretching east as far as the eye can see, the Wind River Reservation includes some of the most productive wildlife habitat in North America. It could be said that the native population here, to a greater or lesser degree, still subsists on the abundance of big game animals that roam the bountiful rivers, mountains, and rolling sagebrush prairies. Although she is as kind as any person you will ever meet, Cathy has the heart and soul of a hunter and is a drop-dead good shot. Every year she packs the family's freezers with moose, elk, whitetail and mule deer, antelope, and the occasional bighorn ram. In 2004 she made national headlines by harvesting the second biggest mule deer killed by a woman in history. Known now as the Keene buck, only a broken tine prevented it from being by far the largest!

For years Marion Doane has been a seasonal employee of the Bureau of Land Management, riding the remote sagebrush and desert country below South Pass and monitoring the impact of cattle grazing on millions of acres of solitary open range. Grazing rights have historically been granted in these vast areas—a certain number of cattle for a given number of days—dependent on the annual relative condition of the range. The impact of grazing rights granted to ranchers on public lands is an ongoing political hot potato in Wyoming.

Marion, in her early forties, is an attractive woman, lean and sturdy with sun-streaked light brown hair. Her apparent quiet demeanor is an expression not of shyness but rather of a confidence and fierce independence that characterizes the self-reliance Wyoming ranch life instills in its sons and in its daughters. She is experienced and authoritative in her understanding of the ecology of northern Wyoming. Marion is known and respected by the ranching community in the area, but if any cattleman wants to argue grazing rights on public lands, he had better have his facts straight or be ready to get an earful. Marion grew up a forth-generation Wyoming rancher, building fences, stacking hay, and working horseback. The historic Doane Ranch is a visible fixture a few miles north of Lander on the drive to Fort Washakie. With a comfortable log-and-wood-frame house nested among old cottonwoods, weathered corrals, log barns, and outbuildings

Freight wagon. *Copyright © Cathy Keene*

dating from one hundred years, it was one of the former quintessential old working cattle ranches in the Lander area. Like many women in Wyoming, Marion grew up subsistence hunting—mostly out of her back door in the

Wind River Mountains. Having killed her first elk at age eleven, she still apologizes that she didn't get another until she was thirteen. Marion is an expert archer, not only as a hunter, but she also has achieved some notoriety as a competitive archer. Regrettably, to definitively demonstrate the presence of certain diseases, the study has employed Marion to "harvest" a dying lamb. A terminally ill lamb can linger for days, wasting away, gradually becoming more crippled. But in nearly every case, death comes in the night from opportunistic predation, making collection impossible. Therefore as a consequence we must select a lamb that is near death and as quietly, humanely, and with as little disturbance to the other sheep as possible, put it down. It has been my unfortunate task to pack a dead lamb before any decomposition can occur and drive some 250 miles to the state lab in Laramie for necropsy. I have often worried about arriving at a trailhead with a dead bighorn lamb draped over my shoulders and the awkward task of explaining my justification to any Wyoming residents who might happen to be there. In this country I would worry that such a trespass might be cause for an immediate and justifiable homicide on the perpetrator—threatened species collection permit or not! Although admittedly, trailside lynchings have become unfashionable, Wyoming, with the full support of its residents, deals harshly with its game violators. Recently, the misidentification of a protected grizzly bear cost a black bear hunter $13,000. Illegally killing any antlered game animal in Wyoming can be punishable with a $10,000 fine.

Marion and her family are the most immediate living relatives of one of the most pivotal characters in all the rich history of the American West. Gustavus Cheyney Doane, although not highly celebrated and almost overlooked in the annals of American history, he was an integral participant in the important events that shaped the West we know today. This remarkable man appeared to be everywhere anything significant was occurring and often was the force that was making things happen. To list just a few of his accomplishments, he was a distinguished Civil War combat officer; provided security for the construction of the Union Pacific Railroad across Wyoming; played a vital role in the campaign to subdue Chief Joseph and the Nez Percé; established the first military fort in Montana, north of the Yellowstone; lived directly among the Crow Indians for several years, creating the famous Crow Scouts that fought so bravely with the U.S. Cavalry; fought in the opening battle of the Sioux

Indian Wars; was the first to officially explore and map Yellowstone; fought in the final campaign to finally subdue Geronimo and the Apaches; led the first official expedition into the Arctic, and on and on. No single individual in the West ever made more real history. The epitome of the career military man, Gustavus Doane was a personality who chose undying resolve and dedication over flamboyance and has never fully received the recognition history owes him. Why Hollywood has never jumped all over this man's life is mystifying.

Cavalry maneuvers. *Copyright © Cathy Keene*

The National Archives in Washington, D.C., is replete with his many contributions that survive in the form of his voluminous and articulate military logs as well as stacks of detailed maps.

John Colter of the Lewis and Clark expedition was probably the first white person to see the Yellowstone country, in around 1806. However, Colter's ravings about an otherworldly wilderness that belched fire and brimstone was dismissed as lunacy for half a century and described humorously as "Colter's Hell." Jim Bridger ventured into this strange land decades later but failed in his only effort to guide government agents into the area. It was Gustavus Doane who first familiarized himself with this astonishing landscape and brought the first literate descriptions to the attention of the U.S. government. Although constituting only a small chapter in this extraordinary man's life that involved thirty consecutive years of uninterrupted warfare in wilderness environments, Doane is best remembered for his unique contribution in the recognition and preservation of the area we all know today as Yellowstone Park. Gustavus was successful in petitioning the U.S. military as well as Congress, receiving authority to organize the famous Washburn-Langford-Doane Expedition of 1870. In 1871 he wrote his seminal report that resulted in the more definitive exploration known as the Hayden Expedition. Geologist Ferdinand V. Hayden became the official leader of the team that included eminent scientists of the day and famous photographer William Henry Jackson. Doane and his men of course provided all the logistical organization and security, and guided the team through this labyrinth of teeming wildlife and geothermal wonder. Some members of these expeditions literally refused to maintain journals for fear of being branded liars—fearing that people would never believe their descriptions. The immediate consequence of the Hayden Expedition was the establishment by Congress in 1872 of Yellowstone—First National Park of the United States. It is mind-numbing to consider that the creation of Yellowstone National Park occurred years before the Indian wars that would eventually allow even preliminary exploration and settlement in the area. This was still essentially an unexplored wilderness with economic potential that had not been described or evaluated. The creation of this park is an almost inexplicable visionary gesture. Bear in mind that the western expansion of the day was defined entirely by the underlying rapacious and avaricious designs originally set forth by the Jeffersonian economic expansionist philosophies of Manifest Destiny. Even the concept of a national park was unprecedented and entirely unique in the world.

Now I sit on this rocky outcrop, shaking my head in disbelief, staring out 150 miles across this essentially identical wilderness as it remains, in essence, unaltered by the hand of man. This same overlook could be a smoking tangle of urban development were it not for the extraordinary wisdom and generosity of these statesmen in Washington who, of course, recognized that logistics would probably never permit them to ever lay eyes on such a remote and inaccessible wilderness.

Ironically, in the misguided adventures of the summer of 1876, these three—Doane, Shoshone Chief Washakie, and scout Edmore LeClair—

would all participate directly in the complex events that culminated in the Battle of the Little Bighorn. Three relatively small detachments of soldiers, Indian scouts, and cavalry were to unknowingly try to surround and defeat the largest and most well-armed band of warring Indians ever assembled. To further compound the irony, all these three remarkable historical personalities are directly related to the small handful of people involved with the Whiskey Mountain Bighorn Sheep Study. But then, this is Wyoming.

Kathy Pappas has relatives in Nebraska and moved to Lander in 1973. She owns one of those great old houses built in the 1930s or 1940s with multiple steep roofs and dormers, stairways running every which way, arches, pantries, garages, mudrooms, and sunrooms. Kathy is the business manager and bookkeeper for the sheep study, and for members of the study coming down from the field, she is alternately nurse, answering service, housemother, and on occasion, resident psychotherapist. She is unbridled energy and enthusiasm, and her wit is so quick it is frightening. She gets paid as seldom as John and is the glue that holds everything together. When we are not in the mountains, Kathy's home is headquarters, staging area, laboratory, and often sleeping quarters for biologists and friends who are either on their way up or down the mountain. It is appropriately referred to as Mission Control. At Kathy's, a biologist can pull a plastic container from her refrigerator, casually sit down at the dinning room table, and spend two hours sorting through a hundred ziplock bags filled with fecal samples from bighorn sheep, mountain lions, and bears, and she will never bat an eye. "Make sure my cats don't get into that."

Kathy is also well adapted to backcountry living as a horse packer and a backpacker. These days she is committed to the latter and has owned her own string of pack goats. This is a woman who is perfectly comfortable packing into the mountains or the Red Desert alone and drinking up the solitude for a night or two. She loves wild horses and wildflowers but is quick to admit she is made uncomfortable by the company of bears. Her old saddle horse shares the pasture with the goats and now serves principally as an old friend and perhaps the most fortunate of retirees.

Prior to her husband's tragic early death several years ago, Kathy would spend weeks on horse packing trips with her best friend, Gale Washakie.

Every year Kathy and Gale, with their husbands John Pappas and Bob Jacob, would lead a string of packhorses and set up hunting camps miles up in the Wind River Mountains in pursuit of elk, moose, or deer. Kathy does not hunt, but Gale, in the rich tradition of her ancestry, is a great hunter.

Gale Washakie is the great-great-granddaughter of the legendary Chief Washakie. When Kathy first introduced me to Gale in the spring of 2001, she had just returned from Washington, D.C., where she was invited to serve as a family representative, along with others from the Wind River Indian Reservation, in the ceremonial unveiling of a monumental bronze sculpture of the great chief when it was permanently installed in the Capitol Rotunda.

Gale and Bob share a comfortable log home in a Wyoming ranch setting, a few miles south of Lander. Bob is friendly and outgoing, loves to talk packhorses and elk hunting, and complains about the overabundance of grizzly bears that are beginning to plague his camps and fellow hunters. Gale has the dark hair and strong handsome features that distinguish her as heir to her great Shoshone heritage. She is comfortable talking about her celebrated great-grandfather, as well as the many positive changes that we have observed among the local Indian people in the last twenty-five years. (In this part of the country, Indians do refer to themselves as "Indians" and seem to rarely use the term Native American.)

Chief Washakie was born among the Flathead Indians in southern Montana around 1796. His father died in a raid by a band of Blackfoot warriors that devastated the village. His mother fled into the wilderness with her children but was eventually taken in by a village of sympathetic Lemhi (a group of northern Shoshonean people). Here Washakie found a safe and protective childhood but eventually, as a young man, was encouraged to join a group of Bannock who had known his father.

At some point in his early adult life, he came to live with the eastern Shoshones and immediately began to distinguish himself as a great leader and warrior, eventually emerging to become their chief. He died in Fort Washakie in 1900 at the age of 104. Actively leading his people until his death, he maintained his status as unchallenged chief of the Shoshone people for over half a century. There are no known photographs of a young Washakie, but it is obvious from photographs taken in his later years that he was a monumentally handsome man. He, without doubt, was that rare enlightened and charismatic individual who comes along only once in a great while and who by perfect timing and extraordinary circumstance is called upon and allowed to rise to the pinnacle of his potential. If it had not been for Washakie's strength of character and a rare wisdom that must have originated somewhere between divine prophecy and genius, the history of Wyoming, the Shoshone people, and indeed much of the West would be quite different. Washakie was a visionary in the truest sense of the word.

However, in spite of Washakie's willingness to bend to the will of the U.S. government and its specific demands for the disposition of the Shoshones, his people were still forced to suffer depredation, neglect, and hardship, as there was failure by government officials, time and time again, to honor the tenants of their negotiations and agreements. It was only because of Washakie's iron will and leadership that the diverse groups of Shoshones did not in frustration join with other native peoples in the wars that would ultimately spell disaster for so many. The Shoshonean linguistic group involves many diverse peoples geographically and culturally. And although Washakie was technically the chief of the eastern Shoshones, his influence was strongly felt among these other related peoples that he had known so well, such as the Lemhi and Bannock. It was with Washakie's intimate understanding and encouragement that often kept the Bannock from all-out hostilities.

Washakie was ultimately successful in keeping his people alive and living together on a large and desirable portion of their ancestral homeland. From the Sweetwater River in the south to the Wind River and the Owl Creek Mountains to the north and the great Wind River Mountains to the west, Washakie laid out the geographical boundaries and was, over all, successful in securing the heart of the Shoshones' native territory—an area that would be most likely to provide them with sufficient resources for the entire year. Despite the willingness of the Shoshone people to cooperate with and even contribute to the desires of the U.S. government, they would continue to suffer the abuses that have defined the experience of Native American people generally. But, even through the difficulties and grief the Shoshone people endured, and although deaths outpaced births on the reservation for many years, Washakie saw his people begin to successfully adapt, if not actually prosper, before his death in 1900. Nevertheless, even after one hundred more years, his people are still suffering the effects of their original subjugation, internment, and the conspiracy to deprive them of their rich and ancient cultural heritage.

It would be unfair, or at least disappointing, to discuss the living history of Wyoming or even the ecology generally without some reference to the cattle industry, and in particular, to that great American icon, the cowboy. As luck and irony would have it, the Whiskey Mountain Bighorn Sheep Study also has a direct connection to the life and ways of the working cowboy in Wyoming and to that livelihood that has captured the imagination of so many. Economically, socially, and environmentally, cattle and their husbandry have shaped the ecological and historical identity of this country in ways that are visible everywhere. This industry has been idealized, misunderstood, and romanticized on a scale that can only be explained in terms of the importance it represents as a component of our great American psyche and the well-articulated mythology that has emerged. Just as the Wyoming cattle industry has been forged and defined by this rugged land, not unlike the native peoples who are also in many ways the cultural expressions of their ecology, so too is the Wyoming cowboy created from the rigors of this wilderness landscape.

The cowboy is in some way it seems burdened with our society's need to explain who we are as individuals. Every culture must of necessity develop a mythology—a mechanism to explain who its members are, where they came from, and by what means they will proceed into the future—a need to clarify and bring into focus some socially unifying vision of the world.

Overflowing with the classical elements of the mythological journey of the hero, it has been suggested, that metaphorically, Lewis and Clark's triumphant odyssey could be described as America's great voyage of discovery (Swanson, 2002). In the mythological voyage of discovery, typically the hero hears the call to adventure, perhaps through the urging of a great leader or wizard and proceeds to embark on some perilous journey into the unknown. He suffers unspeakable hardship and tribulation; is confronted with seemingly impossible obstacles, strange beasts, and dangerous exotic cultures; and yet with near superhuman endurance, strength, fortitude, and a good fortune that could only suggest divine intervention, is triumphant. The hero is ultimately transformed by the attainment of esoteric knowledge, insight, and revelation—the initiation is complete. One returns triumphant and shares not the wealth of gold and plunder but rather the riches of a newfound wisdom and enlightenment. "Departure, initiation, and return"—Lewis and Clark's journey as a classic mythical odyssey is the perfect metaphor.

If Lewis and Clark's phenomenal voyage could be the mythological vehicle representing our collective cultural identity, then the lonely cowboy, real or imaginary, could represent the mythological model that personifies the American ideal of individuality. The cowboy is thought to possess those universal iconic attributes we as Americans identify with so strongly: independence, self-reliance, physical strength, courage, sacrifice, endurance, and a rugged but iron-clad sense of right and wrong. In some way, each of us is heir to this universal American identity. Whether as myth or reality, the Wyoming cowboy may still exist and is the one who, although unseen and uncelebrated, is truly, as in the thoughtful words of Joseph Campbell, "the hero with a thousand faces."

Part 2

9

DISCOVERING A CULTURE OF WILDERNESS

I blundered upon Wyoming in the late 1970s by accident at an awkward moment in life while hunting for something that I had missed, excluded, or perhaps forgotten. Vaguely, as if from some ancient primal memory, I sensed that some possible refuge might exist in the high country. Perhaps I still entertained some romantic notions about the possibility of a life that could be more meaningful, more significant. Such a refuge might exist where continental land masses collide and grind together—fault block, subduction, and uplift—the strong backbone of the earth. Maybe some ancient and organic part of my being instinctively knew that my prognosis called for nothing less than the eruption and exposure of solid batholithic granite, and I needed therapeutic orogeny on a grand scale. Certainly it was obvious that I needed to be keeping better company, creatures that might express integrity and nobility, beings of uncompromising honesty, like moose, elk, grizzly bears, and golden-mantled ground squirrels. The first casualty of a broken heart is a loss of confidence in the ability to make a decent decision, to merely do the right thing. And so instinctively, like some wounded animal, I was seeking any safe refuge—longing simply for clear air, a vast horizon, and to breathe deeply. Like so many others, grave disappointment had been turned inward, and the vacuum created by so many lost ideals cast a historically healthy person into what had apparently become some bottomless well of darkness and sorrow. Depression is self-consciousness turned septic, and nothing is as exhausting as the pathology of the ever present self. Months of agony taught me only three things— the well is indeed bottomless, it was without a doubt bigger than I, and the only possible way out of such a place is to deliberately choose not to be there. Instinctively I knew only to run like hell—metaphorically and physically. Mine was not a heroic call to adventure but the mere necessity to make a blind retreat.

So within a blurring forty-eight-hour period, I put all my worldly possessions in storage and loaded my pickup with clothes, boots, all the old camping gear I could find lying around, and my old Winchester .30-30 rifle. I had no ideas about the rifle, it just somehow seemed appropriate. The few cramped spaces left within my small truck easily contained my last vestiges of initiative and motivation. Without any particular expectation or destination, the truck left what I had known as home in northern Florida and began heading in a general northwesterly direction, leaving behind a failed marriage, a disappointing academic career, idealistic aspirations, an entire forty-acre farm and house created from scratch—years of gut-busting work—all come to nothing but perhaps a pitiful few dollars in the bank.

A day or two into the trip, I recalled that two friends had moved to some place called Lander in northwestern Wyoming. I only knew that Wyoming lies generally above Colorado and assumed it would be en route to the northern Rockies and British Columbia—a more or less arbitrary destination. With a simple pay-phone call, a brief conversation, and an enthusiastic, "Come on!" I now had at least one safe stopover point on my reluctant odyssey.

Thoreau quoted a shepherd of antiquity: "There are none happy in the world but beings who enjoy freely a vast horizon."

For many of us, unknowingly, section lines are such an incremental part of our lives that they have probably become a part of our neurological architecture. Unconsciously, the "section"—a 640-acre square—must at least contribute to our defining confusion as a species by its inherent geometric inability to conform to an otherwise spherical planet. Cartographers and surveyors are made eternally miserable by the impossible task of dividing a sphere into squares. Their persistence is, if nothing else, commendable, their perseverance praiseworthy. Native American people, with a strong cultural orientation to the circle, have long been puzzled by the white European preoccupation with the straight line and the square. Surely native people understood calculus five thousand years before Archimedes but saw no need to dwell on the obvious. Passing into Wyoming, one can eventually become disoriented, as all reference to section line geometry is abandoned. From the air, the transition is startling.

Three days earlier, in May 1978, it was summer in Florida—hot, humid, buzzing—but then dumbfounded, I drove east beyond Casper, Wyoming, into what appeared to be the dead of winter, leaving springtime somewhere back in Colorado. Greeted by a blinding expanse of whiteness, I began my final leg toward Lander, clearly unprepared. Without the advantage of four-wheel drive I contemplated the 150 miles of apparent uncertainty that stretched before me with no farm, no ranch, no fence, no power lines, no towns, and no self-confidence. Finally, I passed a place called Hell's Half Acre, which appeared to be an aging compound with commercial characteristics including what may have been a single gas pump, perhaps some groceries, and possibly even some motel space, all perched on a large, eroded abyss with all geological origins obscured by billowing depths of heavy snow. Several pickup trucks were parked there beside towering piles of bulldozed snow and all had heavy chains on their tires. Wood smoke curled up from one building offering a warm invitation, but I nervously proceeded like a kid in my first driver's education class. This Florida boy had never driven on a highway that was completely obscured by snow and ice. Not only was mine the only vehicle on that empty highway, it was also apparently the only vehicle in Wyoming without chains. Many miles farther, I ascended a gentle incline of several miles, and just before I reached the summit I was consoled to see a large state highway sign that read PRAIRIE DOG TOWN—2 MILES. I immediately decided to stop for a snack and gasoline and perhaps some information on the highway and weather conditions between there and Lander. Cresting the hill, I was shocked to see the road disappearing ten miles over the next horizon, dividing the otherwise uninterrupted wilderness that stretched in an enormous radius around me. There was, as far as the eye could see, no suggestion of human occupation. As I descended the long slope to more level ground, I began noticing small dark silhouettes peppering the snow on both sides. Suddenly I saw a small bloody casualty in the road and realized I was thoughtlessly speeding through Prairie Dog Town.

The despair that had been my traveling companion then seemed even more imposing in this intimidating winter landscape that I had been totally unprepared for. In less than four days I had left summer on the Gulf Coast, springtime in Colorado, and driven into the unexpected depths of a polar winter. Wyoming appeared to be a lunar landscape blanketed in deep snows and entirely devoid of the green alpine meadows, towering spruce, wildflowers, and the placid beaver ponds I had envisioned. This was not the safe refuge I had anticipated—not some soothing alpine scene from *The Sound of Music* but more like a bitter scene from *Nanook of the North*. "Christ!" I shouted. "This is dogsled country!"

Everywhere I looked there were antelope in small groups of five or six and then occasionally fifty in a herd. Mule deer stood or browsed in snow-covered clumps of sagebrush, and though less abundant than antelope, nearly always visible as darker figures in the pale, featureless landscape. The sun was obscured by low churning white clouds seething before a foreboding blue-black curtain of sky. A steady gale-force wind blew from the northwest while periodic gusts rattled my truck and threatened to send me careering across the other lane into a deep snowbank waiting on the other side. Eventually, a strange-looking irregularity appeared on the distant western horizon—more storm clouds or perhaps something else? An occasional dash of sunlight broke through but was soon swallowed up again by the swirling mists above. Driven by the wind, hypnotic curls of dry snow danced in spirals across the road ahead, while handfuls of windblown snow slid across the windshield from right to left. Sunlight peered out of great low-hanging cottony clouds on the horizon revealing strange irregular forms looming in the distance: the unmistakable ruggedness of a far range of mountains. My heart quickened at the site of so much potentially inaccessible wilderness. Distant faces of black vertical rock with alternate exposures of blazing white ice foreshadowed the promise of great beasts and expanses of remote wilderness—the Wind River Mountains. For the first time in months and perhaps years, enthusiasm and a forgotten sense of wonder washed over me. A warm sense of well-being began to thaw some part of me that had turned to ice, not from the snows of Wyoming but rather from a great winter in my life. As if casting hard, frozen steel in warm waters, I felt a distinct moment when something brittle and binding within finally cracked.

Like a kid at Christmas, to me Wyoming and the Wind River Mountains appeared to be just so many presents waiting to be opened. Proceeding westward, the mountains rose ever more grand and enormous, stretching before me from south to north, from distant horizon to distant horizon. By late afternoon, I dropped over an escarpment and looked down on the little town of Lander sitting nestled at the foot of the mountains in a valley created by a small winding river issuing from the mouth of a great canyon. The river is lined with old cottonwoods and willows, and the town is forested with tall spruce and fir that seem to be spilling off the higher slopes of the mountains. Ranch lands surrounded the town, and everywhere cattle and horses were silhouetted against the rolling snow-covered hillsides. A pall of wispy blue wood smoke hanging low over the snowy village was a reminder that some warm, cozy spot may await.

Sid and Nickie lived in the town of Lander where Nickie worked as a registered nurse in the emergency room at the little community hospital; Sid was a farrier, shoeing horses professionally in Wyoming. Lander is a classic 1890s brick-front main street town, and so directions were not hard to follow and ran something like: "Come into town, turn right on Fourth Street, and look for my brown GMC a few blocks down the street on the right." Two minutes into town and I was there. After greetings and a cup of hot coffee, we stood around the woodstove while I ranted about the weather. Even though it was getting late, Sid wanted to waste no time in my orientation. Sid and I grew up together and so he basically knows what I'm all about. He said, "Get in the truck—you're not going to believe it." I climbed up into his big-wheeled pickup, he locked the hubs, shoved it into all fours, and we drove through town. Following a paved road that heads toward the mountains and the mouth of the canyon, the snow-plowed road ran out, but Sid, without slowing down, plowed through two feet of fresh snow and entered the canyon. The canyon is, in a word, immense.

Sinks Canyon is carved by glaciers, exposing miles of towering cliffs of pale yellow limestone that easily rise a thousand feet, with old-growth spruce and fir surrounding a roaring whitewater river known as the middle fork of the Popo Agie (pronounced *Papohsha*). The river cascades down from miles above, originating in the many glaciers and melting snows of the Wind River Mountain high country. Mysteriously, not far up the canyon, the river disappears into an abyssal hole in the earth and then reappears one-half mile back down the canyon—the Sinks and the Rise of the Sinks. The entire canyon is either on Wyoming state land or in the Shoshone National Forest. Several miles up the canyon, after passing mule deer and my first Rocky Mountain bighorn sheep, I noticed occasional marshy areas surrounding the river that supported partially frozen beaver ponds, which were in turn surrounded by waist-high and head-high willows. Suddenly, enormous black shapes materialized in deep snows—not one or two but a dozen, impossible in stature, improbable in appearance, living vestigial remnants from the Pleistocene—the Shiras moose. Standing above the willows, they browsed on the tender tips, giving willows everywhere a pruned and well-manicured look. This creature may average close to a thousand pounds with bulls sometimes pushing two. The moose ignored us. All my remaining apprehension dissolved in these perfect surroundings, and I realized that I need go no farther. This was exactly the right place, and at least for the moment one journey was concluded and another had just begun.

May in Wyoming is in fact spring, and the deep snowfall from the days before was only one of many minor setbacks in a long, slow process—merely a lingering seasonal ambiguity between winter and summer that is characteristic of the northern Rocky Mountains. The next few weeks and months would be a time of continuous revelation as this wonderful land gradually revealed itself. However, even the next day began ushering in sights and experiences that I could little imagine.

Awaking the following morning with visions of moose droppings dancing in my head, I sprang to my feet, grabbed my camera, and proceeded back up to the canyon so I might add "moose" to my bulging inventory of reference slides. Having had more or less intimate experience with other North American cervids—deer and elk—I was anxious to document and perhaps even interact with a creature that was a complete mystery to me, tall tales, mythology, and reference books notwithstanding. In thirty minutes Sid and I arrived back at the beaver ponds to find two cow moose standing belly-deep, browsing quietly on aquatic vegetation. Cameras swinging from around my neck, I trudged and thrashed through waist-deep snow to the ponds below. The weather was changing as billowing clouds dashed by with stiff breezes blowing straight down the canyon. Warmer temperatures and wind conspired to dislodge great quantities of wet snow from the boughs of tall spruce, lodgepole pine, and fir. Washtub-size heaps of heavy snow slipped from high pendulant branches and fell heavily around me—*ka-whump*! I plowed toward the great beasts feeding only one hundred yards ahead. Moving closer, my pace slowed and I begin shooting film—not knowing when my proximity might force the moose to move away. Yet, with only the most casual glances in my clumsy direction, they continued to feed. They grew ever larger as I neared until I was in a state of disbelief that anything this far from a Nebraska feed lot could be so enormous. My breathing became labored as I struggled at seven thousand feet in deep snow with an excitement that resided somewhere between exaltation and fear. I lay roughly prostrate in the deep snow, fifty feet from two of the Northern Hemisphere's largest wild animals with Sid's final admonition still echoing in my head, "Don't get too close." At last I began to become aware of a chill resulting from wet jeans, boots, and from great gobs of snow that had fallen on my head and down my back. Then suddenly I heard *ka-whump* . . . *ka-whump* again, then *ka-whump* a third time right at my outstretched feet. Realizing that no trees or pendulant spruce limbs were nearby, I removed the camera from my eye and turned to look behind me. The biggest bull moose in Wyoming had just walked up and was now towering directly over me. He stared straight down on me with fierce dark brown eyes set on either side of a head the size of an upholstered lounge chair. I had no recourse but to stare back up into his great countenance and inquisition. I was without question the most humble creature he had encountered in his mighty life. Moose are strange creatures in our eyes to be sure, but I was struck by the realization that there is absolutely nothing awkward or amusing about the appearance or behavior of the North American moose. With a turn of his great black neck and massive shoulders, he walked with tall silver-legged strides calmly back to the edge of the timber. My heart raced—I sat nervous and shivering in the wet cold. I wasn't sure what had just happened. Had I just dodged a very large bullet or was that my first kiss? Could I have just had an audience with God? What fear was this that parted my numbing face with such an uncontrollable grin?

I was absolutely sure of only two things about this moose and our brief encounter. With respect to his appraisal of me, he displayed a conspicuous absence of any fear or intimidation; neither was there, mercifully, any apparent malevolence in his disposition—an inclination, for which I will always be grateful.

Many strange events occurred in that first Wyoming spring, but among the strangest was the inexplicable appearance of my wife, Tommie. We had been separated for many months, and in my estimation things were long since irretrievable and hopeless—estranged. That's one of those underhanded nonwords designed to slide by without notice of the actual brutality implied, like eviscerate, emasculate, disembowel. But far beyond my ability to speculate about the goings-on in the universe, here she was. Perhaps it was the otherworldliness of Wyoming coupled with the calming normalcy of our old friends Sid and Nickie, but without any apparent dialogue or reconciliation regarding the excruciating events of the past year, we seemed to just start living a new life. In some way we both knew that things could never be the same—the old water-under-the-bridge phenomenon. And also, if for no other reason, we had been honest. Honesty is of course, the most vicious and cruel weapon in the arsenal of all the so-called virtues. I submit that more lives have been destroyed by honesty than all the wars in history. As my dear mother never tired of saying, "Take care, the word once spoken takes on a life of its own."

One evening Tommie and I returned to Sid and Nickie's house after a long day of exploring anything accessible by a two-wheel-drive pickup in the Lander area—red rock canyons, herds of mule deer browsing in sagebrush draws, and great expanses of snow-covered mountain slopes dotted with hundreds of grazing elk. While we were there, Sid and Nickie had a visitor. Mark Ramsey was a twenty-two-year-old uncompromising and legitimate born-in-the-saddle working cowboy. Lean, lanky, and raw boned, Mark grinned widely and reached out an enormous hand, extending beyond the edges of his horseshoe-scarred black leather cuffs. Earth stained, hardened, and rough, his hand, not unlike the horse's hooves he had been struggling with all day seemed to swallow mine in his exuberance. Light blond hair jutted out from under a dusty black hat and framed a ruddy snow-burned face with wire-rimmed glasses and intense blue eyes. Mark, with a conspicuous midwestern accent tempered slightly with just a hint of a John Wayne drawl, said, "Well, Joe Boy, what do you think about Wyoming? Bet you're not used to all this snow." (I was nearly ten years older than Mark, but from that moment on he always referred to me as Joe Boy.)

Although Sid had only been in Lander for a year or so, he had already met every rancher within a hundred-mile radius. Like Sid, Mark was also known as a skilled farrier, among a long list of other related professions, and was working with Sid on some of the bigger ranches. Some ranches have large strings of horses that all need to be reshod in the spring, and the two of them could complete a job in one day that otherwise would cause one person to drive long distances back and forth or stay overnight.

We would soon discover that Mark's enthusiasm was infectious and that he had a remarkable way of including people in his life. Before we had finished two beers, we had already finalized plans to hunt, fish, pick up elk antlers and arrowheads; pan for gold; drive six hundred head of cattle thirty-five miles out to their summer range on the Sweetwater; break some horses; cut house logs, corral poles, and firewood; and naturally assuming that anyone can rope, attend a jackpot team roping on a local ranch where he graciously offered to be the "header" if I would rather catch "heels." Unknowingly, I had just met the leverage that would cause the doors of opportunity to fly open all over Wyoming. Mark Ramsey would be a familiar fixture in my life for the next twenty years.

We had only begun to become acquainted with the cowboys of Wyoming when there was a knock on the door. Sid answered the door to find a young Native American woman standing on the porch. Reluctantly, after numerous invitations from Sid, the woman stepped into the house. With a weak and apprehensive voice she asked for Nickie, indicating that she had heard that Nickie was "one of the good ones." We assumed that Nickie had been identified as someone particularly sympathetic to the native people who occasionally end up in the emergency room. Nickie identified herself and listened as the young woman complained that she needed help, but when questioned about the specifics, she became rambling and evasive. My heart sank as I heard Nickie try to console her but ultimately could only suggest that she go to the emergency room across town. With a faded flannel shirt, old jeans, dirty tennis shoes, and an unmistakable mask of sorrow, she was still, with long raven hair and delicate features, a vision. This stunningly beautiful woman, whose difficult life had hurried her youth into some ageless netherworld between sixteen and thirty, could in another time or in another world, have been a carefree prom queen. Her words were difficult to follow and slurred slightly with a shyness that was being diluted by some intoxicating substance—probably alcohol. As I looked down on her young, graceful brown arms, I flinched at the sight of numerous long, thick scars covering her arms and hands.

The realization overtook me that these scars were probably the result of either a long history of suicide attempts, self-mutilation, or possibly even knife fights. Sid offered to drive her to the emergency room, but she quietly declined, turned, and disappeared into the cold night. Nickie was never sure why the young woman had found her or what she was really asking for.

In the 1970s Lander was surrounded by three defining entities: old working cattle ranches, the Wind River Indian Reservation, and the seemingly unbounded wilderness of the Red Desert, the Wind River Mountains, and the greater Yellowstone ecosystem to the north. Any drive down Main Street always featured cattlemen and cowhands pulling horse trailers or driving old wood stake body stock trucks. The dark hair and strong faces of the local native people were always visible, and not uncommonly in springtime, five or six hundred head of cattle would be driven straight through the middle of town on the way to their summer range, twenty or thirty miles away. Drivers just sat patiently in their vehicles occasionally waving to a familiar cowhand while the lazy, bawling crowd passed. Although Lander was a busy little community involved in all the many affairs of any American town, it seemed nevertheless to be all about cowboys and Indians. My motives had been all about solitude and wilderness, but I found the people and culture of Wyoming to be, in a multitude of ways, irresistible.

In many mountain states of the West, roads and highways have been constructed through the mountains like they are on Georgia flat land, providing vehicle access to high country environments. Thankfully, there are no major roads into the Wind River Mountains, and the few dirt roads and unimproved "two tracks" are completely inaccessible until late June or early July. My first forays into the wilderness ecology of Wyoming involved parking on or near a highway and hiking often many miles on foot. Only one paved road circles the entirety of the Wind River Mountains. A loop would involve driving twenty miles south out of Lander, traveling west over South Pass, then turning north and passing up through Pinedale and finally Jackson Hole before turning east beyond the Tetons. The last leg would then entail climbing east over Togwatee Pass, eventually turning south again along the eastern slopes through the Wind River Indian

Reservation, and back to Lander. In good weather, the trip could be made in one long day in a drive of about four hundred miles. South Pass and Togwatee Pass in the north would allow the only direct proximity to actual mountain country. The remainder of the circumnavigation involves vistas gained from distances of ten or more miles from the foot of the mountains. South Pass, some thirty miles south of Lander, provided my most convenient access to the mountain high country for the first few months.

Early spring is the perfect time to begin exploring Wyoming. The Wind River Mountain high country runs for about 120 miles along the Continental Divide from southeast to northwest. It is another fifty miles wide, which would average out to contain some six thousand square miles. Further, these mountains are surrounded by many more thousands of square miles of wilderness, including the more-or-less contiguous greater Yellowstone ecosystem in the north and the expansive Red Desert country to the south. It is almost impossible to grasp the magnitude and vastness of this wilderness without actually flying over a great expanse of northwestern Wyoming. Only then does it become appropriately incomprehensible. With the exception of bears, which of course hibernate, the other great beasts and a multitude of smaller ones must somehow survive the cold temperatures and an accumulation of snow that by spring can pack to over thirty feet. Remarkably, everyone is forced to abandon the abundance of the summer high country with its vast inaccessibility and migrate out of the mountains. As deep snow begins to arrive in autumn, animals come spilling out of the mountains and find forage as best they can on the narrow but grassy lower sagebrush-covered slopes, as well as in nearby drainages, prairies, and deserts. In a period of weeks in late fall, thousands of creatures that would otherwise be dispersed throughout thousands of square miles of high wilderness are now concentrated on the relatively narrow unforested periphery. Herds are visible everywhere. Enormous gatherings of elk, deer, antelope, and large numbers of moose, bighorn sheep, and smaller mammals all convene. And, of course, all their predators have followed the crowds onto open range—coyotes, mountain lions, foxes, wolves, and so on. Everywhere you look there is activity.

After the long Wyoming winter, spring becomes a possibility, however remote, and these exposed and vulnerable species of wildlife are anxious to return to easier times with the solitude and abundance that the high mountains provide. As the melting process begins to quicken, an anticipation and eagerness develops among many of the animals, and they press ever upward, focusing their attention on the zone of the thaw as it slowly works its way up and into the mountains. For weeks and months I too followed this zone of early spring as it progressively melted upward—first on the wide expanses of the lower sagebrush slopes, and eventually up through miles of forested ridges, drainages, and finally by July up into the alpine country above the timberline. It offered the perfect opportunity to explore each zone of the mountain in detail with its particular physiographic and environmental characteristics—the geology, hydrology, fauna, and flora. Wyoming was experiencing winters during these years that were on average much more severe than those of today. Snowfall accumulation was greater, temperatures were considerably colder, and the winter season longer. Mortality or winterkill was more serious during these years, resulting in an abundance of dead animals that were being uncovered and exposed as the warmer weather moved up the mountain. Most animals are stressed from the long winter, and by spring many are desperate for the tender green things that are beginning to appear, and many predators become opportunistic scavengers as weakened animals continue to die, and winter-killed carcasses that have been stored in nature's deep freeze are eventually revealed. Even though snows are still deep and temperatures are quite cold, bears leave the comfort of their winter dens early to take advantage of this winter-stored abundance.

Growing up in the rural Deep South, I was no stranger to bear country, but with the exception of raising and interacting with captive bears while managing a zoo during college, I could count a lifetime of fleeting wild bear encounters on one hand. In Wyoming I would see that many or more in one day. Although black bear attacks are rare, especially in the east, western black bears are considered more unpredictable. Unlike grizzlies, which are generally provoked into a brief mauling by some perceived intrusion or trespass on their sense of space, a black bear attack is nearly always motivated by a predatory urge. It's inadvisable to accommodate a black bear by playing dead. As the zone of the thaw reveals the winter's die-off, a multitude of bears begin focusing their attention in this area. My personal learning curve was steep regarding wild bears, but my eagerness to be in their company was insatiable. I intentionally sought them out and naively felt no fear or apprehension while in their presence. However, bears are at the least shy creatures if not downright snobbish about the company they keep. I found that although encounters were daily and almost predictable, these bears were unaccustomed to the presence of humans and displayed little or no curiosity in my comings and goings and would interact only momentarily before they made a departure. No creature has more highly developed senses or is warier, and so in all but the rarest occasions did I ever see a bear before it saw me. As a result, many of my encounters involved a brief glimpse of a bear's backside.

One of my first adventures on Limestone Mountain involved an early morning trek with Tommie across the long eastern front slope. We arbitrarily pulled off the highway about two-thirds of the way up the timbered portion of the mountain. The eastern slope consists of a confusing series of steep drainages, and the moisture that is concentrated there supports thick aspen and luxuriant stands of spruce and fir that grow up to the low canyon walls bordering the creeks on either side. Creeks are fed by snow runoff and groundwater that dashes or babbles down most of these drainages that are contained by intermittent canyon walls. These small canyons, with walls no higher than thirty feet, will split into progressively smaller canyons and tributaries higher up the mountain. The slopes between the drainages are sometimes broad with dense stands of lodgepole pine but will occasionally open onto solid limestone bedrock with sparse, gnarly limber pine and lodgepoles or open grassy "park" land. (*Parks* refer to dry open areas on mountains that are distinguished from open wet areas called *meadows*.)

With more than one hundred miles of uninterrupted wilderness straight ahead, I thought we would have to hike many miles before reaching truly wild areas. We had only crossed two or three minor drainages that morning when we entered an almost impenetrable stand of lodgepole pines (called *dog hair pines* locally). The narrow but well-traveled game trail through the pines revealed an abundance of fresh elk tracks and droppings, as well as a continuous parade of mule deer sign. It is my unfortunate habit to walk faster than Tommie and get too far ahead. As a result, I like to let her lead the way, setting a pace that is comfortable for her. We had traveled perhaps two hundred yards through the dark, shadowy stand of trees and were approaching an open sunny park just ahead. I suppose I was involved with the concerns appearing around my feet when Tom-mie stopped, turned around abruptly, placed both hands on a four-inch-diameter lodgepole, looked me square in the eyes, and said quietly but emphatically, "Great big bear!" Standing twenty feet away was a bear as big as a Volkswagen. The bear had just left the open park, entered the trees on our game trail, and was now standing and letting its eyes adjust to the shadows. Tommie stood motionless with her back to the bear that was by now beginning to nod its head in response to us. I could only remark, "You'd better turn around—you may never be this close to a bear again." The bear scrutinized us. I looked deep into its wise eyes. Without ques-tion the bear looked deep within mine as we both sought to weigh any significance that might reside in this awkward encounter. Immediately, my scientific mind went to work trying to grasp the relative magnitude of this behemoth. In my empirically inspired state, the only quantitative bench-mark that entered my illogical brain was a garbage can lid. *This bear's head is as big around as a garbage can lid*, I thought. Then, with some distinct but subtle gesture, the bear made an informed decision—some unmistakable reasoning occurred that was devoid of fear or any other apprehension, and it simply turned away. Without ever looking back, the bear ambled out into the sun with fat and muscle rippling across its great brown back and it disappeared. After our breath returned we gave each other a knowing glance and continued silently on our hike with a new understanding of the possibilities. It occurred to me that in a lifetime spent observing and interacting with other species from all over the world, I had never once gazed into the eyes of a wild animal that was so totally without fear for the human species. Although the bear left no doubt about which one of us was the superior creature on this mountain, and I could discern no sense of humility in this bear, I did somehow gather that he was at least permitting us an equal footing. In a matter of a few days, I had met two great creatures that demonstrated that I was walking on new ground and that my frame of reference would now be different.

After a couple of weeks of day hikes on and around Limestone Mountain, I was beginning to get a feel for the area and had reached a certain level of comfort with my abilities to get in and out of the mountains. Interestingly, the few people in Lander I shared bear stories with seemed to be unaware that there were so many bears on this particular mountain. When I delivered a handful of ear tags from various dead elk to the Lander Game and Fish headquarters, the biologist there seemed to be surprised to hear of so many dead animals or so many bears. Part of my cavalier attitude toward these bears was based on a common observation by the locals that grizzlies were in general confined to the more northern reaches of the Wind River Mountains, and I could expect to encounter only black bears this far south. Many black bears, perhaps a majority in this area, are distinctly brown—known as the cinnamon color phase. Even though the brown behemoth we encountered looked radically different from any black bear I had ever seen (and I had raised black bears from cubs), I just assumed the difference was because of my lack of experience with individuals in the five-hundred- to six-hundred-pound range. And I was surely unaccustomed to seeing such big bears only twenty feet away. In addition to all this bear activity, I had close encounters with crowds of elk and mule deer every day. It was not unusual to wander among groups of twenty or thirty elk cows and yearlings in the lower timbered areas of the mountain. All the bulls had shed their antlers by this time of year, and I found a truckload of newly shed antlers and bleached antlers from the previous year. Several enormous moose antlers had also turned up along with many from mule deer. Although I had found no large dead bull elk, I had recovered antlered skulls from younger winter-killed bulls and the head and antlers of a young bull moose. Bones have always been an object of fascination for me, and even as a child, I considered antlers to have a special esthetic appeal. When I tried to explain to Mark Ramsey that I had a large "comparative" collection of mammal skulls back in Florida, he got a vacant look on his face, and after a brief moment of confusion and apparent worry about my strange priorities, just looked away and said in a curt tone, "Well Joe Boy, you can have all mine."

The progression of spring revealed startling images and adventures daily. Limestone Mountain gradually became blanketed in wildflowers that unfolded in an orderly succession as the melting snow slowly crept up the mountain. Even from miles away, the mountainsides would flush with the colors of brilliant yellow and pale violet as the knee-high arrowleaf balsamroot appeared each place the sun struck the ground. Similarly, two species of lupine seemed to carpet all the spaces in between but still allowing for the company of dozens of other more diminutive species—scarlet gilia, silky phacelia, stonecrop, blanket flowers. Small pale blue irises covered all the open wet areas, and in time the grassy meadows and expansive bottomlands became a delicate and smooth, fragile green. Eventually, cold, harsh Wyoming becomes the greenest place you have ever seen. For weeks, every creek, every draw, and the bottom of every canyon rushes with sweet clear water. Packing water into the mountains was unnecessary. Never once did I hesitate to drop down on all fours and drink deeply—no giardia, no cryptosporidia.

Wyoming experiences true synchronicity in its birthing season, and for a few days in spring it seems every female antelope, mule deer, elk, or moose is suddenly with a newborn fawn or calf at her side. Twins are a familiar sight in all species. For a short period it is impossible to trek through the wilderness without encountering wobbly-legged little ones everywhere you turn. By the middle of May, elk have dispersed into a uniform distribution of solitary individuals, and each stands nervously nearby as you pass and admire a mother's new calf. I'd often see large newborn calves lying in the dark timber completely exposed on a blanket of pine needles, still appearing wet and desperately trying to be invisible. All of this activity is of course manna from heaven for predators, but they can only consume as much as they can eat at the moment. Thus, the synchronicity strategy serves to limit the number of meals provided over the course of the birthing period to the fewest number of losses. On several occasions I have seen coyotes trotting along with a dead newborn fawn hanging from their mouth—probably on their way to a den full of pups—a synchronicity designed to take advantage of the synchronicity. But within only a few days, the time of the easy kill has passed. It is safe to be near a mule deer and fawn, and in my experience elk cows are not dangerously protective of their calves, but it is inadvisable to tread close to a moose and her calf. One morning, on the front lawn of the Lander hospital, as arriving staff and patients looked on in horror, a hospital employee was rudely assaulted by a mother moose that ran up from the river. Fortunately, the person was not seriously injured, and such unprovoked moose assaults are uncommon. But when it comes to a moose, you just never know.

In addition to green and flowering plants and a multitude of newborn animals, the melting snow also reveals many other treasures. Wyoming is considered to be one of the great Meccas for geologists who come from all over the world to experience its ancient wonders that truly represent creation laid bare. The upheaval of plutons and fault blocks are confused with the torturing effects of volcanism—they twist and disfigure the land in the most extraordinary ways. This conflagration is overlaid by the beds of great lakes and inland seas that are tilted and then carved away by the gouging of ancient glaciers. Geologically, the big picture of Wyoming is overwhelming in its complexity, and in the most dramatic ways imaginable always presents a magnificent and bewildering conundrum. Try to imagine how the Wind River, in defiance of all reason, can flow north *toward* the uplifted Owl Creek Mountains

And then to everyone's astonishment, the river cuts straight through a monstrous canyon made of some of the hardest metamorphic rock on the planet, exiting out the other side into Montana, as the Bighorn River, where it is joined by the infamous Little Bighorn. It is a mind-boggling riddle, and like all good riddles the answer is impossibly simple. It took geologists many years to recognize that the river is simply older than the mountains. The ancient river cut away the mountain faster than it could be uplifted. I believe that like physics, a true understanding of the development of the earth involves some inevitable voyage into that realm where genius, physical science, and mysticism intersect. Geologists are rarely accused and would never admit to being metaphysicians, but I am convinced that the really good ones probably are.

Scattered up and down this mountain, amid this geographical wonder and the rich veneer of vibrant life, the ubiquitous presence of an equally rich human legacy also resides. For thousands of years people followed these reciprocating snows of fall and spring to access the bounty. What falls on the ground in Wyoming stays on the ground. Biological decomposition is perhaps the least important force at work on this land, and a log, bone, or scrap of leather is more likely to abrade under the forces of wind and sun than to organically decompose. Consequently, the debris left from the flaking of a flint tool four thousand years ago lies side by side with the buffalo hunter's expended .45-70 cartridge from 1880, testifying that they shared the same rocky prominence, an identical and unchanged vision of a wilderness, and perhaps also the same motivation as they waited for yet one more unsuspecting animal to pass. Wyoming's history refuses to abate and simply mixes within a thin dusty lens about your feet. The complex ecology of Wyoming and its many diverse and ancient cultures become inseparable, and are all merely representatives of the symbiotic fabric of this rich landscape. But the litter surrounding one-hundred-year-old elk camps and abandoned mining camps confirm that, indeed, the West was won, not with the six-gun but rather with the can opener.

The deep winter snowpack was beginning to melt well up into the forests, and after a day or two of bad, blustery weather with intermittent snow we got a break in the clouds, allowing us to be on the mountain just after daylight. Tommie was a little weary of our long hikes across the face of Limestone Mountain, so on this particular day she decided to stay on a certain outcrop of rocks just below the tree line. She planned on lying around in the warm spring sun, reading and identifying the wildflowers that seem to pop up the minute the snow melts—shooting stars, harebells, wild irises. The rocky outcrop lies at the mouth of a wide, flat draw as it washes out below a heavily timbered shallow canyon. It is thick and brushy here with densely pruned willows, knee-high buffalo berry, buckbrush, and a prostrate ground-hugging species of juniper. Buffalo berry is gradually deciduous, providing browse for moose well into the winter, and the tinder tips of the shrubs are eaten thereafter. In autumn, these dense shrubs are festooned with red berries that are an important fall food source for bears. In early spring, I commonly find freshly shed moose antlers that will otherwise disappear as the thick vegetation of the buffalo berry returns.

It is always a pleasure to share wild places with a friend or companion, but I am mystified by the predisposition of people who anticipate experiencing the natural world in groups of three or more. And further, the frequencies of the human voice have an almost uncanny ability to carry through a landscape. Humans are relatively blind, distinctly deaf, and project a revolting jumble of chemical and biological scents that are detectable for miles and horrifying to most animals. We have the misfortune of being a repellent to other living things. People wonder why wilderness often appears to be a lonely and barren place without ever understanding that this is an otherwise unnatural condition that we as humans perpetually create in a radius around us. However, in rolling mountainous terrain, a little fresh snow, moisture, and a bit of a breeze, it is possible on occasion for a person alone to experience the natural world as more of a participant rather than a vulgar intruder.

Tommie and I parted company with only abstract plans for reuniting late in the afternoon. I would wander up the mountain through this wide wooded draw, and she would not leave the general vicinity of the rock outcrop. After a few minutes spent meandering upward through thick buffalo berry, sparse conical spruce, and lodgepoles, the draw narrows and deepens into the mouth of a more well-defined but shallow canyon. Here the trees became tall, thick, and shadowy as the canyon offered a still and quiet relief from the breezes moving above. Two inches of fresh damp snow enshrouded the world under ancient spruce in a pale blue calm. Sparkles of snow floated slowly downward as air gently stirred through the tall trees. Rowdy Clark's nutcrackers squawked some distance up the canyon while a nearby pine squirrel chattered wistfully, warning of some objectionable presence. Cold air cascaded down the deepest contours of the draw and enveloped my face in the blue chill that underlies the forest above. The bottom of fresh elk tracks were wet and muddy from the spring thaw, and tracks from snowshoe rabbits, blue grouse, and foraging pine squirrels meandered here and there. Wandering higher in the canyon, I soon found myself in some perfect world where time and space seemed suspended in a place I would choose to never leave.

Ahead was a break in the forest that extended across the narrow canyon from side to side for perhaps fifty yards. Centered in this opening I saw something in the snow that surrounded a large dark prominence. Nearing the opening, I realized that a dead mule deer buck, recently thawed out from the snow, had been attracting scavengers for several days. The area looked as if a two-day football scrimmage had occurred there, and this was the fifty-yard line with mud and blood plowed into the snow by ravens, magpies, coyotes, and the numerous tracks from scavenging bears. The carcass was disemboweled, partially disarticulated, and almost devoid of flesh. A dirty and bloody hide lay in a pile with the scant remains of the hind quarters. A shoulder, neck, and large antlered skull lay nearby and were all but picked clean. The antlers were heavy, brown, and symmetrical with five tines on each side. I felt as if I had been given a precious gift from the earth and began separating the skull and antlers from the neck. A few days of warmer weather had rendered the skull a little wet and smelly but not necrotic and foul. Without hesitation I trimmed off some excess skin and tissue and proceeded to tie the whole messy affair on my daypack. Gratified, I hoisted the pack on my back with scarcely another look around and continued on my way up the canyon. Immediately, the timber closed back in, and I found myself once again engulfed by the cover and solitude of ancient spruce and fir that shaded a clean and unobstructed understory, except for the occasional wooden torso of aged fallen giants. Another hundred yards up the canyon, my mind returned to a rare state of stillness, and this magical world seemed to pass through me unobstructed and unimpaired. A quiet mind is a rare companion.

Then from behind me, a deafening roar emanated from a body cavity the size of a refrigerator—a roar that without question could be heard for miles—a resonating substance and volume surpassing any sound I have heard created in the natural world. At once I was overcome by the magnitude of my stupidity—overcome with all the horrific implications as I struggled to free myself from my pack. Instinctively, my body began running, blasted up the canyon by the storm of muscle and anger behind. The pack hit the ground as I dashed another fifty yards with the expectation of being pulled down at any moment. Grabbing the lower limbs of a great Douglas fir, like some arboreal primate, I found myself in the upper reaches in seconds. My heart pounding in my ears, I gasped for air as some ancient biological mechanism within me anticipated the hot breath and gnashing jaws that draw the familiar closing curtain on so many small-minded one-act plays. A trickle of warm blood running down my arm seemed to speak more to my body's primitive anticipation than to the sharp limb that must have caught my arm on the way up. Hanging in a maze of gnarly fir limbs and needles, my vision was obscured except for a patch of snow-covered ground directly below. I watched helplessly with only the sound of blood rushing through my ears while anticipating the dreadful vision of a great dark form below. No bear appeared, however, and gradually my breath began to slow—I hung trembling and motionless with only the occasional gentle moan of wind moving through my green refuge. Still, no one came, there was only an incongruous silence. My heart slowed but beat in intermittent gulps as the roar of the great bear still resonated within me like the lingering effects of exposure to high voltage. Time seemed to pass in sluggish increments that couldn't be accurately assessed—five minutes . . . ten . . . twenty minutes? Cautiously I began moving down the tangle of limbs, all the while trying to gain some glimpse down the canyon. As my mind began to function again I wondered: *Is the bear simply waiting for me to come down? Is it watching over my daypack and his deer head? Is it too soon to climb down?* Finally I dropped the few remaining feet to the snow-covered ground, now littered with the refuse of dislodged bark, dead limbs, fir needles, and a single diluted drop of red blood. My eyes darted around the canyon only to see my daypack lying in the snow with the mule deer skull still attached and undisturbed. Overcome once again with my vulnerability, I looked down the draw for any hint of movement. I strained for any sound. Only a slight breath of air moving overhead broke the silence. Moving a few feet closer to my pack I began checking for bear tracks but found none. Making what could have been my second great blunder of the day, I carefully moved down the draw, grabbed my pack, and with repeated glances behind, retreated up the mountain.

Over the years I have spent many hours replaying these events in my mind, and I am relatively certain of a few important things about this potentially deadly encounter. Although I had not interacted directly with grizzlies before, I had read about and studied their behavior in books, including the definitive work by Frank C. Craighead, *The Track of the Grizzly*. I knew that grizzlies were inclined to stay and protect a carcass, alternately gorging and resting, and unlike black bears are often tragically disinclined to surrender a carcass to the intrusion of a human. It is this particular situation, and more commonly a mother with cubs, that provokes most grizzly attacks. (A few years ago, Tommie was camping alone in Danali National Park in Alaska and came across a grizzly on a dead moose and immediately left the area. The following day someone came across this same site and was killed by the bear.) Further, I knew that in spite of a complex vocabulary of sounds and communication, black bears do not emit the great territorial roar of a grizzly. Without any doubt, there were grizzlies living in the vicinity of Limestone Mountain. In all likelihood this bear had been observing me the entire time I examined the carcass and retrieved the head of his deer, and although I don't fully understand its motivation, the bear chose to exercise restraint in protecting its prize. I do, however, believe its subsequent behavior was a deliberate communication and expression to me—that I had inappropriately trespassed and it could not let this disrespectful insult go unchallenged. The bear had every right to destroy me and in spite of every opportunity chose not to. Perhaps he had some innate fear and respect for my species that without any real substance in my case intervened on my behalf, and so I will not project any gratuitous motives on this bear. But in any case, I will always treasure this moment and the enlightening instruction the bear allowed me that day.

When I returned to Tommie on the rock outcrop later that day, we found fresh bear tracks encircling the site. Tommie had spent some time sleeping and was totally unaware that she had had a visitor.

Throughout the coming months I would continue to observe grizzlies directly as well as other artifacts and behaviors that are specific to *Ursus horribilis*. At the time it seemed that no one else in the Lander area was aware of this powerful presence, and it was only years later that I discovered that my friend and grizzly bear researcher John Mionczynski was quite aware of these particular bears and was also quietly making observations in this area. His observations included a curious event miles farther up the pass involving a young male grizzly that wandered into John's remote cabin one afternoon without an invitation and, ignoring food, lay down on John's floor and made pitiful vocalizations for twenty minutes. John thought the bear had probably been recently separated from its mother and was desperately seeking out any company. This lucky little bear couldn't have made a better choice.

John Mionczynski's cabin near Atlantic City, Wyoming.

One morning I suggested to Tommie that we drive up to Limestone Mountain specifically to try and find some bears. Parking just off the highway, we began casually moving across the mountain, hiking through one forested drainage after another. Often these drainages are small canyons with limestone shelves or rimrocks exposed on both sides but with intermittent breaks or smaller tributaries interrupting the low canyon walls. Eventually, we encountered one of the larger canyons and made our way along the rimrock until we found a break that would allow us to walk down a well-worn game trail into the wide forested canyon and then climb out the other side. We passed through a thick perimeter of large gnarly white-barked aspen with an understory of buffalo berry on our way down to the small but lively stream running below. As we neared the run of the creek, a great commotion stirred seventy yards ahead of us. A large tawny-colored female black bear and two cubs huffed and then scrambled up the creek with the speed of deer. The bears ran up through big thick spruce bordering the creek and disappeared over a small rise. In an effort to get one last look at the bears, I took off at a sprint to the top of the small hill. As I rounded the top of the rise, the terrain opened onto a thick stand of aspen, and the first thing I saw in the distance was the mother bear running directly toward me. Stunned, I reversed course and ran, yelling to Tommie, "She's coming—get up a tree!" Tommie is athletic and is a former trapeze performer with the Florida State University's Flying High Circus. She took to a tall, heavy fir tree with the agility of a 107-pound cat. I slammed into the same tree at the level of the first limbs and in seconds joined her like the Great Wallenda at the twenty-foot level. The bear continued at a run in what by now appeared to be a full-blown bear attack. She hit the base of the tree with loud popping jaws and great paws extended. She huffed in short angry bursts, alternately swinging her head back and forth—this bear was furious. All at once she broke off her attack and ran in great powerful loping strides back up over the rise and out of sight. We panted in an uneasy relief when the bear reappeared at the top of the rise, running flat out toward us again. Muscle, fat, and fur rippled and tossed across her wide brown back. She was running as if shot out of a cannon. This time she was beyond angry and now seemed to be insane with rage. With jaws and teeth popping loudly, she skidded into the base of the tree, tossing her head, slinging saliva, and attacking the ground with a wide slapping motion of her two outstretched paws. She swung her head and bucked back and forth from front to rear. Mercifully, before she could begin climbing the tree, she once again turned in an unexpected gesture and broke off the attack. With powerful strides, she disappeared for a second time over the rise, presumably to relocate her cubs. Again a deafening silence was punctuated only by our deep breaths when we heard a sound only fifteen feet to our left—the unmistakable scrambling-clawing sound reminiscent of a thirty-pound squirrel. There, hanging at exactly eye level in the spruce tree closest to us, appeared the frightened eyes of the big bear's third cub! The three of us all contemplated a brief moment of mutual assured destruction. Tommie and I then made eye contact, which without a word spoke volumes. We arrived at a speechless accord involving the lesser of two bad options and essentially fell down through the limbs of the fir, hitting the ground running. After a mad dash down the canyon, we stopped in a state of near exhaustion and stared back up the draw with an imminent sense of dread. After several minutes of nervous silence, we continued down the canyon until we found a break and eagerly climbed out to continue on with our hike. I recall the only resulting conversation involved a quiet remark from Tommie, "Well, you wanted to see some bears."

The day proved to be rich and productive with two more bear sightings, bringing our grand total to six bears in one day. Although I had some vague sense of a mission accomplished, I was beginning to think it was perhaps unnecessary if not downright foolish to intentionally seek out these bears. At this rate, my luck with encountering "nice" bears was sure to run out. At least I should probably avoid chasing sows with cubs and try not to rob any more grizzlies of their winterkills. Interestingly, on our return across the mountain four hours later, we were of course hesitant to recross the draw where we encountered the mother bear. We decided rather to walk up the rimrock until we could find a suitable place to cross, far from the area of the encounter. We had only gone a short distance along the rock wall when we observed that the canyon forked above, dividing into two separate drainages. At the confluence of the two drainages a large exposed limestone outcrop formed a thirty-foot-high clifflike prominence overlooking the intersection of the two canyons below. Seated on this outcrop was our mother bear with all three cubs climbing about as she stared incessantly down into the canyon. After four hours, not only had she not left the area but her attention was still on our earlier encounter. We observed from a safe distance with binoculars as she sat watching with a determined and uninterrupted focus. Occasionally she would become distracted as her cubs tumbled about and climbed up on her back, but then in a movement like a double-take, she would resume her obsessive gaze. Needless to say, we gave her a wide quarter-mile buffer zone before recrossing the canyon.

After a long and productive day again spent exploring on Limestone Mountain, we arrived at the pickup with plenty of daylight left. The lower slopes of the mountain and all of Red Canyon below had been without snow for weeks and had at last become dry. As we leisurely started down the grade of the South Pass highway we noticed a narrow winding thread of a road meandering from far down in the canyon. The winding road worked its way miles up the lower slopes of Limestone Mountain and exited through a cattle guard onto the highway. We thought a diversionary exploration might be in order, and so we left the highway and crossed over the cattle guard. The sign read: Wyoming State Game Lands—vehicles restricted to designated roads only. We wandered down a rocky dirt road and across a couple of miles of grass and sagebrush that only weeks before had been a barren, steeply tilted snow-covered mountainside, dotted day and night with hundreds of grazing elk. Another sign read: Entering South Pass Winter Game Range—no admittance December 1 through May 13. Now the grassy mountainside was covered with rich greens and vast rolling patches of wildflowers—a great mosaic of yellow, purple, white, and blue. Western meadow larks, horned larks, and lark buntings lifted up from the low cover on each side of the winding narrow road. Richardson's ground squirrels, least chipmunks, and yellow-bellied marmots alternately scampered for cover as we moved along. Ahead, stratified red sandstone cliffs rose one thousand feet from the green wet meadows lining the bottom of the canyon. In direct opposition to the red rocks, the slopes of Limestone Mountain rose away in the west. Many miles beyond Limestone to the north rose the towering jagged peaks of the Wind River Mountain north fork area in the distance. Northward and farther down the canyon fifteen or twenty miles, Table Mountain juts out away from the mountains in a dramatic horizontal expanse. The base of Table

Mountain forms the termination of Red Canyon and casts its shadow over Lander just beyond. We continued down the serpentine road until we crossed the head of the canyon's main creek and observed a solitary moose in the thick willows and stunted aspen above, browsing below a twenty-foot-deep remnant of packed snow. Crossing the creek, the road turned brick red with the weathered sandstone soils that fill the canyon. At last, arriving at the bottom of the canyon we observed the ruins of some old pioneer cabin with a few collapsed log buildings surrounded by green and productive-looking hay meadows. We passed through another fence and cattle guard and a sign that read: LEAVING WYOMING STATE WINTER GAME RANGE LANDS. Red-rock cliffs loomed up to our right as the road meandered through enormous detached geometric red boulders now resting in the meadows below. With miles of unforested sagebrush and grasslands stretching upward to our left, we followed the run of the canyon creek for miles. The white splashing of golden eagle nests washed down from lofty inaccessible shelving along the vertical red-rock faces of the cliffs above. Antelope in groups of does and fawns dashed across the meadows at impossible speeds and disappeared onto the expanses of sagebrush slopes beyond. Mule deer lifted their heads casually from the lush greenness and stared with a meager curiosity. A series of beaver ponds, partially overgrown by thick willows, obstructed the entrance of a small canyon on our left revealing a tall moose and calf. Both were partially submerged in water while dozens of busy wild ducks puttered about. Separating the road from the green meadows surrounding the creek below stretched a primitive barbed-wire fence with posts fashioned from the gnarly trunks of the scrubby bonsai-like juniper trees that thickly populate the slopes leading up to the red sandstone cliffs. Every mile or so down the canyon we encountered hay "stack yards," enclosed in ten-foot-high elk-proof fences that contained the sparse remains of a cattle herd's winter feed. A few more miles down the road amid all this wildlife and geologic and environmental wonder, sitting at the base of a towering vertical red sandstone cliff and at the confluence of two rushing creeks was a two-story ranch house that had obviously survived at least a hundred Wyoming winters. Weathered log barns and outbuildings surrounded the house with an ancient series of corrals containing a few cattle and a small string of horses milling about. The raw, trampled ground was strong testimony that this was still a hard-working ranch. A rusty tractor and a faded red pickup truck were the only indications that the year was not 1880 or perhaps a movie set from a John Ford western. There is a raw edge, a conspicuous cosmetic roughness to a true working cattle ranch that immediately distinguishes it from some rich man's toy. Stunned by this outrageous setting, I could only speak out wistfully, "Good lord, who in the world gets to live here?"

Red Canyon corrals.

Without knowing, we had just discovered the remains of the historic Boss Tweed homestead at the head of the canyon and this, the old Greenough Ranch. A half mile farther down the road we passed over the Little Popo Agie River bridge and stared for the first time up the river across an expanse of rich hay meadows and onto the great stone jaws of the Bear Trap, a canyon rising like the pillars of Hercules where the Little Popo Agie river tumbles abruptly out of the mountains beyond. Standing by the bridge on the river to our right sat the ramshackle remains of the old Ed Young house. These three entities, Boss Tweed, Greenough, and Ed

Two adult rams on Middle Mountain.

Two ewes and lamb, the great southwest-facing slope of Whiskey Mountain in background.

Three mature rams on Whiskey Mountain.

Ram and ewe during rut on Whiskey Mountain.

Sheep Eater petroglyphs on Whiskey Mountain.
Note possible mammoth on right.

Popo Agie River in autumn.

Lone Ram on Middle Mountain with distinguishing horn configuration.

From the foot of the mountain, looking down on Red Canyon
Ranch—1982.

Red Canyon Ranch from the rim, looking northward toward
Table Mountain. Note ranch complex in center of photo.

Ram on Torrey Creek.

Adult rams on Middle Mountain, working their way up into a pinnacle.

A dedicated migratory event.
Note Middle Mountain in the background left.

Many bighorn sheep concentrated on the great
southwest-facing slope overlooking Whiskey Basin.
Note Middle Mountain on left.

Spring 2009. Ram on Popo Agie River. Perhaps the last surviving ram from the Middle Fork herd.

The author observing sheep on Whiskey Mountain. *Photo by Helge Swanson*

A group of five adult rams with a lone ewe on Whiskey Mountain.
Note Arrow Mountain in the background.

The author at Slingerland Ranch—2007.

Looking west from Middle Mountain camp with
Ross Lake 2,000 feet below.

View from Middle Mountain camp—"The Overlook"—with Ross Lake
below hanging glaciers.

Ramparts and castles on Middle Mountain. One of many
pinnacles on the summit of Middle Mountain.

Two of the large rams on Middle Mountain, that, after three days, refused to leave their fallen comrade.

Approaching Red Canyon Ranch—1978.
"Who in the world gets to live here?"

Young, still speak volumes about the rich pioneer history of Wyoming, and ironically these same canyons, creeks, and meadows would eventually come to occupy a great chapter in the small history of my life.

10

BECOMING A GOOD HAND

For months I hiked and trudged with daypacks and backpacks, slowly following the spring season higher and higher into the Wind River Mountains. Even though I was not a complete stranger to the remote alpine country above timberline, the Winds introduced me to the wildness and the inaccessible reaches that only high altitude can provide. The mountains could lighten my pack load by supplying me with fresh water and rich protein in the form of native cutthroats, fat rainbows, and golden trout. Often traveling alone, the ability to pack light allowed me to stay for many days at a time. The alpine high country provided the solitude and a magnificence I longed for, but these extremes of beauty came with the price of weather and an exposure that could alternate from being merely inconvenient to life threatening. I found this alpine ecology to be dynamic with living things but austere by comparison to the richness and diversity that I had become accustomed to at lower elevations. Eventually, I returned to the zones of greatest opportunity for observation and interaction with the creatures whose company I longed for so strongly—elk, deer, moose, bears, lions, beavers, and of course a nearly endless list of smaller birds and mammals. For months, the high-timbered basins became my home. Beaver ponds with fat brook trout, moose, and nesting waterfowl including goldeneyes, green-winged and cinnamon teal, mallards, and the occasional sand hill crane seemed to harbor my companions of choice and the rich, teeming environment I had longed for. Every rocky outcrop showed the evidence of former seasonal occupants with the remnants of their flint and stone tools and not uncommonly their mysterious stylized caricatures of animals and eerie humanlike forms. Commonly, I observed the bleaching bones of great creatures that had come and gone in this perfect place. How I envied their unambiguous and powerful sense of place and purpose— lives so richly lived—lives lived so deliberately. There was a moment where

I actually thought that I had rather be dead in their world than alive in mine. But by then my world had already changed.

Among the many revelations that came to me that first spring and summer was an almost immediate and unexplainable healing that occurred in a heart and mind that had been mired in a long and tedious pathology—one of the possible results of being a normal human being trying to live a normal human life. Wyoming washed through me in a great cleansing wave, and a strong suspicion took hold that at least for some of us, wild places can be the perfect medicinal antidote to a lifetime of exposure to our own humanity—an exposure that leaves us each stricken and afflicted with our own lives. It has been said that the universe is designed to break your heart, but wilderness may suggest that it is only we who can do that.

One of the recurring dreams in my youth was of an unfamiliar and haunting landscape—a landscape where I was surrounded by wilderness and great beasts but was mysteriously permitted to wander unobserved. Now it appeared there was a real wilderness allowing me to pass through, if not unnoticed then at least with indifference, and sometimes even eagerness. Chipmunks readily climbed up on my knee to share a bite of my apple. The gray jay and the chickadee fed from my hand as the blue grouse perched comfortably on a log a few feet away and drummed for a mate. Noisy flocks of reddish pine grosbeaks would alight nearby in raucous profusion, paying no more attention to my presence than to the elk standing in the thick timber nearby. A moose would raise its great head from beneath the water and briefly look me in the eye before returning to its task undisturbed. From an old rotting stump ten feet away, the mighty goshawk stared with fierce blazing red eyes, concerned only that I might want to share in its prize of freshly killed pine squirrel. At my bidding, the reclusive pine martin climbed down its tree and hopped along my fallen log to within inches, investigating my strange unauthentic squeaking noises. Living things everywhere, large and small, made gestures of admission and acceptance that were, in my state of mind, unexpected and healing. What place was this, where my wildest dreams could be surpassed in such unexpected ways? Who were these great creatures that so readily and without question granted me space in their world, space without conditions and expectations different from their own?

Without any reservation, I knew that through some strange circuitous means, I had found this seemingly perfect place and without a doubt could not, would not, leave. After six months immersed almost every day in this wilderness, never once encountering another human being, I was now faced with the conundrum of how to actually survive in this difficult country. Now how would I support this powerful Wyoming habit that had become without question incurable? How to make a living? After ten years invested in a career as a scientist, it was clear that these skills would be of little use to me now.

But I did possess certain skills, and ironically there was a demand in Wyoming for those skills, which I had acquired many years before—skills that had been dismissed in my previous life as being forever useless. As it turned out, I could put a handle on an old ax or on a new horse. Growing up in the economic and cultural ambiguity of north Florida, like most boys of that time and place I had always worked on the land. Farms, ranches, hunting plantations, wildlife refuges, and national forests had defined my youth. My friends' families were often agricultural people or had large family land holdings. Like so many in his generation, my father grew up a farmer, leaving agriculture as a young man for opportunities in business. When I was fourteen, after years of incessant nagging, my father finally but reluctantly agreed to let me have a horse. With $50 I had saved, he helped me buy a $75 two-year-old stud colt that had never even had a halter on and then washed his hands of the whole affair. My colt had already been assigned the prophetic name Diablo. Many in my group of friends had horses, but even though I had spent considerable time riding I technically knew nothing about horses or training them. No tack of any kind came with my horse and I had no money to buy any. I kept Diablo at a friend's farm. I'm not sure if my father ever even saw my horse. He probably felt he had already seen plenty in his life. I simply went to a local tack shop and bought the cheapest bridle with a curb bit and began "training" my horse. My working corral was a fifty-acre pasture. After spending time luring him in with carrots and apples I would fight and wrestle the bit into his mouth and then lead him down the steep hill of the pasture. My technique then involved swinging up on his bare back, enduring a few crow hops, and then letting him have his head, running flat out a half mile up the hill, at which point I would wheel him around before we hit the fence. This had the affect of so exhausting Diablo that he would sometimes refrain from bucking me off. One time, however, we did fail to make the turn at the top of the pasture and plowed through, pulling down fifty yards of a five-strand barbed-wire fence. The horse's chest was cut and one of my lace-up boots was completely torn off. With my expectation of being thrown off multiple times every day, we taught each other how to ride within a few months. I never did get a saddle, and so by age sixteen I had learned two things: (1) never, ever, let go of the reins when being bucked off, and (2) I could probably ride anything with four legs.

In high school and college it was always necessary to work, often full-time, and so I was resolute about only working at jobs I could enjoy. Among numerous other jobs, I managed a zoo; caught venomous snakes to sell to universities, research facilities, and zoos; trained Labrador retrievers; and, finally, legitimately trained horses. An area plantation owner had imported the first Colombian Paso horses into the United States and was going to introduce the athletic little breed to the world. He imported over 120 brood mares, most of which were selected entirely on the basis of conformation with little or no regard for any previous schooling. Many were as wild as deer. Several of the most famous Paso studs in Colombia were obtained at no small cost, mostly from the region of Medellin. Hired to manage this whole extravaganza involving the finest facilities and some two thousand acres was the eminent western horse trainer and authority Dave Jones. Dave is world famous as a trainer and handler of horses in the western tradition. Dave is also a prolific writer, an excellent photographer, and author of several definitive books, including the seminal standard reference *Practical Western Training*. Scarcely a horse magazine has sold a monthly edition in the last forty years that did not include an article by Dave. Dave is also renowned for designing a unique western saddle. Dave Jones was a big-boned, hard-core, dyed-in-the-wool cowboy, never without handmade cowboy boots and hat, and he always, as he pulled a cinch up tight, squinted through the smoke of a hand-rolled Bull Durham cigarette hanging rakishly off one side of his lips. A former champion roper, he has even become known in the world of cowboy music, composing and belting out with a great baritone voice old standards like "The Strawberry Roan." He has traded songs and saddles for years with the likes of cowboy performer-songwriter Ian Tyson.

Without any invitation, I showed up unannounced at Meridian Meadows looking for any kind of a job—mucking stalls—whatever. Dave and the owner, Colin Phipps, happened to be working with some horses in the arena when I arrived and immediately asked me if I had any qualifications. My response was, "Not really, but I can ride most anything." Without further discussion they put me on the rankest stud in the barn named *Sin Vergüenza* (Without Shame). We tore around the arena like his tail was on fire—it probably wasn't pretty but I stuck like glue. The next day I started to work as a hand, and months later formally agreed to become Dave's apprentice. I came to love Sin Vergüenza as the finest horse I ever knew. We had an arrangement—I wouldn't hurt him, he wouldn't hurt me, and we both liked chasing cows and feeling the wind in our face. My new job involved riding and training all day, every day, along with all the other responsibilities of an outfit involving large numbers of animals— feeding, stall mucking, corral and fence mending, tack repair, trimming and shoeing over four hundred feet, floating teeth, stacking hay, worming and doctoring calves, and so on. I learned proper techniques of breaking and training, proper riding techniques, and the best ways not to get killed. I was given my own young horses to bring along under Dave's supervision, plus we systematically broke every brood mare to ride and in many cases tried to teach each one a skill, either calf roping or cutting cattle, so eventually I became handy with a rope and became proficient at "turning back" calves and yearlings—the really fun part of cutting cattle. We trained some of the most famous cutting horses in the country including champion quarter horse stallion King of Clubs and his son, Steel Helmet, owned by August Busch—the beer guy. Of course, one is called upon to "husband," which means responding to animals' various needs, including giving shots and medications to horses and cattle and occasionally pulling a calf or foal from a mare or cow in distress. By this time in my life I had built miles of fence, become proficient with tractor work using backhoes and front-end loaders, and still a horse could drag me on my back for fifty yards but I never let go of the reins! When I finally graduated from college and left to begin working full-time as a field archeologist, I had gained a lot of ranching knowledge but at the price of many broken bones—some more than once. The young man who took my place had his ear torn off on a corral fence, and the next young man who followed was eventually killed by a kick to the head. If you work with large numbers of half-ton animals every day you are going to get hurt—there are no exceptions to this rule.

And so, upon coming to Wyoming ten years later, it appeared that all these extracurricular activities that I thought would never serve me again had inadvertently endowed me with certain advantages. Ironically, this itinerant scientist now had prospects in the Wyoming livestock industry.

After Tommie and I concluded that we would definitely not be leaving Wyoming, we set about trying to make some sort of living arrangements. After several months, we could not continue to impose on Sid and Nickie's hospitality, and we had no interest in living in town. After considerable discussion, Sid and Nickie expressed their preferences to be out of town as well, so we entertained the possibility of finding an old abandoned ranch house and making renovations. Every old ranch has all its successive houses, barns, sheds, and equipment standing around everywhere. Typically, a ranch contains the original and inevitable log house of the late 1800s, then the newer and somewhat improved wood-frame house from the 1930s or 1940s. Then in many cases a contemporary ranch house in wood or brick has been added. Occasionally, the culminating structure of the smaller family operation is the ubiquitous double-wide. A similar chronology exists in transportation, with the classic bone yard of every successive old wooden wagon, Model T Ford cars and trucks, ancient wood-bodied stock trucks, and a complete progression of rusty, worn-out tractors and their old Rube Goldberg assortment of strange implements and attachments. Almost every ranch in the area had at least one abandoned old house. Because of the lack of humidity in Wyoming, many of these houses are quite sound even though livestock may have occasionally wandered in and out.

After asking around a couple of ranches, we were directed to the Rick and Jane Bieber Ranch, the Bar-B-Bar, several miles south of Lander. The Bieber Ranch backs up to the Little Popo Agie River and is a classic small family ranch that might run a few hundred head of cattle and enough irrigated hay meadow to keep them alive through a winter. The ranch was originally built by the pioneering Anesi family in the late 1800s, but eventually wound up in the ownership of "Big Steve from Riverton." Although this man owned and operated this ranch for decades, he was still known far and wide not as Steve or Big Steve or Steve from Riverton but like one big word—Big-Steve-from-Riverton. And, naturally, he was not actually from Riverton. However, Steve was in fact big—everyone got that part right—lean and sturdy from a lifetime of hard work, and he was enormous. He had only in recent years sold his beloved ranch to Rick and Jane and was an almost daily fixture as he could not seem to stay away. We gave Rick and Jane a call, and they were delighted that someone might return the old house to a livable state and invited us out any time to take a look. Sid and I both had experience building, and so the four of us optimistically climbed in Sid's big truck and drove south out of Lander to explore the possibilities. Rounding over the crest of a hill six miles south of Lander, we could immediately see the Bieber Ranch set back a half mile off the highway and up against a backdrop of rugged rocky ridges with the river canyon dropping off behind. The ranch sits nestled among old cottonwoods, surrounded by lush green rolling hay meadows and a small apple orchard perched on a slope nearby. The ranch complex was the typical cluster of weathered houses, barns, sheds, and corrals. Nearby, an old crudely engraved granite boulder by a small turnout on the highway reads: IN MEMORIAM—D. R. BARR, JEROME MASON, HARVEY MORGAN—KILLED HERE BY INDIANS—JUNE 27, 1870. The nearby drainage running under the road and climbing west up the lower slopes of Table Mountain is known as Deadman Gulch. We pulled off the highway to the east and followed the gravel driveway up to the ranch and stopped at a ragged white-picket fence and an abandoned wood-frame house that we immediately recognized as a viable candidate for residential salvation. Jane, thirtyish, red haired, and dressed for a day's work on a ranch, met us at the truck with the most perfunctory greeting imaginable and concluded her one-sentence introduction with, "I need some help." We of course said, "Sure, what do you need?" Rick was out somewhere working, and Jane was alone dealing with a heifer that was having difficulty delivering a new calf. We hurried into an old log barn and immediately saw the rear end of the heifer and that her calf had presented a nose and one hoof but not two. This is not a good sign—meaning that the other leg was probably twisted back out of position. Jane already had a come-along out and a stainless-steel chain, but the more delicate aspects of calving were obviously out of her immediate area of expertise. The distressed heifer was straining, groaning, and tied to an old wooden milking stanchion, so Sid

Bieber Ranch.

and I got to work, knowing that if the calf had been in this position for a long time it could soon die if it was not dead already. I held the tail back while Sid reached up inside the cow past his elbow and struggled to locate the calf's other leg and drag it out with the other one. This is unpleasant for the heifer; she was entirely unappreciative, resentful even, and so the three of us all fought and groaned with each other. At last Sid got the leg around and we could finally see both little pink hooves. Then we cinched up a small chain around both front feet, attached the chain to the hook and cable of the come-along, and then tried to find something immovable to securely attach the whole contraption to. We chose the entire corner of the log barn. Making sure the head of the cow was securely fastened to a central log support in the barn, we began taking up the slack in the come-along. At last we started actually pulling on the calf, which of course the heifer found blindingly painful. The legs of the calf began extending out of the cow but the head refused to pass through. The heifer obviously couldn't dilate enough to allow the head to pass. There was no alternative but to bring all of the mechanical advantage of the hoist to bear on the calf and the heifer. The heifer bellowed, the force of the come-along literally pulled her hind quarters off the ground, and she toppled over on her side in a great floundering struggle. Her eyes rolled back and she roared and groaned in pain—the strain on the calf's hooves seemed to be enough to pull them loose from the bone. We cranked on the hoist as the cow fought and stretched across the dirt floor of the barn. Finally, the wet head of the calf emerged, the heifer bellowed, the barn groaned and cracked as the log corner gave way in a loud snap. Just at that moment, the calf began to slip free and came slopping out in a great heaving pile of bloody afterbirth and amniotic fluid. We pulled the calf's face free of some membrane and her nostrils began dilating and pulsing for air. Releasing the chain from the calf's front feet, I looked up and saw Tommie and Nickie's faces, pale and grimacing with sympathetic pain and obviously in some state of empathetic maternal horror. Nickie, revolted and aghast, blurted out, "Oh god, I will never have a child!" I laughed out loud and said, "Oh, sweet home on the range."

In minutes the heifer was up, and although still not altogether appreciative, she seemed quite pleased with the overall results and held no apparent grudge toward us. She began eagerly examining and cleaning her new calf. A hush filled the barn as shafts of afternoon sunlight filtered through a hundred years of dust still suspended weightless in the air. What appeared to be the scene of a heinous crime was at once transformed to one of serene bucolic bliss. Phenomenally, the calf soon lifted its head up looking around, and its soft little pink hooves were undamaged. The four of us (cow, calf, Sid, and Joe) had, however, managed to break the corner of a one-hundred-year-old log barn, so Sid and I began making repairs with sledgehammers, crow bars, and a wet, messy come-along.

The old Bieber house needed plenty of work that literally involved shoveling some dried sheep manure out of the living room, but in a week of hard work, a few gallons of paint, some replaced window panes, and a lot of caulk, we had a serviceable three-bedroom house. Amenities included an old functional coal furnace in the basement, a good mudroom (arguably the most important room in a Wyoming ranch house), and Sid's good Jøtul woodstove installed in the kitchen. Out the back door of the mudroom stood a small but well-constructed squared-stone building with fine engraving over the door reading: ANESI.

We had an arrangement with Rick and Jane involving renovating the house at our expense, and they in exchange would receive no rent for six months. Everyone was happy. Rick is perhaps one of the most likable men I have ever known and simply expects to work hard, seven days a week, twelve hours a day. Jane and the kids, Anita and Keith, are delightful, so it was always a pleasure to help out around the ranch any way we could. Typically, ranches do not have many full-time employees because many jobs are strictly seasonal. On a ranch, work comes at you in storms—calving, branding, spring cattle drive, irrigation, cutting hay, stacking hay, fall roundup, winter feeding—big jobs but sometimes lasting only a few days or weeks. As a result many ranch hands are itinerate. Also it is common to work for barter—we will gather and stack a thousand bales of your good grass hay for fifty bales to feed our horses. And more importantly, often the price of living a rancher's life is learning to live and work without a supply of actual cash. Let me fish in your river and hunt your elk and I will stack all your hay for the next ten years!

Immediately, Rick put Sid, our friend Mark, and me to work stacking his last cutting of hay for the summer. Big round bales had not become fashionable at that time, so we drove a wagon across the hay meadows gathering small square bales (which are not square at all) and alternately transporting them to the stack yard. Hay is never covered in Wyoming, and a yard is simply a small fenced lot that excludes deer, elk, and cattle but provides access for pickups and tractors. Stacking hay in good uniform, tall, rectangular piles is a feat bordering somewhere between architectural engineering and a skilled art form, and in almost every case the amateur's stack will eventually collapse and fall over. Naturally in Wyoming a stack yard is visible for miles and so every cowboy or rancher who passes a collapsed haystack is sure to smirk as he drives by and think: *dude*. Between the connections of Mark, Sid, and Rick, it was only a matter of a few weeks before word got around that willing new hands were available, and soon I was getting calls for all manner of ranch work. Roundup was beginning and cattle were coming into ranches by the hundreds and thousands. The weather was getting chilly by October and November, and so I found myself cutting and separating hundreds of cows and yearlings in snow and occasionally on frozen ground—horses, cows, calves, and cowboys slipping and sliding around, ass over tea kettle.

Sweetwater country.

Most ranches maintain a string of working horses, so all I needed was to buy my own saddle. A guy might lend you his horse but he'd rather not leave you alone with his saddle. Rick Bieber, of course, had to round up his cattle as well, which were on an allotment of a Bureau of Land Management range stretching twenty or thirty miles to the east and south called Government Draw and Cedar Ridge. This area is a convoluted sagebrush desert with a maze of red-rock and juniper ridges, cliffs, and canyons. Rick would load me and a good blood bay cow pony named Coffee, then trailer us fifteen miles south before daylight, unload us just off the highway, and I would make a wide sweep out through the draw and pick up any cattle bearing Rick's brand. Coffee and I would drive what cows and calves we could find in a general northerly direction. After dark and a hard day's ride, Coffee and I would finally drive the cattle across the river onto the ranch, close the gates, and unsaddle. Most cowboy work, I soon found out, is done alone, and so it can be a solitary business—before daylight to after dark—providing endless opportunities for contemplation and introspection. I never met a working cowboy who did not show the inevitable signs of a thoughtful mind. And when a man or woman comes in after a long twelve- or fourteen-hour day riding in the Wyoming sun, you can actually see the daylight in his eyes—I swear! Forget all that Hollywood stuff about chuck wagons, campfires, and guys sitting around playing guitars—maybe once in the entire history of the West did a guitar wind up on a cattle drive—and you can bet the cattle drive lasted longer than the guitar.

Chuck wagon. *Copyright © Cathy Keene*

Wyoming is vast, and as a result, orientation is maintained not by one's immediate surroundings, which are often confusingly similar or altogether unfamiliar, but rather by geological structures many miles in the distance. Government Draw, for example, is geologically complex, labyrinthlike, but every time you come over a rise you see the Wind River Mountains that are ten miles to your west. Also, the Little Popo Agie River lies in the same direction, and the Owl Creek Mountains and the Washakie Needle rise up one hundred miles to the north. Rising behind you twenty or thirty miles to the south, the pale chalky face of the Beaver Rim escarpment is always evident. In this country it is common to have no idea where you are, but you are never lost. Older cattle always know where they are, and once you get them moving, they understand the plan and often even know the best route to travel whether they are being driven in or driven out.

Mark Ramsey often cowboyed for the Yellowstone Ranch thirty miles south of Lander, headquartered in the Beaver Creek Basin below Beaver Rim. The Yellowstone was at that time owned by Wyoming Governor Ed Herschler and was by far the largest outfit in the area. The Yellowstone ran thousands of cattle in the remote Sweetwater country of the Red Desert and the Great Divide Basin The Yellowstone ranch range lands involved around a million acres of rugged high desert wilderness, and a cow could drift for one hundred miles by roundup time in the fall. Mark worked for manager Ken Ballard, along with a crew of several other good cowhands. The Yellowstone Ranch, because of its size and its remote high-altitude desert characteristics, had a reputation for being a hard-core working ranch with a bunch of no-nonsense cowhands. Ken Ballard is a big, good-looking, square-jawed professional cattleman, friendly and charismatic but with an almost mythical reputation for occasionally being trouble in a bar. A former champion bronc rider, Ken even once competed in the national finals in Madison Square Garden. I never knew Ken to be anything other than a really nice guy, but one of the first things I heard when I started working in the area was, "Don't ever mess with Ken Ballard." I never did.

Mark Ramsey knew what a real cowboy was and had strong opinions about that definition. The real working cowboy is a highly skilled professional who has spent a lifetime honing his many varied abilities, and there are but a few really good ones. Contrary to the advice of that old song, you can't just "get yourself an outfit and be a cowboy too." It was interesting how careful people were in using that term when referring to a hand or a cattleman. In a country where hundreds of people worked in the cattle industry, I only heard Mark refer twice to a man as a real cowboy—one was Ken Ballard and the other was one of Ken's contemporaries, rancher Doug Salisbury. Mark could spot a wanna-be five miles away. He had great respect for Ken who became eventually more like a big brother than a boss, and I observed a similar respect toward Mark. During roundup, we wouldn't see much of Mark for weeks at a time, except periodically he would show up all wind burned and dusty just to check on everybody. Mark cultivated an enormous network of friends that he somehow managed to keep in contact with on a regular basis. Hunting season starts in early fall, and outfitters often have big strings of horses and pack mules that need to be shod, and in spite of the busy season, Sid and Mark would still occasionally find a day or two for shoeing horses.

Mark was always grabbing me for a day's work here or there, and it wasn't long before I had been introduced in one way or another to most of the old working ranches in the area. My first full-time job offer was working for Jerry Spence's Thunderhead Ranch near DuBois, and occasionally worked on other ranches including Bill Macintosh, Johnny Lee, the Ellis Place, Willow Creek Ranch, the Ruby Ranch, Walt Shearer, Sherlock, Hancock, and Red Canyon—Mark either knew or worked for almost everyone in the area. Additionally, one place or another would often host a jackpot team roping on weekends, where hard-working ranchers could get together on a busman's holiday and have a little social time. Lander is home to the oldest paid rodeo in the United States—a tradition that still persists on each Fourth of July weekend. Almost every Sunday, throughout the warmer months, and with weather permitting, there was an official jackpot roping at the Lander Municipal Rodeo Grounds. Teams of ropers would come from a radius of a hundred miles or more to compete. I would occasionally participate in the local ropings, but the big rodeo ground events were too much pressure for this hand.

Throwing a rope well is a skill that must become hardwired, seemingly part of someone's DNA. It seems that kids start throwing ropes in Wyoming before they can walk, and like ballet dancers (forgive the analogy) they are the ones who can become the real masters. But of course in a country where everyone starts throwing ropes before they can walk, it is simply taken for granted. People who start in their late teens and twenties can catch a steer or a calf but never with the congenital facility that comes with learning to handle a rope in childhood. A good roper possesses an ability that borders on the mystical. Without exaggeration, I have literally thrown thousands of ropes and caught not hundreds but thousands of cows, calves, and horses, and yet when I see the real masters work their magic, it never fails to boggle my mind—the rope becomes not an extension of the arm but of the will.

By working on the various ranches in the area and attending some of the social events like team roping and brandings, I gradually came to know many of the members of the ranching community. It would be a disservice to these kind people not to mention how readily and eagerly I was welcomed into this group of hardworking people. I was never once made to feel unwelcome or like an outsider, even though my southern accent was always an immediate tipoff and I would occasionally get a friendly "You aren't from around here are you?" Often people were curious about my degree of handiness around horses and livestock and were puzzled when I tried to explain that the land of palm trees and tourists actually had prairie country and arguably raised more cattle on one ranch than could be found in the whole state of Wyoming. I came to know these people working on the land—ranchers, cowhands, farriers, brand inspectors, horse traders, saddle makers, outfitters, and stock truckers. Over the years I had been around a lot of horse people and agricultural people—people in riding boots and big hats—but it was clear that the cowboy culture in Wyoming was, of environmental necessity, defined in completely unique ways. There is a lingering authenticity in the cattle business and the cowboy's life that I have never observed in other ranching environments. The country demanded it—never permitting changes to occur in the way things had been done for over one hundred years. Weather and the wilderness terrain that characterize this country requires work to be done almost entirely on horseback in rugged, remote areas involving literally thousands of square miles. Working with cattle in Wyoming can require people to be in a saddle from daylight to dark, in rough weather conditions, and in isolated environments month after month. Working cowboys were still living like this, year in and year out, and there were still those who had never known another job. On average, Wyoming range lands will support about one cow for every fifty or sixty acres. To operate a modest outfit of a thousand mother cows can involve hundreds of square miles of grazing land, and it is not uncommon for one ranch to maintain a hundred miles or more of fences. Ironically, most fences in Wyoming are built not to keep animals contained but rather to exclude them from hay meadows and winter pasture that in summer must grow an entire winter's feed. In fact, Wyoming range law specifically states that it is a landowner's responsibility to fence stock off their property if they do not want it grazed.

Lightning and winter snowpack are devastating to fences. It seems impossible but packed shifting snow can flatten a half mile of mountain fences like a bulldozer. Lightning can run along a fence and cut the wire at every staple like touching each one with an arch welder. One cowhand can spend solitary weeks in spring riding and repairing fences where no vehicle could ever go. Many fences in Wyoming are quite old and have been in place for more than a century, making annual repairs feel like a seasonal walk through time. You suddenly catch yourself digging a rusty staple out of a gnarly 120-year-old juniper fence post and making yet one more splice with barbed wire old enough to be in a museum collection. You see where a lonely cowboy performed the exact same task one post down the line—but over one hundred years before.

Having grown up and worked among commercial fishing communities along the northern coast of the Gulf of Mexico, I soon began to observe distinct similarities in the two traditional lifestyles. A cowboy working alone on open range or mountainous country is much like the solitary fisherman, always drifting slowly along on some great expanse and always at the mercy of the elements—freezing rain, snow, powerful winds, and of course, lightning. Historically, since the days of the big cattle drives of the late 1800s, more cowboys have been killed by lightning than all other causes combined—ask rancher and writer Gretel Ehrlich—a horseback lightning strike victim herself. Further, a small boat at sea and a rider on a wilderness range must

Juniper fence post.

be completely self-contained and self-reliant. All the bare essentials for survival must be on board, but space and logistics will allow for nothing more. The two livelihoods share the same fundamental reality: Every day life hinges on the best gear—a good outfit plus a lifetime of skill and the good judgment to use it wisely. And unavoidably, when dealing with boats or horses and the unpredictable variables of weather and circumstance, sometimes life or death is purely a matter of dumb luck. Being violently thrown into the rocks or into the water and seeing your outfit disappear over the

Shoshone women preparing game. *Copyright © Cathy Keene*

horizon can be a similarly dreadful and hopeless prospect for waterman and cattleman. It is possible for any crabber on the bay or any cowboy on the high desert to just have one bad day. If you are lost in a frozen fog at sea or a whiteout snowstorm in the sagebrush, the consequences can be the same. Whether you are setting a gill net or riding ten miles of fence, when the squall comes up there is no shelter—often as far as the eye can see—and both steel-shod horses and boats have all of the unfortunate characteristics of a lightning rod. You just stare down the barrel of nature's loaded gun, pull your hat down, your collar up, and hope the lightning does not strike the most conspicuous object in a five-mile radius.

Autumn in Wyoming is an exciting and active time, a time when everybody is eagerly up to something. Horse trailers are busy hauling things everywhere—moving cattle and horses, going hunting, returning from hunting, or carrying huge loads of hay or firewood. Everywhere you go, the question is not, "Are you going hunting?" but rather, "Have you gotten your elk yet?" Many people prefer elk meat to beef. Elk meat is lean and tender without the strong gamey flavor that people often find objectionable in deer. When butchered and completely deboned, a good bull can yield over two hundred pounds of the finest meat. Elk have always played a strong role in the economy of Wyoming—past and present—with many people depending on the rich source of dietary protein supplied by elk and other species of big game. Moose are highly prized as a food source, but hunting is strictly regulated and permits are hard to obtain. Elk are abundant—in some areas overabundant—and so for a small fee every Wyoming resident is eligible for a general elk permit. In addition, other special elk permits are issued on a lottery basis for areas where elk numbers need to be reduced. An adult elk can eat close to fifty pounds of vegetation in a day, and populations can irreparably devastate their range in no time if they surpass the carrying capacity of the habitat. Many Wyoming residents depend upon wild game all year, and out-of-state hunters and the outfitting business constitute a major source of revenue for the local economies. Here, hunting is not thought of as a sport but part of the livelihood and economy, and for many residents it is simply part of what you do to live, like cutting firewood. It seems that most everyone has a mandate to disappear into the high country for a few days in the fall and pack the family freezer for the year. Few employers would have the nerve to suggest that an employee's disappearance in the fall was inconvenient or in any way inappropriate. In Wyoming, there shall be death, taxes, and elk hunting.

Family elk camp. *Copyright © Cathy Keene*

Similar to the catastrophic overabundance of zucchini squash in the rural South, the only reason anyone ever locks car doors in Wyoming in October is to prevent someone from putting yet another ten-pound package of fresh elk meat in the front seat—although, admittedly, probably no one would ever really be inconvenienced by a package of good elk meat. If you are the least bit squeamish about animals dying in the name of nutrition, you are probably living on the wrong planet in general, and, specifically, you might want to avoid Wyoming in the fall. In the cooler months of autumn the entire state is abuzz with large meaty animals being transported in every direction. It seems every third pickup is loaded with an elk or a couple of deer and antelope, not to mention the stock trucks that are moving cattle by the thousands to market. There are several game processing businesses in town, and most people do not find unusual or offensive large dead animals hanging and being processed within sight of the main roads. In the fall, people are scrambling to accomplish all of this critical economic activity before the deep snows come to the high country.

That first fall and winter was a time for exploring new possibilities and a new world. The only real reservation I had about life in Wyoming involved my inexperience with really cold weather. I had lived and worked in snow and freezing weather, but the ramifications of forty or even fifty degrees below zero were impossible to comprehend. There was little question in my mind that such temperatures could not be fooled around with or taken lightly.

Immediately I was instructed to have the customary heating element installed in my truck's engine block, which eventually would be connected to an extension cord every night. Even motels in Wyoming supply every parking space with an electrical connection. It appears that should you attempt to start a car in forty-below weather, the motor may be damaged or destroyed as temperatures dip past the ratings of the antifreeze.

Further, certain articles of clothing are nonnegotiable. Besides all the typical long john stuff, down layers, and weatherproof shells, "pacs" are essential for the feet and are standard and universal on almost every Wyoming foot. Pacs consist of a rubber-bottomed boot with lace-up leather uppers, often with fleece or coyote fur around the top, ostensibly to exclude snow, and with a removable one-half-inch wool felt liner worn like an inner bootie. The liners are pulled out at night to dry completely.

Pacs are about the only thing that will keep your feet warm in subzero temperatures.

Almost everyone outside a town uses wood heat in Wyoming. In a ferocious winter that can last for seven months, any other heat is too expensive and dangerously unreliable. If the power goes out or the gas doesn't flow on a forty-below night, you will not be merely uncomfortable. So the acquisition of firewood begins in summer as soon as the mountain forests are free of snow and accessible, and by fall you will need a wood pile the size of a small mountain. But having used wood heat my entire adult life, I find the entire process completely satisfying. I love to split firewood. And feeding a woodstove on a cold night is a most gratifying activity.

During these years, forests had already begun dying and dead standing trees were available for firewood by the tens of thousands in the nearby mountains.

Work was still available as winter came on, and I actually found time to do a little hunting for the first time in many years. The winter of 1978 proved to be one of the coldest in a hundred years. For a time, it was suspected that I may have overcompensated for the possibilities, and in my exuberance, oversupplied us with firewood. However, we soon realized that you can never have too much firewood in Wyoming. By mid-November, Wyoming was experiencing below-zero temperatures every night, and for eight straight weeks in December and January, day or night, the temperature never rose above the zero mark. The frost line plunged to eight or ten feet. Hundreds of people lost running water and sewage for the rest of the winter. Frozen ground has the peculiar properties of stone and of plastic and cannot be overturned or broken with shovel, bulldozer, or blasting. Summer is the only time for building roads, pouring concrete, digging foundations, or digging graves. Working outside all day in fifteen degrees below zero proved to be a possibility if no wind was blowing, but even on a still day, twenty below became at some point unbearable and eventually dangerous. In these temperatures, any exposed skin gets superficial frostbite within minutes, and like chronic sunburn, can have a similar long-term effect. Wildlife suffered that winter, and antelope numbers were especially hard hit with thousands dying throughout the state. One group of over three hundred was found frozen up against a fence south of Lander.

Wyoming is transformed into a startling new world in winter. The activities and excitement of autumn gradually give way to an extended period of cold white resolve. Life is slowed by a viscosity of the spirit that seems to be increased in all living things. Cattle are eventually turned into the confines of hard frozen hay meadows and the stack yards are gradually emptied in a perpetual daily ritual. The numbers of cattle sustained in Wyoming are not, in general, determined by the amount of grazing and range land available but rather by the amount of hay that can be grown in the short summer months. The hay that is grown in summer must sustain the entire herd for half a year, and buying hay to feed cattle has never been a viable way to stay in the ranching business. After moving from the lush pastures of the southern states, an ironic observation about the cattle industry in Wyoming became obvious. There couldn't be a country more unsuitable for raising cattle.

People are often surprised if not appalled to find that animals in this country are almost never provided with shelter even in the most brutal winters, but surprisingly, as long as good alfalfa and grass hay is readily at hand, they all seem to prosper in a state of confined and contented resolution. Horses respond with a thick six-inch covering of downy fur that causes the finest chiseled horse to look like a model for some Pleistocene cave painting in France.

The land becomes perpetually white with the accumulation of successive deep snows that never seem to melt, and for months Wyoming can resemble any winter scene north of the Arctic Circle. A rolling pale blue and white winter landscape is broken only by the occasional frozen ranch complex and the distant silhouettes of herds of large slow-moving creatures—horses, cattle, elk, deer, and the occasional moose standing among willows hidden beneath puffy billows of blanketing snow. A deep, rutted, muddy trail through the snow marks the daily reciprocating route taken from ranch to stack yard to cattle and back—no matter how cold the temperature, how strong the wind, or how deep the snow.

In winter, the towns of Wyoming can begin to resemble small islands of refuge, stranded in a desolate white sea of motionless drifted snow—like choppy waves frozen in place. Highways are commonly closed for days with wind and deep drifting snow preventing all vehicles from either coming or going, while anxious truckers are often stranded and sit idly waiting for things to improve. Occasionally grocery stores are emptied of fresh produce, and once again the inhabitants of Wyoming lay down their six-guns and quickly draw the can opener from their drawers, even if the contents may be frozen solid.

With only wood heat in a house, the extremities such as bedrooms can become quite cold in the night, so heavy down comforters are a standard feature in many sleeping quarters. We went so far as to purchase an enormous moose hide from the Lander Tannery that completely covered our full-size bed and hung down over the sides all the way around. A moose hide can be six inches thick and heavy enough to flatten you in your sleep, but you will never wake up cold. When the wind blows seventy miles per hour on the Gulf of Mexico, it makes the national news. The wind blows seventy miles per hour once a week in Wyoming it seems, and, without a word, people just pull their hats down tight, lean into it, and go feed the stock. Commonly we would wake up in the old Bieber house to find long white darts of fine snow stretching out across the floor from cracks around the doors and around the fireplace, forced in by the pressure of gale-force winds. On more than one occasion, drifts would be so deep against the house, we would have to climb out a window and grope around for a snow shovel.

To my great surprise, this southern boy came not to dread or tire of winter in Wyoming but rather to discover it as a rich and beautiful season—a constant feast for the eyes as well as the spirit. Most fortunately for man or beast, the colder the temperature plummets the more immobilized the air becomes, until at twenty degrees below zero the air becomes suspended in a quietude, a stillness that is so unfamiliar as to be otherworldly. There can be a sense of the wondrous in the Wyoming winter that is somehow bound up with an air that sparkles with suspended minute icy particles, like a sorcerer's mixture of fairy dust and diamonds floating about you everywhere—an obvious symmetry between the equally unexplainable forces of gravity and magic. On the coldest mornings, hoarfrost will mysteriously appear and cover every object, limb, or line, with a perfect weightless and feathery frosting. Every small branch will be enshrouded with an enormous shimmering ephemeral cloak, like a frozen blend of gossamer, spun glass, and goose down, waiting in a breathless cold for any miniscule perturbation that will liberate and send a billion sparkling particles floating slowly to the ground. The only sound for miles is the deafening crunch of the frozen snow beneath your big boots and your own warm but borrowed breath as it freezes instantly upon returning to the world.

11

RED CANYON

Our first fall in Wyoming was cut short. Unfortunately, Tommie suffered a medical emergency, and so we chose to return back east for corrective surgery. We had to leave not only Wyoming but also our new blue healer puppy, Minnie, with Sid and Nickie, but Sweetwater, the pet crow I had raised from a chick, made the trip home with us. My pet kestrel had already been returned to the wild, and he never made a backward glance. Worried about Tommie's health and saddened to leave our new life, the situation was sickening in the truest sense of the word, but we were resolute about returning as soon as circumstances would allow.

Leaving Wyoming was a painful but unavoidable decision, but we kept in touch with Sid, Nickie, and Mark, as well as many of our new friends. Mark would always conclude a conversation like a doctor offering advice on a serious diagnosis, "Well you just better get back out here, Joe Boy." After completing some business matters that involved severing our few remaining ties back east and getting Tommie healthy, we finally returned to our new home early in the summer.

A few things had changed. Sid and Nickie had separated—she moved back to Lander closer to the hospital, while Sid continued living on the Bieber Ranch and shoeing horses when opportunities arose. We moved back in with Sid, and within days it seemed as though we had never left, although there was no question that our former puppy was now his cattle dog. My first objective was to visit the Lander car dealership where I ordered the first factory-made, four-wheel-drive Toyota pickup ever sold in Wyoming. Included was a small camper top, some oversized snow tires, and a really good set of chains. Now I could actually go places with the consolation and prospect of returning. Because there are few vehicle trails in the Wind River Mountains and even though there are laws prohibiting off-trail travel, people are always pushing the envelope on a vehicle's ability to negotiate rugged terrain. People do lose vehicles in these mountains, and on several occasions I have found cars and trucks dating from the twenties to the present that lay rusting in the bottom of some remote mountain draw. Similarly, the all-too-common and unfortunate litter of more than a half century of aircraft wreckage remains forgotten and unrecovered. Middle Mountain's Bomber Canyon is obstructed by twisted scraps of aluminum, mangled propellers, and four hulking radial engines that were tragically deposited there in the 1940s by a B-17 and its crew. Ken Ballard told me of the mangled remains of a .50 caliber machine gun that, for years lay across the horse trail leading up the canyon.

Available jobs in those days were usually confined to oil rigs and mines, which mercifully were few and far between, and of course to the ranching business, which seemed to always be in need of a willing pair of hands—hands that could enjoy some measure of contentment without ever knowing the feel of large amounts of cold hard cash. There was still plenty of cutting, bailing, and stacking of hay to be done, and by fall I was again helping with roundups and separating cows and calves for fall sale. At that time ranchers agreed that a break-even price on a calf or yearling was around $0.80 a pound. Prices during these years were near historical highs and when bought by contractors or sold at auction could bring between $0.75 a pound to as much as $1.20 per pound. One dollar was about what a rancher could expect on a good day. A contractor is a buyer who represents speculators on a futures market and provides the rancher an opportunity to lock into a previously agreed-on price and therefore avoid the otherwise capricious whims of the daily livestock market in the fall. Mark and I had a beer one Saturday night with rancher Doug Salisbury at the old Atlantic City Mercantile saloon and asked him how he came out with the sale of his calves, and he quipped, "Well the contractors offered me $1.05 last summer but I held out for $0.75—want to buy a ranch?" Profit margins in the ranching business are notoriously low, and although most ranches were owned outright after many generations, still many ranchers had to borrow money every year and were often deeply in debt. From my perspective, the interesting common denominator that seemed to define ranching in Wyoming was the ironic equation that although these people owned thousands of acres of good land, hundreds of head of livestock, and barns filled with tractors and other expensive equipment, no one seemed to have any money. Ranches were all operating on a shoestring budget and many survived from year to year on the edge of financial disaster. Most ranchers would be the first to admit that the livestock industry in Wyoming is a definitively high-risk business with relatively poor returns even in a good year. However, most ranchers are born into this life and understandably grow to love it. It is common for ranch employees to be compensated with only a modest amount of actual cash but also with many other gratuities—housing, horses, use of vehicles, gasoline allotments, free beef, access to chain saws and abundant firewood, and of course hunting and fishing privileges.

That fall I began doing some serious elk hunting with the urging of Mark and some of his friends. Typically, we would trailer the horses up into the mountains before daylight and spend the day going our separate ways on horseback, often in an expansive wild area known as Maxon Basin. Mark killed a large 6 x 6-point bull elk that year, and his friend Mike Ruby and I helped him pack it out of the backcountry. For our efforts Mark gave us each a big box of elk meat and eventually awarded me the antlers. Many sets of elk antlers have passed through my hands over the years but those antlers still hang on my wall today. Lander had an unofficial big buck contest sponsored by a local taxidermist involving no prize other than the right to a little bragging. Mark and I harvested the two biggest deer recorded that year with mine edging out his by a small score. For years Mark refused to talk about it. More importantly, however, we managed to pack our freezers with fine elk and deer meat and supplemented our groceries all year with wild game.

Growing up in a family and a culture with a rich hunting tradition on the Florida Panhandle, I look back now and realize that I had the good fortune of being taught well by my father and his friends. We were all taught to hunt with respect—never waste a bird or an animal, rigorously obey game laws, and always resist any opportunity for greed—not because you were likely to get caught but because it was the right thing to do; it had as much to do with personal integrity as with the management of a particular species. In those days a man's character was determined in some measure by how well he hunted (with "well" having little or nothing to do with how many animals a person killed). As I matured, however,

I became increasingly disenchanted with hunting as it developed in the Southeast, and a new ethic seemed to evolve in the contemporary hunting culture. Although certainly not universal, a pervasive attitude of disrespect for the land and the creatures living on it seemed to replace an older, more highly evolved sensibility. Even more important, it seemed that there was simply an overwhelming pressure by too many hunters on a rapidly diminishing resource of wild game. I gradually began to perceive many hunters as insensitive if not downright profane. However, upon moving to Wyoming I began seeing that most people had a healthy attitude toward wildlife stewardship and hunting. Ranchers had a powerful respect for the abundant wildlife that shared the range with their cattle and recognized that they had every natural right to share the land and the resources. Conservation was not so much a part of the consciousness but rather a part of people's heart and soul. This country lacked the overwhelming pressure and competition on animals that I had witnessed earlier in my youth, and it was again easy to view hunting as an appropriate and healthy thing to do. Once again I felt honored to be a participant in this most ancient and vital human tradition. Ultimately, the hunter's motivation is irrelevant to an animal that is killed, but for many, the description of hunting as a sport is not merely demeaning to hunter and prey alike, but more importantly constitutes an overwhelming misunderstanding of the significance of the process. The trivialization of hunting by the definition and application of the word *sport* logically forces the nonhunting public to view hunting as irreconcilably unwholesome and impossible to understand.

To kill and be killed is the predicate upon which all biological life is founded. It is the ironic but universally unifying principle of all living things—that for a thing to live another thing must die. Most people in our current civilization choose to ignore the inherent unpleasantness of this conundrum and are merely content to let others kill their animals for them. At least once in a lifetime, every human who eats a hamburger or a prime rib should have to put a bullet into some unsuspecting cow's head to get some idea of the magnitude of the terrible sacrifice that has been made. Vegetarianism might be easier on our conscience, but a great Taoist teacher once said that in desperation the cabbage screams as loud as the rabbit, but we just cannot hear it. However, any conscious person who truly experiences the gravity of killing another living thing for food or any other reason knows that it is not something that is done for amusement. Sooner or later every true hunter has this pivotal moment of realization. As you see this magnificent bull elk lying dead at your feet, it becomes overwhelmingly clear that your bullet has not only rendered a few hundred pounds of meat and placed some extremely large antlers into your possession, but without question something phenomenal and important has also been lost in an ambiguous bargain that always tugs both ways in the ethical balance between profit and loss. All cultures throughout human history that have depended upon hunting for life have without exception acknowledged the ancient and sacred relationship that is implicit in our universal necessity to sacrifice a life so that we might be sustained for yet another day.

Fall graduated into winter. One cold day in January—one of those cold and snowbound days when you refuse to leave a twenty-foot radius around the woodstove—I loaded the stove one more time and leaned back in a chair and read the Lander newspaper. Tommie was at her job in town and Sid was out. After catching up on new proposed game regulations, dire predictions for future cattle prices, and the possibility of the state's airlifting hay to some elk herds starving in deep snows up near Jackson, I turned to the classified ads. The Lander classifieds were often filled with obscure treasures and occasionally revealed interesting artifacts like old wood and rawhide snowshoes, horse sleighs, dog sleds, old bear trap saddles, or granddad's buffalo hide overcoat. After cruising through the fun stuff under the miscellaneous column, I turned to the real estate section. Land prices were still relatively low during these years, but small, affordable parcels have always been scarce. My eyes glanced past the "For Rent" column, but not before the words "Red Canyon" caught my eye—"Old two-story log house for rent, seven bedrooms, $300 per month." We weren't looking for another house to rent and certainly not a two-story house with seven bedrooms, but it suddenly occurred to me that there was but one house in Red Canyon. The first time I saw this beautiful old ranch house I said, "Good lord, who in the world gets to live here?" These words now echoed in my head. Still, the prospect seemed unlikely, since I knew that house had always been the manager's house on the Red Canyon or Slingerland Ranch. But if that could in fact be the Red Canyon house, I would at least enjoy an opportunity to see the interior of the old place. Immediately, I surrendered to my curiosity and picked up the phone. A man answered and introduced himself as Henry Slingerland, explaining that indeed the Red Canyon Ranch house was for rent. He went on to say the house had always been the manager's house, but he had become tired of dealing with disappointing employees. They seemed to never work out, and, exasperated, he was going to assume all those responsibilities himself and just rent out the old house. After a brief introductory conversation on the phone, he invited me out to take a look. Finding the opportunity irresistible and just needing an excuse to get out of the house, I got into the truck and broke through eighteen inches of fresh snow to get to the highway, then turned left, and drove another five miles south. Arriving at the Little Popo Agie River Bridge, I took a right and began driving a snow-covered gravel county road that hugged the slope paralleling the river. The river was nearly frozen over, with the surrounding hay meadows and a couple of small ranches all virtually buried in snow. The road eventually zigzagged through the cut that the river had made in the red sandstone of the canyon. The warm red color of the vertical rock faces stood in stark contrast, almost in contradiction, to the cold blues and whites of the surrounding world. Soon the narrow confines of the red rocks opened back up to the expanses of frozen hay meadows and the great rising slopes of the Wind River Mountains thrusting up ahead to the west. Embedded a half mile ahead in this great uplifted expanse was the gaping mouth of the river's canyon with vertical limestone cliffs rising abruptly on either side—the Little Popo Agie Canyon—the Bear Trap. Leafless ancient willows and cottonwoods revealed Henry Slingerland's tidy ranch complex with wood smoke hanging low in the mouth of the canyon. Turning left over a river bridge I headed south, up Red Canyon with its vertical rock faces towering above and to the east. Immediately I saw the old ranch complex less than a mile ahead. Pulling into the driveway, I approached the house and stopped in front of two small log buildings with log barns and corrals surrounding me to the right. There appeared to be no one around, so I climbed out of my truck and began looking about. A creek surrounded by thick willows flowed down Red Canyon just behind the house and joined another creek flowing from the west that was obviously being discharged from another narrow rock-walled canyon at the foot of the mountain. One hundred yards up this creek stood a cow moose and calf, belly deep in snow-covered willows and browsing peacefully. Immediately behind the house and fifty feet from my truck, a porcupine browsed four feet up into the top of a willow bush, clumsily eating tender buds and ignoring me completely. Three quarters of a mile up Red Canyon to the south, a herd of fifty or more cows and yearling elk grazed on the lower mountain slopes above the hay meadows. Above them, perhaps another quarter of a mile, two big bull elk slowly trudged up the mountain, gently swaying their heads under the weight of their massive antlers in a slow rhythm from side to side. I looked across the backyard of the house, and my eyes followed the towering red cliff face up to the highest ledge, and there, hundreds of feet above me in perfect silhouette, an enormous mule deer buck stood majestically, as if surveying his royal domain. The entire scene was so outrageous that I felt as though I had been set up—as if the deer, the porcupine, the elk, and the moose were planted—meant to make the whole package irresistible. I thought, *This has got to be the rarest place I have ever seen.*

A faded red pickup slowly crawled up the canyon road through the snow toward the house. Eventually pulling into the parking area next to me, Henry Slingerland slid out of the truck and hopped out into the slush. Not at all the picture of the salty cowpoke, Henry was topped by a well-worn and dirty John Deere baseball cap, a heavy brown canvas jacket, faded jeans, and scruffy lace-up boots. In his midsixties, short and stocky, Henry appeared to be a wiry stump of a man—muscular, gnarly, and strong. He greeted me with a barely detectable or perhaps contrived sense of pleasure. After a few polite exchanges, he immediately wanted to know what my interest was in his ranch house. I launched into a comprehensive synopsis of my entire life, all of my motives for being in Wyoming, with particular emphasis on the more interesting and significant highlights of my varied experiences. The whole dissertation was concluded in less than a minute. With a conspicuous disregard for my esthetic motives for wanting to live in Red Canyon, Henry focused on the ten-second chapter of my life story in which I summarized my academic experience. His interest seemed to mysteriously suggest the notion that his approval of potential renters might hinge on their academic credentials. Eventually, Henry confided in me that he too had an appreciation for the beauty of this place but only admitting to it after finally warming up to me a little bit.

Henry Slingerland had a reputation for being withdrawn from the ranching community and for being gruff, and by all reports, difficult to work for. My first impression substantiated all these character features, but as we talked I began to recognize that although he was obviously a strongly opinionated man, he was probably a thoughtful, intelligent person and at least without the outward signs of an unreasonable personality.

The old house was indeed remarkable and rambling with seven bedrooms, not a foyer but a lobby, an enormous living room with a fireplace, and a great picture window. Known as the Greenough place, it had been built with square, hand-hewn dovetailed logs in the late 1800s, and it is rumored that for a time it may have been a stagecoach stop between Lander and South Pass. Eventually the logs had been covered with chicken wire, smeared over with concrete, and whitewashed in an apparent effort to make it appear more civilized. Age was again beginning to reveal itself on the corners and around the foundation of the log structure. The picture window in the living room looked out onto vertical red-rock cliffs, and framed perfectly in the middle, perhaps five hundred feet up the cliff face, was the ragged woody debris and telltale white splashing of a golden eagle's nest. Now I was thinking, *This is ridiculous.* The large kitchen was equipped with the necessary chimney for a woodstove and also had a walk-in pantry lined with old oak cabinets. All the cabinet doors and their brass-latch hardware were of the type seen on the typical oak ice boxes that one might expect to find in any antique store. Opening one of the cabinets, I saw that they were indeed constructed like the old ice boxes with slightly corroded galvanized metal linings. Centered in the back of every cabinet was a curious square wooden block with a handle. Pulling on a handle, I was surprised to find that the block was a plug that merely sealed a square opening to the outside of the house. Then it occurred to me—the refrigeration system involved merely letting in the cold outside air at night and then replacing the plug in the morning to contain the cold air and ice all day. Further, a door was provided in the pantry on a north-facing wall to allow entry to a small screened-in enclosure where a side of beef or an elk could be hung for daily use. There was a full stone-walled basement that looked somewhat like a wine cellar in a great castle. The house had functioning bathrooms upstairs and down with big cast-iron, claw-foot tubs. Although in desperate need of an industrial-scale cleaning, all in all the house was wonderful.

Henry and I stood outside in the snow talking for quite a long while as I questioned him about his ranch and he quizzed me about my affairs. He was especially curious why someone with my career experience would be doing ranch work, and I tried to explain that it involved a love affair with the country and a necessity to be in Wyoming but also the need to some-how make a living in the bargain. The concept was within the range of Henry's esthetic sensibilities, and he seemed to express an appreciation for my motivations. Within a short time the two of us made some sort of con-nection. In spite of Henry's cool facade and an unwillingness to engage in the most rudimentary social pretense, there was something about the man that I could not help but like. I'm not sure what qualities Henry found ad-mirable in me, but he began inquiring about the experiences that had pro-vided me with the abilities to adapt to ranch life so readily. After listening to me ramble a few minutes about my background in large animals, farm equipment, and building a house or two, Henry asked me bluntly, "Do you think you would like to try to manage this ranch?" My jaw dropped at the suggestion and I began immediately to explain my overwhelming lack of qualifications. Without hesitation, I explained that I was no cowboy and certainly not a career rancher or cattleman. Henry seemed content that I was a good horseman and could throw a rope or pull a calf, but oddly, he was more fixated on the fact that I had a degree from a major university, an experience that from my perspective seemed to render me supremely unqualified for any useful employment in Wyoming. Henry may have tired of cowboys and was merely looking for someone who might be there on any given Monday morning to do another week's work.

After explaining my living situation with Tommie and Sid, Henry be-came interested that Sid was handy with livestock, farm equipment, and was a professionally trained farrier. Henry then explained that Red Can-yon was predominantly the cattle operation with relatively little good hay meadow, and that the real hay operation was twenty miles east of Lander, just beyond the little community of Hudson. He then suggested that Sid could run the hay operation with another hand named Don. In addition, the herd was wintered there, calving season would be beginning soon, and Sid and I could live in the old bunkhouse until calving was complete.

That night I shared the news with Tommie and Sid, and without much discussion we all agreed that the prospects sounded inviting, depending on the variables of hours, responsibilities, salaries, and so on. The next day I met with Henry again and told him of the favorable possibilities, and we discussed the variables. With Sid and I signed on as full-time employees, the arrangement would involve free board for all of us at the big house, including some money for renovation with me performing much of the labor. In addition to two woodstoves, the ranch would pay for supplemental heat from a propane gas furnace. Working hours would begin promptly at 7:00 AM, and the workday would normally end at dark. And Henry made it clear: that meant you were in the saddle or on a tractor at seven, not just standing around the barn with a cup of coffee in your hand. If circumstances would allow, I would get half a day off on Sundays, but I should expect to work seven days a week much of the time. I would receive one beef a year, which I could slaughter for meat, or I could take a live heifer and gradually start my own herd. The ranch bought gasoline in bulk so I would be allowed a certain number of gallons per month. I would provide my own saddle and tack, but Henry would provide a string of working cow ponies and preferred that we not bring any more onto the ranch. An exception was made with Sid's horse Joey after we explained that he was a light eater and an easy keeper. Salaries would be set at $1,000 a month.

I began interrogating Henry about my various responsibilities and obligations to the ranch with reassurances that he would be there to tutor and offer advice on the rigid timetables of the various activities and the many intricacies of managing a ranch. Though I didn't know it then, the truth was that no one ever managed a ranch for Henry Slingerland. All he really needed was a dependable hard-working hand.

At one point, as I gradually became overwhelmed by the unimaginable magnitude of what I was about to undertake, it became necessary for me to ask about the actual size of the operation. Asking a rancher how many acres he owns or how many cattle he runs is like asking an ordinary businessman to simultaneously pull down his pants and tell you how much money he has in the bank. My thoughts were that under the circumstances it would no longer be an unforgivable breach of etiquette and would now be necessary and appropriate. "Henry," I said in my most professional managerial voice, "how large is this ranch and how many cattle do you run?" Realizing that the question was timely and one of necessity, Henry got a look on his face that was not an actual grimace but one that might be seen perhaps on a patient in a doctor's office just prior to some unpleasant procedure. Henry's eyes narrowed as they darted ever so slightly from side to side, though, other than me, he was miles from the nearest human being. He then lowered his voice and said, "The ranch involves about fifty thousand acres. I can run a thousand cow-calf units, but it's too stressful on the land, and so now we run between seven and eight hundred pairs with less than fifty bulls—guys around here always run too many bulls." He concluded my uncomfortable inquisition with, "We have to keep up with about a hundred miles of fence."

After briefly turning pale and experiencing a swoon that rocked me back on my boot heels, I began to contemplate the dimensions of this new undertaking, this new direction in my life. The prospect was so overwhelming it was comical. However, one thought kept coming to mind again and again, *This could be a terrible mistake, but if you don't take advantage of this outrageous opportunity, you might regret it for the rest of your life.* And so, I agreed to Henry's offer with the one caveat that I absolutely do not work on farm machinery or do engine repair, especially diesel—to me it was all mechanical mysticism, and in my estimation the possible spawn of Satan. And so with this single compromise, we had an accord. Tommie, Sid, and I immediately began preparations to move from the Bieber Ranch to Red Canyon.

12

SLINGERLAND RANCH

Within two days we had hauled all our possessions by horse trailer from the Bar-B-Bar Ranch to Red Canyon. After installing both of Sid's woodstoves—one in his bedroom and the big one in the kitchen— he went on to Hudson to get things under way there while I cleaned and made repairs on the house. In a week we both hit the ground running full-time for the Slingerland Ranch. Indeed, during the next six months I took two days off, which Henry found to be decidedly inconvenient on both occasions.

As we gradually settled into a routine, Sid drove to Hudson almost every day or stayed at the bunkhouse while I began preparing Red Canyon for the eventual return of the cattle. Obviously, the roundup and separation of cows and calves the previous fall had left the corrals in a bit of a mess, so I worked for a couple of days replacing corral poles and nailing boards back in place. Henry then informed me that it was time to begin riding and repairing all the fences before the herd could be returned. Most of the cattle would be held at the ranch until it was time to be driven out to their summer grazing allotments. It is also during this period that all new calves must be branded, bull calves castrated, ear tags installed, Ralgrow hormone tabs injected under the skin of the ear, and inoculations given for infectious bovine rhinotracheitis (IBR) and bovine viral diarrhea (BVD). Calves born with the buds of horns showing must be dehorned, which involves applying a circular cup-shaped branding iron around the hairline of the new horn that serves to arrest any further development. Cow horns are not decorative, and any mother cow with these weapons still intact represents a serious threat to a cowboy's life and limb, especially during calving season.

It was impossible to anticipate how the majority of my time would be spent in the performance of my duties, but my suspicion was that I would be working horseback only on occasion. I was wrong about that. For the next few weeks and months, the vast majority of my time would be spent in the saddle. The ranch owned a string of good, experienced working cow ponies, and I immediately bonded with a big, strong proud-cut sorrel gelding named Sport. We became inseparable while Sid took up with a smart hardworking buckskin with a phenomenal Roman nose, named, of course, Bucky. Sid's horse Joey would relieve Bucky on occasion. Sport and I were saddled and under way by 7:00 AM each morning, and Henry never failed to be at the barn before that, checking on things and giving instructions for the day's activities. After completing repairs on about twenty miles of hay meadow fences, Sport and I would trudge up the mountain behind the ranch every day until we hit the Shoshone National

Sid Johnson and Minnie at
Hudson Ranch, 1982.

Forest boundary fence. Starting where we left off the previous day, we would ride all day making repairs. Once again I found myself exploring the draws, ridges, and canyons of Limestone Mountain. Sport was a seasoned mountain horse, and when my attention lagged he never failed to alert me to the presence of a bear, elk, moose, or the many other creatures that we could encounter, including coyotes, deer, antelope, bighorn sheep, and even the occasional mountain lion in the distance, bounding away up a rock face.

Typically we would work our way up the mountain at first light and ride the forest boundary fence line, which was a time-consuming mess because of the crushing effects of heavy drifting snows and the aftermath of the occasional lightning strike. I found myself having to dig ancient staples out of one-hundred-year-old fence posts to complete repairs. (There were no new staples on the ranch, and Henry got incensed by the extravagance when Sid and I bought ten pounds of new staples at the ranch supply store.) By late afternoon each day, Sport would haul me back down the mountain, and we would drop onto the hay meadows several miles up Red Canyon. From there we would have a leisurely ride along the brushy canyon creek back to the ranch.

Late one afternoon we plodded along the creek after a long day, gradually working our way back home, when suddenly a great commotion stirred from down the steep embankment of the creek. Something like a careening high-speed truck caused the thick willows to thrash and shake violently just below us, causing Sport to panic into a spin as I hauled back on the reins. The powerful horse then lunged forward, slamming me back across the high cantle of my saddle seat. As I barely recovered, Sport again wheeled around abruptly just as an enormous black shape came plowing up through the nearly impenetrable creekside vegetation. A bull moose appeared in one single great leap onto the hay meadow only a few yards away. With the dancing staccato sound of four terrified hooves, the horse spun again and seemed to draw close to the ground like pressure applied to a coiled spring, ready to explode upward in flight. With long bounding strides, the equally terrified moose began running across the hay meadow, retreating toward the lower slope of the mountain a half mile beyond. Suddenly Sport's ears drew back like an angry cutting horse, as if possessed by something demonic. Somehow, perhaps instinctively, we found ourselves at a run behind a moose that was rapidly gaining ground in the distance as some unexplainable force seemed to come over us both. I don't know if my spurs were involved, or if it was Sport's love of the chase, but before we could think about motives or consequences, the big horse released all his bound-up tension and turned on the afterburners, resulting in a flat-out race between horse and moose. Sport rapidly gained ground, pulling into a roping position just behind and slightly to the left of the great beast. With big chunks of mud kicked up and flying in our faces, we escorted the moose at a strong gallop across the wet green meadow three hundred yards to the fence at the foot of the mountain. The moose strode over the barbed-wire fence with barely a leap and started straight up the steep slope. Sport and I pulled back and watched panting as the moose ran another quarter mile before stopping and staring back inquisitively. It is not my custom—in fact, I would never do anything to intentionally harass any wild animal, let alone a moose whose company I try to cultivate. But even though this innocent moose that had been peacefully lying down, possibly even sleeping in the willows, was probably as horrified as we were, somehow Sport and I reacted to what seemed like a moment of life-and-death terror with some sort of primeval response—perhaps even a knee-jerk sense of retribution. I never tried to explain it. Extending all possible apologies and appeals for forgiveness to the moose, the shameful truth is that Sport and I were somehow exhilarated by the whole affair. Sport moved with a new-found spring in his step for the next few miles back to the ranch, while I sat a little straighter in the saddle. If horses could grin, Sport would have been all teeth. And me—well, I think the opportunity to run like hell with a big bull moose just proved to be irresistible.

Calving season was getting under way and after completing repairs on corrals and fences at Red Canyon, I moved temporarily to the Hudson facility and shared the bunkhouse with Sid. Calving in Wyoming is a problematic time. Calves that come in from summer grazing must be sold immediately in the fall for it is never cost-effective to continue feeding artificially. Grazing allotments on government range are defined by a certain number of cattle that are allowed to graze for a certain number of days. Thus the growth of a calf and its eventual weight and sale price is determined in large part by how early in the spring it is born. An older calf is usually a heavier calf, and calves are sold by the pound. The catch-22 is that the earlier a calf is born the more likely it is to be caught by early spring blizzards that invite mortality through freezing and disease. It is always a gamble to let the bulls in with the cows too early. If the coming spring is mild, the lucky rancher can sell older and heavier calves in the fall. If the spring is bitterly cold, the rancher stands to lose many calves, with the surviving calves often unhealthy and slow to put on weight. It is common to see cows and calves in Wyoming that were born early and have completely lost their ears to frostbite. Calving season is a critical, deadly serious operation that perhaps more than any other phase of the cattle business determines the ultimate success or failure of the ranch. Calving losses are inevitable, but in most cases must be limited to 10 percent or less. Ideally, the herd is all bred back simultaneously so that calving can be confined to the shortest period possible. During the calving season the pregnant cattle are kept in relatively small enclosures of not more than several acres and watched over carefully day and night. Further, old cows are culled annually and replacement heifers are selected each year from the calf crop to maintain a stable herd population. The young heifers are bred for the first time at one year and are often confined separately during the calving season because of the likelihood of the first birth's being difficult.

Calving season is the most stressful time for a ranch hand and is a seemingly endless, tiresome, and often miserable affair. Calves that are born in blowing snowstorms or extreme cold must be gathered up at birth with the mother and brought in and sheltered until the calf becomes dry and strong. The daylight hours involve constantly riding or walking through the herd, while nighttime requires setting an alarm and riding through the herd at least every two hours. It is a strange but unfortunate fact that a herd of cows will go days without delivering a single calf, but when the blizzard arrives, inevitably ten cows will calve at once. Getting a wet, cold, newborn gathered up and coaxing its mother to follow to a barn in the darkness of a freezing spring blizzard goes beyond mere unpleasantness and can be suggestive of some cruel form of torture. Trying to "pull" a calf by yourself, in the dark and in below-zero weather, can make you wonder if life is actually worth living, as your afterbirth-soaked jeans and gloves freeze to your skin. Mother cows can misunderstand your best intentions and become dangerously protective of their new calf. That spring Don was nearly killed by an angry shorthorn (a breed of beef cattle) that attacked him while he tried to catch her new calf. The cow knocked him down on the ground and repeatedly tried to butt and gore him in the shallow confines of an irrigation ditch. Don was out of commission for several weeks with broken ribs, and we found that many of our shorthorn cows displayed similar aggressive behaviors when we attempted to handle their calves.

Sleep is snatched in two-hour increments, and every day all the boss wants to know is not how many successes have you had but "How many calves have you lost?" A good fall calf could bring $500, and at that rate the bone pile starts looking like a stack of sad little $500 bills. Before long you find yourself giving mouth-to-nose resuscitation to a stillborn calf, then skinning it out like a sock, stretching the bloody hide over some previously rejected orphan, and then praying for adoption. Fortunately that spring

Sid and I limited calf mortality to slightly less than 10 percent, and Henry seemed pleased with the outcome.

As soon as calving was complete, we started preparing the herd for the spring drives to the summer range on either Bureau of Land Management lands or in national forests. Ranching on wilderness range lands and cowboying is a solitary business and couldn't be farther removed from rodeos or country and western music. Most days a working hand will not see another human being from dawn to dark. One of the few exceptions to this is spring branding. Branding time is an opportunity for neighboring ranchers, ranch hands, and families to come together and turn a grueling few days of work into a hardworking party that lasts just one. However, Henry preferred to confine our brandings to Slingerland Ranch personnel only, which always included Henry's lovely wife, Nan, as well as Don's wife, and Tommie. That spring, a couple of college boys hitchhiking through Wyoming saw the activity from the highway, wandered down, and offered to give us a hand. Sid and I roped and dragged calves in, the boys held the calves down, and Henry, in billowing clouds of white smoke, applied the brand → S (pronounced Spear S). Don, an older, experienced cowboy, performed the necessary surgical castrations with a pocket knife. Sid clipped in the calves' new ear tags while Nan administered immunizing injections and implanted Ralgrow in the ears. (Growth hormones can add 10 percent to the final weight of a calf, and in many cases is the difference between a profitable year and a loss. Tests reveal that the hormones are completely metabolized and eliminated in only a few weeks, although the practice remains controversial. These days, Slingerland calves grow to 700 pounds without growth hormones.) During branding, adult cows and replacement heifers were run into the "squeeze shoot"—a trapping enclosure—where ear tags were installed, replaced, or upgraded. Even young calves are surprisingly strong, and handling older calves can be strenuous. After spending your day at a branding, you're covered in manure, dirt, and blood, with the smell of burned hair and hide permeating your clothes and your sinuses. The physicality and brutality of a branding resides somewhere between a day-long football practice and a day at the Spanish Inquisition. Mercifully for the calf, however, the whole affair is over in seconds, and the confused and appalled creature is sent bawling back to its mother. Sid and I joined other

Slingerland Ranch branding crew 2009. Right to left: Big Mike Zabinski, Joe Hutto, Travis Lucas, Tom Lucas, Richard Gould, Mitch Woolett. *Photo by Nan Slingerland*

brandings in the area that spring, including the Bieber's and the Willow Creek Ranch's with ranch owner John O'Neil and most of the neighboring Day family. Fried Rocky Mountain oysters were prepared in abundance.

Eventually, after calving, branding, and all other preparations had been made, it became time to begin moving cattle. Henry met me at the Hudson Ranch one afternoon and said we would begin dispersing the herd by initially driving cattle directly from the Hudson location. We were to cut out 175 pairs—350 cows and calves—and herd them due south to Beaver Rim. The Hudson Ranch is located in a small river valley east of Lander that is surrounded for many miles by open, rolling prairie land. Except for the cottonwoods and willows along the river valley, there is not one tree within the hundreds of miles that the eye can see—just a rolling mix of short-grass prairie and sagebrush desert.

Henry and I stood on a high ridge just above the river valley and a mile south of the ranch as I nervously tried to understand exactly what he wanted me to do with these cattle. He pointed to what appeared to be a dry mountain range twenty or thirty miles to the distant south and said, "Take them out there, drive them across Beaver Creek, and leave them." I stared out across uninterrupted rolling expanses of desert and prairie wilderness without a single road or jeep trail in sight—literally hundreds of square miles—and tried to grasp Henry's vague instructions. In frustration I inquired, "Where exactly do you want me to drive them?" Henry got a quizzical look on his face, as if he had discovered some sort of grave mental impairment in me that up to now I had managed to conceal—one that would perhaps prevent me from seeing an entire mountain range—an impairment leaving me with an inability to grasp the concept of "over there." He just pointed emphatically to the distant southern horizon, as if addressing some sort of imbecile and said with annoyance, "Just drive them over there—shove them across Beaver Creek and let 'em go!"

Driving large numbers of cattle across miles of open range was one activity I lacked confidence in, but not wanting to further alert Henry to my ineptitude, I merely asked if we should get started the following day. He suggested that if we wanted to cross Beaver Creek before dark, we would need to start moving out around 4:00 AM. Sid and I spent the remainder of the day cutting out cows and calves and of course being cautious not to put the wrong cows and calves together.

The following morning we were joined by Sid's girlfriend, Jenny, and before any sign of daylight, we had all the cattle rounded up and began moving them slowly south—first crossing the highway and holding up some early-morning traffic, then pushing everybody through a gate in the highway fence. Care must be taken when moving young calves for the first time. If large numbers of calves become separated from their mother's side, they may suddenly panic and stampede back to the ranch, creating a pandemonium that could take half a day to resolve. This is the only behavior that cattle display that can approximate the familiar Hollywood fantasy of the stampede. Walking continuously all day is unnatural for cattle, and except for the occasional walk to and from water they typically walk only as fast as they can graze. When cattle are on the rare occasion inspired to run it is only for relatively short distances. In fact, on steep terrain, cattle become so tired after only a few hours that it becomes necessary to literally push them with your horse to get them moving—known as punching cows. Fortunately, the older cows have a perfect recollection of the summer ranges and will tend to get in a steadfast migratory mode and know precisely where they are expected to go.

By midday, Sid, Jenny, and I were well out into an open expanse of prairie, far from any evidence of civilization, visual or otherwise. Jenny is no stranger to cattle drives and knows all the ins and outs of horses and cattle. She was one of the many horsewomen, cowgirls, I would meet. Many women in Wyoming grow up with a rope in their hands just like boys. Gender roles in this part of the West have always been blurred.

As the desert stretched out before us and the cattle moved on toward the horizon, a strange sensation washed over me. The scene was suddenly devoid of any suggestion of time—no roads, no power lines, no vapor trails in the sky, and no particular year on the calendar—only desert, prairie, and sky with cattle and horsemen in big hats and dirty chaps, moving steadily toward the horizon. How many times had this event been repeated, perhaps now more like a ritual than a tradition, reenacted amid such open expanse and vastness and yet always so hidden from the eyes of civilization? The only sounds were the squeaking of leather saddles and the occasional moan and bawl of the cattle carried by a cool prairie wind. A horned lizard scampered between rocks. A pair of golden eagles soared to the east. A solitary antelope buck stood on a ridge to our west and calmly watched our latent and almost imperceptible progress. I wondered, *Is this really what we do or is this just another performance, calling for yet another few nameless extras in an ancient but nameless drama? When will time and circumstance lower our final curtain?*

By dusk we had moved over twenty miles, forced 350 head of cattle across a muddy, meltwater, swollen Beaver Creek without drowning a calf, and then in a seemingly unnatural act, just rode off and left them. Following the creek eastward, as if we knew where we were and how we got there, we saw headlights and a pale fog of dust coming down a dim outline of a two-rut road in the distance. As Don wheeled the trailer and pickup around, we arrived simultaneously like some sort of scripted choreography and calmly loaded three tired horses. The three of us, exhausted, nodded silently in the darkness of the rattling truck as we were gradually transported back through time and into some semblance of a civilization that was distinctly unwelcome.

While Sid continued watching over a few late calvers at the Hudson place, I returned to Red Canyon to make the few last-minute preparations for the return of the remaining cows and calves. This was after all a cattle ranch, but with the exception of a few horses wandering here and there, the absence of livestock was conspicuous. With only the occasional whinny or nicker from the few horses milling about, the constant gurgle of spring runoff in the canyon creek, and the perpetual wind hissing softly through dried yellow grass, Red Canyon Ranch was oddly hushed with the incongruity of an abandoned sawmill. But finally, the powerful moan of the big diesel engine of the tractor-trailer stock truck containing the remaining cows and calves from Hudson could be heard for miles coming up the canyon as it strained back and forth from one gear to the next. Soon a great cloud of orange dust boiled up from down in the run of the river. The massive truck crawled and groaned slowly up to the ranch, then pulled into the parking area, and began wheeling around to gain access to the chutes. Sid followed, driving an old, faded red two-ton stock truck with a blunt bulldog nose and a rattling wood stake body, packed tight with last year's heifers. In an hour, all the cows, calves, and heifers were unloaded—the heifers corralled and the cows and calves turned onto the dry lot—a temporary small holding area of a few acres. Again the diesels growled and rattled back down the canyon and disappeared in the distance. At last I was left alone with a hundred disturbed and agitated animals. Cows roared and bellowed while calves bawled in an effort to become once again sorted into matching pairs. I found myself motionless as a chorus of deep voices echoed and reverberated off the vertical red walls of the canyon that rose directly above us and stretched for miles from north to south. Chills ran up my back, as if the ghostly hollow moaning was somehow being transported from another age and was now being heard again through the deep cavernous well of time. And so, like the hauling of anchors, the casting off of lines, and the unfurling of sails, at once this great lumbering vessel groaned, growled, and was brought to life—under way again. Life was breathed into the great billowing sheets, and I felt ancient shrouds and lines take up a strain.

As we continued driving cattle off to their various summer ranges, often many miles away, the remaining cattle were watched over carefully for diseases affecting young calves that often occur in spring. Many calves develop a form of diarrhea that cattlemen refer to as *scours*, which if left untreated can lead to dehydration, wasting, pneumonia, and death. Every day the herd must be examined by horseback, and calves showing signs of sickness must be roped and administered a large antibiotic bolus tablet orally. Treatment of sick calves must be repeated for several days. By the time the last of the herd has been driven to distant summer ranges, most calves have been roped and handled several times. It is phenomenal, but eventually, after caring for so many hundreds of cows and calves, a hand learns to recognize each individual cow and calf. "Oh, there's old D-21 and her white-faced, lumpy-jawed dink. And there's A-12. Remember, she's still got a slick (unbranded) calf; better bring her in."

Summer comes slowly to a mountain ranch, and heavy periodic snowstorms add to the likelihood of sickness in younger calves throughout the spring. Temperatures can plunge for a few days after these events, threatening calves even further. Some breeds of cattle—Herefords in particular—have pink udders, and on occasion, bright sun reflected off deep snow will sunburn the udders causing cows to find nursing painful and to ultimately refuse milk to the calves. In this case all the pairs must be rounded up and corralled—the cows milked by hand twice a day, and the milk then artificially supplied to the calves. It is but one of the ranchers' many potential nightmares. Additionally, Hereford cattle, with pale eyes, have a predisposition in these higher elevations to develop a condition known as cancer eye. Herefords have become widely unpopular in Wyoming, particularly on high country ranches, although some still find the handsome breed irresistible.

Many heifers were late to calve and were kept nearby in the lot closest to the house. Typically, Sid and I would alternate with our alarm clocks and check the "girls" every two hours in the night. One stormy night in a state of fatigued semiconsciousness, I was walking through the heifers in a blinding windblown snowstorm when I kept feeling a tug on the back tail of my jacket. I turned with my flashlight to find a hungry yearling elk chewing on my coattail in a desperate effort to find food. It is common for elk to take up with cattle in winter, but if their numbers swell they can negatively affect a rancher's winter reserves of feed. Occasionally the game and fish people will intervene and offer assistance. In Red Canyon, however, the agency was less sympathetic, suggesting that we had brought the ranch to the elk.

After cattle are dispersed in the spring, ranching begins to look more like farming, as the hay meadows become the primary focus of attention. By the end of June, moisture in the form of precipitation becomes increasingly unlikely, and most Wyoming hay meadows are supplied with water by gravity irrigation. Usually, on the more elevated mountain ranches, a headgate installed on a creek or river high up on the mountain directs a specified amount of water down to the highest point of the ranch. Shallow ditches are then carefully engineered, surveyed, and dug, snaking back and forth across the contours of the hillsides at a perfect incline. Small sheets of plastic tarpaulin are installed with a few shovelfuls of dirt to form temporary dams that flood a given stretch of hillside. The dams are moved on average twice a day, starting at the lowest point of the meadow and gradually working back up the hill. After reaching the highest point of the meadow, the dam is moved back to the bottom of the hill and the process starts over. Irrigating takes some thought and a little ingenuity, and the challenge is to not leave any dry spots on a meadow while simultaneously trying not to overlap too much water with the next placement of the dam.

Prairie rattlesnakes are not found in the Wyoming high country, but the canyons, prairies, deserts, and the lower sagebrush-covered slopes of the mountains often support a sizeable population. It is not uncommon for every rattlesnake on a two-mile sagebrush-covered mountainside to eventually make its way to the lush wet abundance of the irrigation ditches and hay meadows below. Prairie rattlesnakes are relatively small, averaging less than three feet, but they are ill tempered, and in most people's estimation, infuriating in their perfect camouflage of the indistinguishable blend of sagebrush and Wyoming dirt. As a result, heavy boots are essential when irrigating. On warm early spring days, a hundred may appear coiled in the sun on rocky outcrops in the area of their winter den or hibernarium. On the hay meadows it is not uncommon to encounter ten in a day as temperatures increase. Mercifully, prairie rattlers are easily annoyed and often have the accommodating predisposition to rattle incessantly as you approach, making them easier to avoid. Even though they serve to keep damaging rodent numbers in check, some ranchers are disapproving and resentful of rattlesnakes. I find them in general to be rather good company, and a day spent irrigating with rattlesnakes is a decidedly richer day.

Wyoming ranches are not laid out in big convenient squares like ranches in other parts of the country but rather often look like contorted spiders on a map, as their properties conform only to the damp and meandering fertile waterways. No one would bother to homestead the dry sagebrush and sparse grasslands, which were generally considered valuable only as open grazing lands.

As I gradually came to know the land in the area, its rich history also began to reveal itself, not only by the evidence that seemed to be lying everywhere on the ground around my feet and by the strange petroglyphs carved into the red rocks, but also by the rich written and oral histories that have survived to the present.

For at least ten thousand years, Red Canyon supported a continuous aboriginal population, and, more recently, some of the oldest ranching activity in Wyoming. But perhaps more significantly, it has served as a corridor and thoroughfare for humans and wildlife throughout the millennia. Red Canyon provided the main passageway north and south from the Indian lands and soldier forts of the Wind River Valley to the Oregon Trail, the Army posts, and the gold mining communities of the South Pass area.

The William "Boss" Tweed homestead at the head of Red Canyon was one of the first ranches in Wyoming Territory and was not only the first to introduce sheep and cattle into the area but also supplied vegetable crops to the miners of Atlantic and South Pass cities. Boss Tweed was an ambitious young immigrant from England who settled in South Pass during the early days of the Gold Rush of the 1860s. His wife, Sarah, was the first white woman to live permanently in the South Pass area, and their children were the first whites to be born in South Pass City. The Tweeds built the second permanent log structure in the burgeoning tent community that would become a thriving boomtown. South Pass City would eventually support saloons, banks, and hotels before being largely abandoned in the late 1880s. The weather on the pass can be inhospitable even during the summer, so Boss acquired property in the more temperate elevations of Red Canyon. He began grazing the first permanent herd of sheep in Wyoming and raising a few cattle. Sheep have always been a

Covered wagon. *Copyright © Cathy Keene*

fixture on Wyoming range lands, and resentment by cattlemen has been largely exaggerated. But then when I was riding toward Sweetwater Station one day with Mark, he mindlessly looked to the West at sheep grazing on a distant mountainside, looked back to the road, and mumbled the quiet observation: "Prairie maggots."

In addition to selling beef and wool, Boss Tweed also operated a truck farm to supply the demand for goods in South Pass City and Atlantic City as well as other smaller mining communities. Tweed maintained a store and butchering operation in South Pass and supplied whiskey, tobacco, vegetables, dry goods, firearms, and ammunition, as well as meats—wild and domestic—including beef, bison, elk, antelope, and even dog meat at $0.03 a pound! As the ranch in Red Canyon grew, he eventually began providing lodging and supplies for pioneer travelers, traders, stagecoaches, and the many soldiers traveling between the forts at Lander and South Pass. Most of the Boss Tweed homestead was purchased by the state of Wyoming and now constitutes a large portion of the South Pass Winter Game Range.

Down the canyon, the Greenough Ranch was built around 1870 by a man named Wiesbrod and is more or less contemporary with the historic Ed Young place lying on the river at the mouth of the Little Popo Agie Canyon. Greenough acquired the ranch from Wiesbrod in the 1890s and constructed the existing house, but the ranch was eventually sold to world

Carrissa Saloon, South Pass City, 2002

champion bronc rider Bill Wilkinson in 1948. The Slingerland or Red Canyon ranch was created in a merger of several ranches. Henry purchased the Ed Young place on the river in the 1950s and eventually acquired the Greenough and the Hudson Ranch in a deal with Wilkinson and another lifelong Wyoming cattleman named Frank Cady. Frank's son Duane is a professional rodeo clown and was one of the first cowboys I met in the area. I had the privilege of meeting Frank, a true Wyoming cowboy and legend, many years later while studying bighorn sheep.

Ed Young was a tough and innovative rancher who survived raiding Indians and some of the most brutal winters in Wyoming history, and he created a profitable working ranch from scratch. He was perhaps the first to introduce apple growing to the high country of Wyoming, and his orchard with many of his original heirloom varieties still produces an abundance of sweet apples for Nan and Henry today. Fort Stambaugh was established to protect travelers on the Oregon Trail from hostile Indians, as well as miners working claims on South Pass. Stambaugh was eventually abandoned in the 1880s after the gold mining operations gradually

Fort Stambaugh logs—Slingerland barn.

played out and miners began leaving the area. Ed Young salvaged the well-constructed log buildings from the fort, transported them to Red Canyon, and reinstalled them at the mouth of the Bear Trap. Nan and Henry now live in a comfortable two-story, hand-hewn log house constructed from the logs of the former officer's quarters. A substantial log barn and some smaller log buildings were constructed from Stambaugh logs and placed on the same site where they remain in perfect condition today.

I eventually had the pleasure of meeting another local living legend, a real Wyoming cowboy and rancher named Corky Facinelli. Nan introduced us, suggesting that Corky had firsthand knowledge and personal recollections of some of the interesting history of Red Canyon. Corky grew up on the old Boss Tweed place in the earlier years of the twentieth century and arguably knows more about Red Canyon than anyone living today. Only the stone foundations and a few charred timbers remain at the Boss Tweed site, but Corky and I spent a day reminiscing and walking around this and several other sites in the canyon, kicking up old ax heads, cartridge casings, and horseshoes. After he showed me the general layout of the old Tweed place and the locations of some Indian fights that occurred in the immediate area, we drove back down the canyon. Crossing the river, he pointed out the site where the Shoshones pitched their tepees and camped when he was a boy. Corky vividly recalled that some of the Shoshones were occasionally employed to watch over the sheep herds grazing in Red Canyon. However, Corky and another boy were assigned the task of killing antelope and supplying the Indian camp with fresh antelope meat because the Indians did not have a strong cultural connection with domestic sheep husbandry. If food supplies became depleted, they would simply start killing and eating the sheep.

A cricket common on the open sagebrush and grass prairies of this part of Wyoming wanders about during the day as a solitary individual but is often seen in great numbers. These Mormon crickets are shiny, black, and robust, suggestive of some bizarre genetic cross between an ordinary black field cricket and a Sherman tank. Apparently, the Shoshones considered Mormon crickets a delicacy and would smash them up in great numbers into a sort of edible paste. To this day Corky cannot forget the repulsive sound of thousands of Mormon crickets scrambling around in the baskets of the Shoshone women who would spend hours collecting them.

At some point Corky pointed to a flat-appearing prominence overlooking the river and said that was the probable location of the bench where a Shoshone scalp dance was held during the early Ed Young days. Today that prominence is a productive irrigated hay meadow on the Red Canyon Ranch, still referred to by name as "the bench."

It has been said that the universe abhors a vacuum. After only a couple of years it seemed that Wyoming had rushed in and filled some great empty space within me. This working scientist from Florida became immersed and assimilated into high deserts and windswept mountains, new cultures, and old ranches. At some point I began to realize that things that once appeared different or strange were now becoming ordinary, familiar, a part of any normal life.

One day at noon while running a ranch-related errand in Lander, I found myself grabbing a bite to eat with a friend at one of the better restaurants in town. Without a thought, I walked in with boots, spurs, shotgun chaps, and hat, and naturally, because this is Lander Wyoming, no one even looked up. Midway through the meal it occurred to me that in my former life this attire would probably be deemed inappropriate if not outright jaw dropping. Another day I brought a visiting friend down from the high country after he had spent a week on a bear hunt. Exhausted and thirsty, we thoughtlessly walked into the only downtown Lander convenience store wearing revolvers, and the clerk behind the counter casually looked up and said in a detached voice, "Uh, you guys probably shouldn't be wearing those in here." Not even realizing that we were wearing sidearms, I was suddenly stricken with an arresting sense of confusion. As we walked outside to put our guns away, I thought to myself that this was probably odd in any other culture, and I certainly don't think of myself as a gun-totin' kind of guy. Having always found handguns to be unreasonably dangerous and generally undesirable, I was left with the startling realization that Wyoming had apparently slipped up on me from a blind side. I suppose the pistol had become a familiar tool of necessity, not unlike a carpenter's hammer hanging on a nail apron.

I never for one moment thought of myself as a cowboy, but it was apparent that necessity and an infectious life were causing me to look and behave differently. Once I was overcome with a brief recognition that I had at last, unknowingly perhaps, become a different person. It was not while throwing ropes, riding bucking horses, or branding calves, but it was a more subtle moment in time. While driving a load of replacement heifers from Hudson to Red Canyon in the old stock truck, I was traveling on the lonely Lyons Valley road when I passed another similar stock truck coming from the opposite direction. Two cowboys were also hauling a load of cattle and casually gave me a knowing wave, perhaps even a sympathetic wave; at any rate some expression of camaraderie was exchanged. For a brief instant I was overcome with a distinct feeling that somehow I had in some way managed to become a legitimate part of this small but persistent culture. As the truck radio ironically blared out Willie Nelson singing "Mamas don't let your babies grow up to be cowboys," I thought to myself, *What have you gone and done—Joe Boy?* There was no question—this was not what my mama had in mind. However, it was only a brief and passing moment that was soon overcome by my more defining lack of any real personal identity.

Working hands. *Copyright © Cathy Keene*

While having a beer one day with Mark Ramsey in the old Atlantic City Mercantile saloon, he inquired about a person that he felt had no business in Wyoming. Mark expressed strong opinions about what sort of person should or shouldn't live in this country, and he was particularly disturbed by, and disapproving of, this individual. Mark declared, "Why would a guy like that want to live in this country?" At a loss to explain, I replied, "I don't know, Mark, I think maybe he just wanted to be a cowboy." The words had not yet completely passed my lips before Mark blasted, "He couldn't be a pimple on a cowboy's ass!" Recoiling a little, I laughed out loud at the analogy but simultaneously worried where I might reside on Mark's rigid continuum between cowboy and ass pimple.

A working cowboy is forced to confront life each day on the most fundamental level. Ranching, in its most basic sense, is about turning the cold hard earth into cold hard cash. As a financial reality, that transformation from the most basic of natural resources to the fiduciary abstraction of liquid monetary currency is the economic equivalent of getting blood out of a turnip. The cowboy is truly a highly skilled craftsman, but his tools are the most basic—ropes, leather, wire and shovels, hammers, handsaws, and a good folding knife. His hands are hard and scarred, and like old saddle leather, cracked and browned from sun, wind, sweat, and frost. His fingers show the history of a thousand busted knuckles, and he is never without at least one bruised and blackened fingernail. It is a lucky cowboy who retains all ten fingers. The medium he finds expression in is all about dirt, lodgepoles, rocks, old leather, and rough stock, mud, blood, barbed wire, and rusty old tractors that absolutely must start on a forty-degree-below-zero morning. Every day is an exhausting and uncelebrated act of sheer will where he expects to do the hardest thing he can possibly do as hard as he can possibly do it. He will do it today and he will do it tomorrow and he will nearly always do it alone. Invariably, at some point he will find himself actually risking his own life so that someone else's water will get down the ditch or so someone else's animal might live another day. And the only job that will ever be acknowledged is the one that didn't get done. Every day, he is simply expected to turn stardust into living things.

13

THE LAST WYOMING COWBOY

A good working cowboy is a person who not only has to be multi-talented and highly skilled in many areas but also adaptable, aggressive, and possess a wide range of serviceable tools, that is, a good "outfit," including saddles, tack, pickup truck, horse trailer, carpentry tools, chain saw, and horseshoeing equipment. And yes, most are pretty handy with a gun. Many people fit that description in those days but I think most people in the area would agree that Mark Ramsay fit the profile in a most defining way, displaying a certain confidence, proficiency, and expertise in all he undertook. He was without a lot of formal education but could be considered without question a highly intelligent person with an insatiable curiosity for new things, new ideas, and the goings-on with new people. And even on occasion, Mark could be found with a "good read" sticking up out of a back pocket or a saddlebag. I would drag the strangest assortment of people into this country from my former life—scientist, artists, doctors, lawyers, Buddhist monks, whomever—and invariably Mark would, after perhaps a little initial suspicion, find common ground, gain their respect and admiration, and become eventually best of friends.

Like most good cowboys, Mark had excellent tools and fine gear. In twenty-five years, I never new him to be without a string of good working horses and often a couple of fine mules. He sat on good saddles, his horses wore good tack, and his mules bore their load on good oak crossbuck packsaddles and fine handmade calfskin panniers. He had a work ethic that would shame a Lutheran dairy farmer, but the line between fun and work was always blurred by Mark's enthusiasm; he was always demonstrating that he could make a living at both. Thoreau wrote, "Let not to get a living be thy trade but thy sport." Mark could have been his inspiration. He could turn the dirtiest day's work into an event you wouldn't want to miss. Like so many who have grown up only knowing a life derived from the bounty of the land and the creatures living on it, Mark was driven by the most natural and innocent presumption that the earth would provide him with a living. He was always imagining new ways to mine, harvest, collect, hunt, fish, and gather from the natural world. He transformed the necessity to scratch out a living into a rich life that made other men envious, and he could do it with a box of bullets, a chain saw, a bamboo fly rod, a good horse, a strong rope, or a backhoe. There were few economic opportunities that the environment of Wyoming offered of which Mark did not avail himself. He even mined a little gold and for a time cut dead standing spruce and lodgepole pines commercially for house logs. Always mysteriously finding ways to make things happen—an industrial-scale rabbit-out-of-the hat capability—he turned up one day with a twenty-year-old bulldozer to be used as a log skidder and an even older log truck that not only could he miraculously keep running, but when Sid would get the choker chain caught in the dozer winch, Mark just magically produced an acetylene torch and cut it free. The dozer was eventually trapped in deep snows in the mountains for nearly six months. When the snow finally melted enough in the spring, Mark returned to the frozen dozer, built a pine-log fire under the crank case, tinkered with the engine for a few minutes, and fired it right off. When ranchers had a nuisance problem like coyotes or beavers, Ramsey was always there. He owned an old Savage .250-3000, which was probably made in the 1920s; it was one of the first rifles made to push a bullet at 3,000 feet per second—which is fast. Using an ax or sledgehammer, he would drive a one-inch-diameter round bar of steel into a beaver dam, pull the bar out, and stack dynamite up in the hole and leave one stick protruding above the rest. Then he would back off, lie down, and take careful aim, squeeze off a shot, and the high-velocity bullet struck with enough energy to detonate the dynamite. Voilà—no more beaver dam—and in addition, Mark had seized a golden opportunity to make a really loud noise. By his own admission, he had an unhealthy fascination with all things "loud, fast, and dangerous."

Always willing to try something new, Mark's aggressive self-confidence made him appear fearless. A former Vietnam helicopter pilot named Jim settled in the Lander area in the seventies, and if he lacked any common sense he made up for it with some ready cash. Ranchers were being plagued by coyotes as their numbers began to soar, and, coincidentally, in those days a good winter Montana pale coyote pelt could bring as much as $125. Mountain coyotes are commonly believed to be larger and often possess thicker and more desirable pale furs. Jim owned a small helicopter and decided to hunt coyotes commercially. He needed some fearless soul to shoot while he maneuvered the helicopter through the steep and treacherous mountain terrain with a dangerously thin atmosphere. Mark was an immediate candidate for the job—loud, fast, dangerous—perfect! On several occasions they would pick up so many coyotes the helicopter could not lift off without "jumping" the overloaded contraption off a steep incline to provide a little more "air." Predictably, they soon crashed the helicopter with a load of coyotes but managed to snowshoe nine miles out of the high country in the dead of winter to a road. It eventually occurred to Mark that it was illogical for the other guy to be making all the big bucks, there was no reason he couldn't pilot an aircraft, and since he was Mark, he was sure he could probably do it better. He soon appeared at the Lander airfield seeking a flying lesson. It is unclear how many lessons Mark took to solo, but surely it was only the minimum. Then in true Mark Ramsey fashion, he got a ride to the Casper airport 150 miles away, and after having purchased a thirty-year-old Piper Cub for $7,000, he flew it back along the familiar highway to Lander. In the dead of winter, he took the doors off the plane and with his shooter, Monty Hitshew, began hunting coyotes. His strategy was to shoot the coyotes from an elevation of one hundred feet or less, make note of the locations, and then retrieve them by snowshoe, horse, or snowmobile. The old plane's engine burned so much oil that he would have to land on a road or highway every twenty minutes or so and add some. The professional pilots at the Lander airfield were taking bets on whether Mark would survive the winter. But out of necessity and with nerves of steel, Mark became an extremely competent pilot, but one who always chose to take risks. In Wyoming, the terrain, altitude, and wind create conditions that are notoriously dangerous for any aircraft and every pilot. Local taxidermist Bill Miller confessed to me one afternoon that perhaps the only time he has come close to crying in his adult life was during one afternoon he spent elk antler hunting from Mark's plane. He said Mark would come into the mountain on a dive and make the sagebrush shudder in his wake. But winter in Wyoming is typically downtime for a working cowboy, and Mark had found a way to fill the gap.

Elk shed their antlers every spring and immediately begin growing replacements that are completed in only three or four months. It has been suggested that elk antler development could represent the most rapid formation and completion of such a large quantity of structural biomass in the animal world. A large mature bull can grow over twenty-five pounds of strong, dense, bonelike antlers in about twelve weeks (Murie, 1951). It is common for mature bulls to herd after breeding season in groups of thirty to fifty individuals. Limestone Mountain and South Pass would always have large bull herds wandering around through the winter and spring. As the bulls began shedding their antlers in March, Mark would fly every day, find a particular herd of bulls, and mark their specific location on a topographic map. When the last of the bulls had shed, Mark would get on his horse and follow the daily wanderings of the herd from point to point on the map and find all the sheds that were dropped along the way. If one typical mature bull antler can easily weigh ten pounds, and if thirty bulls drop twenty pounds of antlers each, at a value of $7 or $8 a pound—well, do the math—that $4,200 from one bull herd is a cowboy's fortune. Combining the antler value with one hundred or more prime coyote pelts, at a minimum value of $50 each, the addition of an airplane to Mark's "outfit" was definitely improving his winter outlook.

Mark Ramsey and Jiggs, 1985.

Mark often worked for outfitters in the fall, wrangling horses and mules and taking hunters far into the backcountry in pursuit of elk, deer, moose, or bears. He, of course, raised his own pack mules and had packsaddles, large canvas wall tents, and most of the gear necessary for his own efficient elk camp. His hardworking dependability, his charismatic personality, and his mastery and competence of all the requisite backcountry skills made Mark a natural candidate for a professional outfitter. However, he was not licensed, and the outfitting business requires buying an expensive "area" outfitter permit. These permits are in short supply, plus it is necessary to jump through various legal, bureaucratic, and insurance hoops that he found inconvenient and annoying. Mark was fiercely independent and resentful of the slightest intrusion into his life by anything governmental. Although not an outlaw, he probably thought he was as competent as anyone and certainly more so than any politician in determining the difference between right and wrong. Once I was asked by some of my friends who were coming to hunt with us if this guy could be trusted. I replied that I would trust Mark Ramsey with my life and then jokingly followed with, "He has never stolen a thing in his life and he would never shoot you without a good reason." However, any Wyoming resident can serve as a guide for any out-of-state hunter, and in those days the law seemed to be unclear about the extent of the service a guide can provide so long as no significant "gratuities" were involved.

For years I had been taking friends into the backcountry on expeditions that sometimes involved hunting, fishing, or just backpacking through the high mountains, depending on the time of year. Following the Slingerland Ranch years, I became a sort of Wyoming connection for a number of old friends and friends of friends from back east. Mark and I decided that we should all throw in together and go ahead and do things correctly—Mark's way. I could throw a diamond hitch on a packsaddle and generally keep guys out of trouble, even stumble onto an elk once in a while, while Mark would provide the horses, mules, and most of the camp gear. The two of us would pack into the backcountry, select the perfect location, and spend several days setting up a comfortable camp. This would involve pitching large canvas wall tents for sleeping as well as a larger one for a kitchen, complete with a collapsible woodstove for heat and Coleman stoves for cooking. By packing in 2 x 2 pieces of plywood, handsaws, nails, and bailing wire, we could cut dead lodgepoles and fashion shelves, pantries, and an accommodating table complete with a checkered tablecloth. Folding aluminum and canvas stools and wooden cots would keep everyone comfortable and off the ground. Our camps were always dazzling in their esthetic location and efficiency,

Joe and Mark at Elk Camp. *Photo by Harry Knight.*

and the idea was to create a sense that everyone was stepping back in time. It would be my responsibility to hire a cook and organize a small group of guys to fly into the Jackson airport, seventy miles from our camp. We would then all drive to the trailhead where Mark would meet us with the horses and then pack everybody into the camp a few miles down the Snake River. Our first year I brought an old friend and former Buddhist monk with backcountry backpacking experience to serve as camp cook. In spite of fifteen-degree mornings and pesky grizzly bears, Harry chose to sleep outside the tents every night "under the sky." During our first night sleeping at the campsite, we were exhausted from a 4:00 AM start and a day spent packing in all the camp and erecting tents. We hadn't constructed the corral yet, so the horses were tied on a short picket line right outside the tents. Annoyed by his accommodations, one of Mark's horses, Jiggs, began incessantly pawing the ground in protest. We lay in a state of semiconscious torpor for an hour listening to coyotes howling and bugling elk, desperately trying to ignore Jiggs when Mark, exasperated, finally bellowed at the top of his voice: "*Goddamn it,* Jiggs—*shut up!*" Just below us on Glade Creek, a grizzly answered with a roar that would have been audible for miles in the still mountain air. We all became very quiet—with nary another peep out of Jiggs. Thereafter our camp cook still never slept in a tent, but he may have become one of the first Buddhist monks ever to habitually sleep with a loaded rifle inside his sleeping bag. There is nothing like a seven-hundred-pound grizzly to put your spiritual priorities in perspective—Harry apparently preferred to become one with the universe but not with the bear.

Prior to the hunting trip we would all settle on a cash figure that would help pay for a ton of groceries, plus the camp cook, and some money to buy new or improved gear for the year. If anyone asked, we owned the gear jointly but left it in Mark's safekeeping. The idea was to help Mark get into the outfitting business. I was in it for any excuse to get into the wilderness. We only hunted on public lands, and every game warden and outfitter for two hundred miles knew Mark personally, as well as the beautiful but grizzly-infested country where we were hunting. (This was an area where Yellowstone Park had been customarily releasing problem bears.) So, although we possibly raised a few eyebrows, no one ever suggested that we could be bending the letter of the law. Clearly, we were just a bunch of buddies out trying to get away from the road.

Many young people find the lure of the Rocky Mountain West irresistible. You see them throughout the spring and summer months—usually college age, maybe out on their own for the first time. Invariably, their faces are smooth and rosy red from a few days hiking or backpacking in an exotic mountain terrain, and their eyes wide, beaming with astonishment and enthusiasm for a world that has surpassed all their expectations. Their curious hats and clothing speak of another world and their soft, smooth hands speak of another life. Any given night they may be seen standing in any old Wyoming bar, staring in wonder at a hundred years of history hanging dusty and faded on the smoke-stained walls that surround a curious mingling of burly oil roughnecks, craggy veteran mountain climbers, and weathered cowboys. Looking at these young faces always begs the question, Will this be the one who cannot, will not, leave, or will this be just another one to treasure a passing memory? However, the majority seem to get their fill and in weeks or months, or perhaps in some cases a year or two, begin looking in other directions. For a few, the necessity to live on the edge of the wildness and vastness that the Rockies provide is overwhelming—their appetite is insatiable. My predisposition is for the latter, and now there can be no question that I will never get enough. After so many years, a yearning for the Wyoming wilderness still takes on the proportions of an obsession. All the experience gained only serves to illuminate the proportions, the magnitude of the remaining wilderness that will never be explored. It is not a frustration but a consolation that one lifetime is woefully inadequate for the task.

After a few brief years in Wyoming, inevitability overtook us and Tommie and I separated permanently. Tommie had found a new life in another culture as a technical rock climber and mountaineer, and I began making changes too. Although there were things about ranching that suited my personality, I was only willing to invest myself in such a life if I could own my own place—a financially unrealistic dream. So I began working full-time as a wildlife artist and writer. Coincidentally, during the 1980s cattle prices began to suffer from a permanent reduction in worldwide demand for beef, and the operational costs of ranching began to skyrocket. Old family ranches began to go under left and right. By 1990 the new demand for real estate created a hungry market as destitute ranchers foundered, and their ranches sold for a fraction of their potential value. Many former working ranches all over the West, particularly the more beautiful ranches in the wildest locations, were gradually bought up as "hobby ranches" for the very wealthy, and tragically many others were bought, broken up, and subdivided into the familiar forty-acre "ranchette." Nan and Henry Slingerland foresaw this inexorable onslaught, and in a gesture of great wisdom and generosity, sold Red Canyon Ranch at a small percentage of its actual value to the Nature Conservancy. Today the ranch is preserved and operated as an "ideal, environmentally friendly Wyoming cattle ranch," exercising a healthy and sustainable land-use strategy. It is the Nature Conservancy's goal to demonstrate ultimately that ranching must be an integral partnership with the ecology. If ranching degrades water quality and range lands, then the carrying capacity for wildlife and cattle is irreparably sacrificed. The equation is brain-dead simple, but the tendency to squeeze the last dollar out of a piece of land in the short run is irresistible for a goat herder in east Africa, an indigenous logger in Brazil, or a failing rancher in Wyoming. Unfortunately, it appears that common sense and conservation are luxuries that will always be casualties of fundamental human need.

Upon the death of my father and the need to care for an aging mother I was forced to leave Wyoming and attend to things in northern Florida, where I stayed for many years. However, I still found months each year to immerse myself in the country I loved. It was clear that I was never fully awake or alive in any other environment. Mark and I continued our fall hunting camp activities for several years, and summers became opportunities for experiencing the high altitude. I gradually lost all touch with Wyoming ranch life, although I would occasionally drop in on Nan and Henry, who retained several hundred acres of the original Red Canyon Ranch. Mark was always there to keep me up to date on any significant changes that occurred, socially, economically, or environmentally. I even managed to entice Mark to leave the West for the first time and venture into the culture and ecology of north Florida for a few weeks. He had never seen an ocean, and one morning he found a cold March storm surf on a barrier island impossible to resist. Abandoning his red cowboy boots on the beach, we entered the cold, raging water with all our clothes, laughing and whooping like children as we were pummeled by ten- and twelve-foot breakers. Mark later made analogies to bull riding, and we were both so sore the following day we could barely walk. However, north Florida proved to be claustrophobic with its suffocating overgrowth of vegetation, and Mark was further disturbed by a conspicuous overabundance of people. Mark was highly approving of airboats, however, which met his loud, fast, and dangerous criteria. He also approved of the brilliant red cardinals at the bird feeder and fresh Gulf seafood, but he was simultaneously mystified that people living in such a botanically rampant environment would voluntarily choose to have additional plants in the house.

Over the years I never observed any real compromise in Mark's approach to life, but he was all too aware of the rapid changes that were occurring in his beloved Wyoming. He continued with ranch work, hunting coyotes and elk antlers, and meeting the demand for miles of new lodgepole buck-and-rail fences. Buck and rail had become popular because it's safe for wildlife, conveniently free standing, and bisonproof to boot. (Bison are notoriously disrespectful of wire fences.) However, Mark was becoming increasingly bitter and resentful with all the cultural and economic changes he observed and perhaps was worried how he might persist in this new world. We found ourselves ranting and raving over the disappearance of ranches and the abundance of fabulously wealthy landowners as we nursed a beer or cup of coffee in the old Mercantile bar. Once in a reflective moment I asked him, "Mark, listen to us—are we being the old timers complaining about the good old days like every other generation as it becomes overtaken by the next?" Mark paused briefly and then mumbled something like, "Maybe so," but then offered proudly, "Well Joe Boy, one good thing about this country—it'll still get you killed!" Not feeling the necessity to pursue that line of conversation, I simply acknowledged that I understood. People have historically traveled long distances and continue to go to enormous effort and extremes to die in extraordinary ways in Wyoming.

Mark became less itinerate and eventually found an old one-room log building out in the desert near the Sweetwater River that he simply picked up with the help of a few friends and hauled into Atlantic City. He installed the more than one-hundred-year-old cabin on Rock Creek downstream from the Mercantile and chinked the logs with trimmings from his coyote hides. Heat was provided by an ancient but rock-solid industrial-grade woodstove that he somehow recovered in typical Mark fashion. There he brought four- and six-inch dry lodgepoles out of the mountains and built his crossbucks and rails for fences. He dug a veritable cave in the hillside behind the cabin and lined it with a huge ten-foot-diameter steel culvert. He then welded up a steel door and mounted the thing like the entrance to a Fort Knox vault. He proudly opened the padlocked door for me one afternoon, and there I observed a securely protected treasure consisting of two well-used saddles, some calfskin panniers and tack, a Winchester .30-06, the old Savage .250-3000, a few hand tools, and two fifty-pound bags of sweet feed. To bring me up to speed on his new industry, he grabbed a chain saw, ax, hammer, and a handful of twenty penny spikes and set about building a set of crossbucks in less than five minutes. It was still Sunday, however, and so retiring the chain saw, we made immediate emergency plans to catch some browns and rainbows out on the Sweetwater.

Soon after coming to Wyoming it became clear to me that I would be writing about the environment and people. At some point, however, the nagging urge developed into necessity as the human and environmental ecologies began changing into something radically different and in some cases unrecognizable. Those familiar and defining American icons, the cattle ranch and the working cowboy, as well as the wilderness ecology that had defined them all, seemed to be slipping into obscurity, or were at least being redefined in a most disappointing but perhaps inevitable way. Were people aware? Did people care? I worried that most people had no idea that such a culturally iconic and defining life had all but slipped into history in a single decade.

However, it became increasingly obvious that the artifact that most clearly defined the people and culture of Wyoming was not actually the cow but rather the horse. The horse more properly sustained the identity of the people and their intimate ecological relationship to the land. Native American people have always viewed their ponies as a form of wealth, and even today reservation grazing lands seem to support more horses than cattle, although even after thirty years, a decent horse can still be bought for about $700. Horses here are always easier to get than to get rid of. Of course, not everyone in Wyoming owned a ranch or worked on one, but many more people found the horse to be a tool of necessity in this vast country. For literally hundreds of years the horse was the common denominator between a rugged wilderness of mountains and deserts and its people. Not only ranchers but most people who needed access to the land were dependent on the horse. Every game warden and forester used the saddle horse and the packhorse as a means of simply doing their job. The need to hunt and pack out large quantities of meat was nearly always met and facilitated by the horse. Even into the 1990s many loggers customarily used a team to gently skid house logs off the steep, inaccessible slopes of the mountainsides. Today only a few horse loggers remain, like Jack Malmberg and Woody Barmoor, and, curiously, new national forest policies are throwing bureaucratic obstacles in the teams' way. Teams of draft horses are a low-impact and efficient way of managing forests by using them to remove the thousands of highly combustible but valuable dead-standing "beetle kill" trees that are prized for house logs. Fuel for forest fires is reduced. Sport fishermen employed the horse to reach the rich, productive waters of the high alpine lakes. Outfitters kept the art of horsepacking alive, employing and educating successive new generations of wranglers in all the necessary backcountry skills. Outfitters have probably produced and sustained more real working cowboys than ranching. A horse trailer at a trailhead is becoming an increasingly rare sight in much of the Rocky Mountain West.

By the mid-1990s a new tool was redefining the way people saw and related to the wilderness of Wyoming. Without a conspiratorial word or any overt inimical design, insidiously the all-terrain vehicle (ATV), or four-wheeler, slowly replaced the horse as the vehicle of choice. In a few brief years, the ATV changed a culturally and environmentally defining tradition that had spanned four hundred years. People in the Wyoming backcountry look and behave differently as a result, and much of the backcountry environment looks and feels and has become a different place. Trailheads are crammed with ATV trailers. What horseman would be foolish enough to head up a mountain trail before daylight with ATVs by the dozen buzzing past in the dark? Now a burgeoning industry that is an integral part of every small-town economy has become an enormous genie that will never again be contained. ATV enthusiasts have become a large voting constituency and a powerful lobby for ever more lenient restrictions on access to wild areas and for the proliferation of new roads into otherwise inaccessible forest lands. Abuses by ATVs have proven to be impossible to police, and the temptations are obviously irresistible as a spiderweb of new trails indicate that many riders will leave designated roads with impunity. The customary $100 fine for leaving a designated trail merely represents a cheap and easy license for any rider driving a $7,000 machine. Many have chain saws on board so no obstacle can obstruct their path. Formerly pristine wild lands are now literally *abuzz* and crisscrossed with sportsmen gaining access to wildlife, or even more troubling, simply using Wyoming's wild places as cleverly designed obstacle courses, with no respite for wildlife. Ironically, an ATV is much gentler on a mountain trail than a four-wheel-drive pickup truck, but unfortunately an otherwise useful tool that is not without virtue has become a travesty careering out of control, and Wyoming will never be the same. Invariably where these activities occur, wildlife habitat is degraded, and the negative effects can be clearly demonstrated in any public use area. Forest and wildlife managers are hamstrung by the so-called multiple use definitions created to define our public lands and national forests over one-half century before the ATV was even a concept. Teddy Roosevelt, Olaus Murie, and Aldo Leopold have long since rolled over in their graves. ATVs quickly became the leading cause of severe injuries among children in Wyoming and in much of the West. *Wyoming Wildlife Magazine* staff writers Chris Madson and Cody Beers published cover articles several years ago, one titled, "ATV, Scourge of the West." The backlash was enormous. Both writers received hate mail and multiple life-threatening phone calls. Cody's entire family was threatened with murder by an explosives expert. No Wyoming politician, forest, or wildlife manager with an instinct for self-preservation would now have the courage to speak out against this pernicious infection, although in private I have never once heard one of these professionals speak out in their defense. Wyoming game wardens have no jurisdiction to enforce abuses by vehicles on national forest or BLM lands! Legislation, regulation with teeth, as well as law enforcement have been slow to come, or one could argue are nonexistent. So far only our designated wilderness areas are technically immune from this plague. As Cody reminds us, "In Wyoming, you can park by the road, walk half a mile, and you are in wilderness—or you can drive your machine five miles off a trail into the backcountry, walk half a mile, and you are in wilderness."

Other areas of the Rocky Mountains have been loved almost to death. Wyoming has maintained its integrity and virtues in large part because without paved roads, ski areas, upscale shopping, and rubber tomahawks (Jackson, Wyoming, excepted), people have stayed away in droves. When I was considering writing this book, I consulted Mark. After numerous exhaustive, emotional, and even painful conversations, Mark and I eventually unanimously concluded that I should not write a book about Wyoming, agreeing that Wyoming could ultimately suffer from this kind of attention. And so one morning over coffee at the Highwayman truck stop, Mark and I drove the final nail in the coffin of the Wyoming book. No question—it was dead.

Once again I left Wyoming to head back to north Florida. Neither Mark nor I are men of letters, and since Mark had never had a telephone, it was typical for us to go long periods of time with no communication.

Perhaps three or four months later, one winter evening after midnight, the phone rang. It was Mark calling from a snowplow he was working in a raging blizzard on the summit of the South Pass highway. "Joe Boy, I've been thinking about this thing a lot—you need to write this book," Mark said emphatically, like we were picking up a conversation from an hour earlier. "You mean the Wyoming book? I thought we had put that to rest," I said. Mark then said, "Wyoming is going to hell and people need to know what we're losing, and you can't possibly make things get any worse!" Recoiling a little, I muttered something about that not being such a good idea, and Mark bellowed, "You need to get your ass back out here and write that book!" Unconvinced by Mark's sudden declaration, I mentioned our reasons for letting the idea go, but I would be back in a few weeks and we could kick the idea around a little more. With that, I told Mark to be careful on that snowplow and I would see him soon.

A month later I got a call from Tommy Peters, a mutual friend and manager of the Hitching Rack Restaurant and bar. As soon as I heard Tommy's voice I somehow knew it was the bad news I had dreaded for years. Mark had gotten a call from a rancher in the Sweetwater country south of Lander in a remote desert area known as Bison Basin. Coyotes had been decimating his spring lambs, and he wanted Mark to fly out and try to eliminate a few. In blustery wintry weather, Mark and Monty flew out over the high desert as they had so many times before, but they never showed up at the ranch and never returned to the airport. Another pilot eventually flew the route toward the basin and found Mark's plane nosed straight into the ground. Mark and Monte had been killed instantly. The exact cause was never determined; a backhoe was driven out to the lonely stretch of desert, and the plane was buried on the spot. Within six hours of hearing the terrible news, I was on the road heading to Wyoming with a broken heart.

Three long days later, I crossed the border from Nebraska into Wyoming and immediately began perceiving a conspicuous vacuum. It was impossible to imagine the Wyoming that I had always known without a Mark Ramsey. After his forty-four years, the man and the country were somehow inseparable, and the void was palpable—like trying to imagine Wyoming without elk and grizzly bears. As I pulled into Lander, a pall of sadness seemed to hang over the little town, and I spotted a Lander *Journal* newspaper with a picture of Mark's plane on the front page, nose crammed straight into the prairie, tail pointing upward toward the sky. I visited with

Tommy Peters briefly at the Hitching Rack where we shared our disbelief but also some element of inevitability born of Mark's insatiable exposure to risk. That was when I ran into John Mionczynski for the first time in a long while and retrieved a copy of my book on the wild turkey in Florida from my pickup and dropped it on his table.

The following day a memorial service was held for Mark and Monte at the local Elk Club. Not surprisingly, it seemed as though everyone within a two-hundred-mile radius was in attendance. Anyone passing through Lander might have suspected that the governor of Wyoming had died. Observing the many hundreds of sad faces in the big room, it soon became obvious that these two men's lives had indeed been thoroughly interwoven with the widely dispersed community and ecologies of northern Wyoming—a most common thread. Mark had an infectious personality, and it was clear just how far reaching his effect on other people's lives had been. Women adored Mark and men learned to love and admire him. Mark seemed to possess some unique quality of spirit that was contagious—his humor, wit, and hand-forged self-confidence could take control of a room like an irreverent anarchist running for office. It was not always easy being Mark's friend, and women seemed to pass through his life with some predictability. He had a confrontational personality and on occasion would intentionally try to push you to your philosophical and emotional limits. He considered it his responsibility, if not his pleasure, to give your cage a good rattling from time to time as he called into question anything you considered truthful or sacred. We certainly had rough spots throughout our twenty-five-year friendship, and even though I loved him like a brother, I was among a much larger group of brothers who were exceedingly grateful we never had to fight him. He never missed an opportunity to appear hard as nails, but without fail, eventually, some evidence of a sensitive and kind heart would escape through his rough exterior. If Mark ever truly got out of line, it might have taken a year, but eventually you would get, not necessarily an apology, but at least an acknowledgment. Ironically, it was probably Mark's ultimate caring and generosity that wove his complex tapestry of relationships together.

A real cross-section of Wyoming's culture was in attendance at the service, but naturally the ranching community was probably best represented. It eventually occurred to me that there were only a few familiar faces, and

I began wondering about the many ranchers and cowboys I had known so well all those years before. With the demise of the ranching industry in the 1980s and 1990s, had they all left the area? Where were all those faces I had seen while branding calves, hunting elk, or drinking a beer at the Merc on a Saturday night? Why had they not come to say good-bye to Monte and Mark? Gradually, as I looked around the crowded room, the many grim middle-aged faces began to take on a faint familiarity. There they were—the young, strong eager faces that I had once known began to appear as mature, dignified older men. There was Mark's good friend Mike and his father, Bill Ruby, now a silver-haired older gentleman. One of the last times I saw Bill, he was fifty-eight and riding a bull at a Lander rodeo. I hadn't seen Mike Ruby since we spent a day and a night helping pack one of Mark's big elk off some remote backcountry mountain. And there was Chuck Brodie. Had I seen Chuck once since we spent long days together with Mark on our horses riding Maxom Basin, Freak Mountain, and Indian Ridge two decades earlier? Chuck taught me that in Wyoming a rifle scabbard always goes behind the saddle and never in front. It seemed as though a paradox was at work here. How could this vast country visually appear so unchanged while so much time has slipped by unnoticed? And doesn't that in some way characterize the paradox of Wyoming? How equally unrecognizable had I become? Where is the strong young man they once knew?

Wooden coffins covered with garlands of prime coyote pelts and elk antlers—so many grieving people—how is this possible? As I left the building, I saw Nickie outside.

Over the next few days I managed to make contact with old friends, and one by one, each expressed a common sentiment. Not only had we all lost a dear and valued friend, but something perhaps even more transformative had occurred. Almost without exception, every person recognized that something definitive and irreplaceable was now lost. No human being I know would dare take on the daunting task of trying to be a Mark Ramsey, but nevertheless, I think many of us have a need to know there is still someone like Mark in the world—one extraordinary person who simultaneously defined and was defined by the wilderness of Wyoming. The man and the ecology of Wyoming were inseparable. It seemed as though a certain authenticity had finally and irrevocably slipped from our grasp—a symbolic end of an ancient tradition culminating in one extraordinary individual. But then Mark would have hated all this sentimental crap.

A short time later, a celebration was held at the old Mercantile Saloon in Atlantic City where a big crowd of Mark's friends gathered outside. At a designated time, a small plane similar to Mark's, flew down Rock Creek at low elevation directly in front of the bar. As everyone cheered, Mark's ashes were released over the creek, but then with an appropriate irreverence they blew right back into the plane. The crowd roared as the plane cruised down the creek, billowing ashes like it was on fire.

Although life is changing in Wyoming, and the true working cowboy may be riding into a final sunset, there are still a precious few hardworking ranches that will always need good help. This country demands that branded cattle be driven many miles out onto open summer range lands in spring and rounded up in the fall, and every working horse must be trimmed and shod. Many hardworking outfits still need at least one good hand. Somewhere out there, there must be a few men and women who are riding horses and working cattle every day and haven't heard the word— that a special way of life has finally died. They are not trying to rope calves from a four-wheeler, and they don't wear a hand-tooled leather holster for a cell phone. They probably haven't had time to come to a town, sit down, and reflect over a cold beer with a few old friends or burn perfectly good daylight at a rodeo. This is still a land where a cow can drift for a hundred miles. And so, surely, there are those who will ride alone through an unbroken rocky sagebrush wilderness—those who will choose to live within a landscape that few can even imagine. They will ride alone on a sturdy, willing horse and on occasion slowly scan a full and unbroken horizon, saying to themselves once again, "Good lord, this is what I get to do." Consider that they may be one of those rare survivors who climbs out of a saddle and into a bunk dead tired every night, secure in the recognition of having reconciled that most fundamental bottom line, a bottom line that lies balanced between heartbreak and a life well lived, a bargain between the wages you earn and the price you are willing to pay.

Part 3

14

FACING THE FACTS

There has been an unspoken presumption that the rich, some would say sacred, landscape of the remote Rocky Mountain West was possessed of some inherent immunity to a changing world. But it appears that even this obscure ecology, with its great creatures and its seemingly iconic cultures, may at last be in peril. We are reaching the inevitable vanishing point that appears as a perspective on every horizon. For unlike so many other places on our planet, here the landscape and its people have always coexisted in parallel. At last however, this vast and ancient passageway, this wondrous thoroughfare, unknowingly disappears behind us and begs the question: Is this in fact our choice as humans, or have we merely lost our way?

A disturbing paradox hangs over Middle Mountain and much of the high mountain west that casts an ominous shadow. In spite of this mountain's perennial integrity and splendor, a sickness is occurring here that causes the heart to ache. Everywhere you look, amid this glorious setting, the suspicion that something must be wrong is now inescapable. In my first summer, almost without exception, all the bighorn lambs I saw showed signs of disease. Even the larger, more robust lambs were often hacking and shaking their head in probable response to a compromised immune system that perpetuates chronic respiratory infections and possibly the proliferation of lung worm infestation. Even by late summer, many were still noticeably weak and lacked the usual enthusiasm, play, and vigor that normally characterize the behavior of young lambs. Yet more disturbing were lambs that continued to display signs of some progressive crippling illness throughout the summer. Again and again, I saw small backs that were bowed slightly and eyes that appeared swollen. They limped and stumbled, and even though the mother held back behind the group in its various wanderings, the gimpy little lambs had trouble keeping up with the ewe.

In a particularly wet summer in 1998, the herd experienced a cata-strophic die-off with almost 100 percent mortality in lambs. And obviously this resulted in virtually an entire year with no new lamb-bearing ewes— a reproductive hole in the breeding population that will reverberate for nearly a decade. In the following years bighorn sheep numbers continued to decline at a frightening pace. Rapidly accumulating data now strongly suggest that the difficulty may reside in changes that have occurred and are continuing to worsen in the alpine atmosphere. In 2000, my responsi-bilities included not only testing and recording the pH or relative acidity occurring in the high country precipitation, but also the summer runoff of melting snow and ice. Precipitation from each rainfall or snowfall was collected, measured, and recorded in terms of dates, accumulated amounts, and the relative pH of each sample. Further, a clean sample from each event was collected for future reference and more exacting laboratory analysis. Normal rainfall should be on the slightly acidic side of neutral, which is around 7.0. Remember, these values are exponential, and so pH 6.0 is ten times more acidic than 7.0. Throughout the month of July, in disbelief, I rechecked my samples again and again as I recorded values in the range of 3.8 to 4.2! As I serviced the forage selenium test plots with this acidic solu-tion, I wondered how quickly selenium availability might fall to zero.

All plots had been carefully clipped at the beginning of the growing season, and each soil or forage sample was tested for selenium availability. Soil and plant samples were also taken at the end of summer. If nothing else, this study has demonstrated that the chemical changes occurring in alpine soils today are radical and mind-numbing in their complexity and implications.

The nomenclature is the all-too-familiar and tiresome term *acid rain*. The term acid rain is a simplistic epithet that in reality involves not merely a good dosing of nitric or sulfuric acid, but also a veritable witch's brew of accompanying chemistry including the entire spectrum of heavy metals resulting from fossil fuel and other industrial emissions. Each time a drop of water falls, these mountains are being doused with a chemistry that includes not only acid in the form of nitrate and sulfur compounds, but could include mercury and other toxic elements that can continue mi-grating up the food chain. It is the snow, rain, and glacial meltwater from these mountains that feed the Wind River in its entirety, and the Wind

River in turn fills the Boysen Reservoir seventy miles to the east before it is discharged into the Wind River Canyon. Research has demonstrated that heavy metal levels are elevated and mercury warnings already exist statewide. Pregnant women are advised not to eat any walleye pike from many reservoirs in Wyoming. During the summer of 2004, I collected hair samples from bighorn sheep in the Wind River Mountains. Subsequent spectrometry analysis revealed that some samples contained concentrations of mercury that approach the levels that human mothers can begin to expect serious developmental changes in an unborn fetus. Without any previous research it is impossible to know if bighorn sheep are less vulnerable to these toxins, or perhaps more. It seems an impossibly cruel irony that the primary means of ridding toxic mercury from any organism is by the body's application of the vital mineral, selenium. It would be logical to assume that although the research has yet to be funded, the larger trout that populate the glacial lakes just below Middle Mountain may be supporting elevated levels of mercury, and the eagles and ospreys that feed on the trout and then nest nearby would be accumulating high levels as well. Researchers in other areas of the Rocky Mountain West are focusing on hydrocarbon deposition precipitating from the burning of fossil fuels, the production of plastics, and the dire consequences of related compounds and by-products such as polychlorinated biphenyls (PCBs) and polycyclic aromatic hydrocarbons (PAHs). We are unaware of any similar scientific interest being shown in this area of the Rocky Mountains.

In conversations with two eminent PhD researchers in related but separate fields, each expressed in almost identical language the same dire description of the overall phenomenon occurring in the northern Rocky Mountains: "We are quite possibly watching an entire ecosystem in collapse."

The same acid rain over fifty years ago began destroying the boreal forests of Soviet-dominated eastern Europe, sterilized the pristine glacial lakes of eastern Canada, and decimated the ancient spruce and fir forest of our own Appalachian mountains throughout the 1960s and 1970s. It is the same acerbic solution that continues to etch and erode the great artistic and architectural monuments of Egypt, the Mediterranean, and Europe, until today many are all but unrecognizable. That same *anthropogenic* (having its origins in human activity) fossil fuel and industrial pollution found its way to the pristine heights of the northern Rocky Mountains in the 1960s and 1970s, contributing to a die-off of timber that continues rampantly today, and as of 2009 many boreal forests in the northern Rocky Mountains are experiencing 90 percent mortality. In the past five years we have lost many times more trees than were lost in the great Yellowstone fires of 1988 without even a raised eyebrow throughout the nation. The standard excuse doled out by various government agencies is beetle kill. The mountain pine bark beetle is endemic to the Rocky Mountains and has evolved with these forests like fleas on dogs. Bark beetles should not kill healthy trees, which have a natural resistance. Just as sick bighorn lambs always die of predation and almost never from their disabling illnesses, in a similar way, stress of some kind allows trees to become infested by bark beetles, and the insects then become the actual agents of death. The West is in the midst of a ten-year drought. It is believed that drought may be a contributor to beetle infestation. But the infestation began decades ago and was rampant throughout some of the wettest years in history. Further, it is no coincidence that the trees most affected are often those in the highest elevations and commonly on north-facing slopes—areas that experience the most moisture, are the last to loose melting snow, and never experience more than a few weeks of significant drought. Parts of the northern Wind River Mountains and the Absorkas may be at the time of this writing experiencing the most catastrophic tree die-off in recorded history, following a year of some of the highest registered rain and snowfall amounts in a decade. A month in the fall of 2008 that I spent surveying tree mortality along the slopes above the Buffalo Fork River just east of Yellowstone revealed nearly 100 percent mortality in trees over one hundred years old, with younger individuals succumbing by the millions.

Atmospheric pollution, much of it in the form of complex nitrate compounds, is being expressed in ever more dramatic and disturbing ways. The graph of this concentration has been rising worldwide since the turn of the century, but for ten years has risen exponentially across the globe until now it is suspected that soils in many areas, and particularly the soils in higher elevations, may have even reached *absolute nitrate saturation*, and further absorption may have become a chemical impossibility.

The subject of nitrate deposition is a complex and disturbing one. Although various atmospheric phenomena can be natural and cyclic, like global temperature fluctuations and levels of atmospheric CO_2, there is no natural global precedent for nitrate buildup in soils and water. These build-ups have never been discovered in ancient glaciers throughout the world or in the geological record, implying that global nitrate deposition is probably unprecedented in the history of the earth and entirely anthropogenic in origin. In the words of chemist Bruce Mincher, "The low pH of acidic rainfall can be buffered by the effects of karst or limestone soils, but most mountain soils are made from granite and have less ability to compensate. Nitrates themselves are only lost through leaching, and with high rates of deposition, can accumulate in soils, resulting in eventual saturation."

Soil scientists from the University of Wyoming making observations for most of a decade have gathered data that corroborates findings from other scientists, including Dr. Mark Williams from the University of Colorado in Boulder, and are now beginning to suggest that total nitrate saturation may have already occurred in many areas of the Rockies. If so, much or all of the Northern Rocky Mountain high country, including Middle Mountain, has probably experienced a similar accumulation, contributing or even accounting for the vulnerability and mortality seen in so much of our subalpine forests. Just as we have seen in most boreal forests around the world, particularly in the Northern Hemisphere, these effects should now be entirely predictable and probably at this point in time irreversible.

It is possible that an even greater threat now looms over our subalpine forests with the more recent introduction of deadly levels of ozone contributed by a vast sprawling oil and gas development just west of the Wind River Mountains known simply as the "Pinedale Anticline Development." The World Health Organization has recognized concentrations of ozone that surpass fifty ppb (parts per billion) to be a danger to human health. Our own Environmental Protection Agency has liberalized the acceptable limits on America's atmospheric contaminants and recommends seventy-five ppb as a safe limit. Readings on the western slopes of these mountains have been spiking above 120 ppb, with some of the highest readings near the continental divide of South Pass. Ozone readings tend to spike in the evenings and at night when the stomata of conifer leaves are open, making trees of higher elevation particularly vulnerable. Possibly, no single atmospheric contaminant is more deadly to conifers than ozone. Pinedale, Wyoming, is now experiencing atmosphere that more closely resembles that found in Peking, China, than a small town in the northern Rockies.

Catastrophically high levels of nitrates, plunging levels of pH, and ozone levels that are off the charts strongly suggest that the bark beetle is not the real problem. And even though we have been collecting rain and snow for most of a decade that more closely resembles lemon juice than rainfall, only now has any government agency begun to express an interest in the chemical properties of high altitude precipitation in the Wind River Mountains.

Acidity in the form of nitrate compounds alters the relative pH of the tundra earth but also, among many other ills, may introduce large amounts of free nitrogen that can create organic bedlam in a soil chemistry that is normally defined by a narrow range of variability in pH and nutrients. Oxides of nitrogen—like nitrates—are powerful and reactive nutrients in soils, and in delicate alpine environments the micro fauna and flora that define and control soil chemistry can be thrown into chaos. Endemic microorganisms like bacteria, fungi, nematodes, as well as other invertebrates might alternately either proliferate out of control in these new nutrient-rich soils or become devastated by an alien chemistry that is inhospitable or outright toxic. Interestingly, studies in the Appalachian mountains regarding the imminent extinction of the native hemlock by the "wooly adelgid" insect, have found that even small applications of nitrate fertilizer will actually weaken a tree's immune response and insure infestation and eventual mortality. Logically, it would appear that alpine plant diversity is being altered, as some species may proliferate in a chemically redefined and nitrogen-rich environment, while others, intolerant, could begin to disappear.

One of the objectives in this study is to explore the effects of this acidic deposition that along with other complex changes occurring in mountain soils may be causing selenium to bond with compounds of iron or oxygen, sequestering Se in a chemical form that is unavailable for uptake by the alpine flora. Plants may no longer absorb selenium, and so Se availability to herbivores, large and small, can be reduced or perhaps eliminated entirely.

By the end of July during the summer of 2000 the needles of every little krummholz tree on Middle Mountain began turning brown, and by the middle of August, all appeared to be dead, as if an invisible fire had swept across the mountain tundra. A few trees would put out weakened new growths the following spring, but many were completely dead and are gone forever. By the end of summer, with some form of rain or snow almost every day, my clothes were faded beyond recognition, bleached out by the acrid precipitation.

15

LEAVING MIDDLE MOUNTAIN

This summer on Middle Mountain has quickly come and gone, and it seems the few months I have lived here have passed in the blink of an eye. Daily log and journal entries stack up in volumes and represent the only indication that an entire season has somehow passed, and it has been months since I have seen another human being. Although green rolling summer pastures have uniformly turned to a somber brown with nighttime temperatures well below freezing, a brief seasonal ambiguity between warmer days and true winter lingers on. Evidence everywhere suggests that the bite of winter is beginning to nip at the heels of the Wyoming high country.

This evening a gentle wind and mild temperature momentarily hold winter at bay. Rare in any season, a soft, almost balmy breeze floats lightly across the mountaintop. My many busy furry companions seem to appreciate the moment, not in terms of a much-deserved respite from powerful elements but rather as an opportunity to preserve calories while making last-minute preparations for a rapidly approaching winter that will last the greater part of a year. As the sun settles toward the jagged horizon to the west, I find time to climb out on my familiar precipice below my camp. Tonight the skies are stratified with clouds that reveal an infinite variety of color seemingly awash in the complementary possibilities between orange and purple. I settle comfortably into the spongy tundra earth. The setting sun glows warm on my face and seems to sparkle through my eyelashes, while an accommodating smooth granite backrest surrenders its collected warmth to my weary back. As the wind occasionally settles to an unexpected soft, gentle breath, the many rushing waters in the chasm below offer up a soothing whisper. Two species of chipmunks scurry about without any apparent resentment for my idleness. One of the least chipmunks climbs across my legs, stops, and cautiously wags its small tail like a snake being charmed, and seems to offer only a passing glance into my eyes. Several others forage within a three-meter radius. The much larger golden-mantled ground squirrels harvest material close by, and if not as accepting of me, at least do not have to feign their indifference. Three pikas and a fattened marmot scurry back and forth across my little bench of tundra sod enjoying the warm evening sun.

A movement below us brings all the busy activity to a momentary pause. We stare straight down on a golden eagle soaring fifty feet below us. Its broad sun-drenched back and wings are braced against a supporting thermal that rises against the warm rock wall and suspends it more than two thousand feet above the canyon floor. The eagle's southwesterly flight across the face of the mountain is deliberate and unwavering, except for an occasional wary glance from side to side. In complete silence the great bird disappears around the face of the cliff. My companions return to their chores. The marmot, however, remains statuesque and seems to stare wistfully for a few moments longer. The mountain swells to my right, obstructing my immediate view down the cliff face. A large form appears silhouetted thirty feet away on the precipitous skyline of the ledge. A young bighorn ram has arrived unseen from somewhere along the cliff face and stands as a dark, powerful presence, motionless. Unconcerned with the little society that we offer on the precipice, he plummets straight down the vertical rock face beneath and disappears. He is immediately replaced by two adult ewes and a lamb. Surprised but not startled, they stand, all sharing a single precarious boulder, and examine me. Satisfied that I am the same peculiar but harmless creature that has been their quiet shadow all summer, they also dive down the face of the cliff in obvious disregard for the thousand-foot drop that would await any misstep they should make. I hear only the occasional tinkle and clatter of dislodged pebbles as they bound from one narrow outcropping to another on their route down the sheer face of the mountain. A few minutes later they all appear without ceremony one hundred feet below on a narrow grassy ledge and begin calmly feeding. My sun and windburn lips widen in an involuntary smile while moisture of unknown origin fills my tired eyes. Some unfamiliar buoyancy seems to relieve the normal tug on my limbs and spirits. But then perhaps it is the logical nature of elevation to eventually give way to levitation. In stark contrast to my normal disposition, my mind becomes motionless. As if careening downhill for most of a lifetime, my mind comes to a halt. Stunned, my internal prosecutor calls for a recess and only my senses seem to remain—sight and sound, the fragrance of this wild place carried by the gentle wind across my face, the warm earth cradling my back. Is it possible that all the work and trials, all the heartaches and disappointments that life offers in such abundance could possibly fade into irrelevance in exchange, in a grateful and willing bargain, for this one peculiar moment? As if now I will be able to say, *Oh yes, maybe this is what all the fuss has been about.* Without offering any real understanding, the moment feels like it may be the only thing that has ever truly made sense. After a few pleasant moments, my mind finds the opportunity and the vacuum irresistible—it rushes in. Could it be that life is not so much about longevity, acquisition, attainment, and the accomplishment that is facilitated by patience and perseverance? Could it be that life is measured more properly by our few fleeting and defining moments—those rare, shining, and illuminated occasions? Whether we live twenty years or one hundred, could it be that only our most shining moments are preserved? Is it only those shining moments that in turn preserve us?

Eventually, as with the colors of sunlight, my busy companions disappear, and the more customary sting of cold blue mountain air begins to retrieve the warmth that has filled my face. Wandering up a familiar but steep incline to my campsite, and without a glance backward, I reflect on sunlight, tall mountains, the mystery of living things, and the humility that accompanies gratitude.

September has arrived and a new season taken hold of the mountain. The spirited frenzy of life that has entertained and accompanied me all summer has vanished in the blink of an eye. In an instant, it seems the bountiful rolling green pastures have turned, not into the cheerful yellow thatch of wheat straw but rather more like the dark sepia of an old oxidized apple, a moody and ominous brown. Nights have become consistently cold, snow flurries are a daily event, and daytime temperatures hover around freezing. Morning temperatures average in the low teens, although this morning, following six inches of fresh snow, the thermometer dipped below zero for the first time. All my many familiar companions disappeared days ago, and apparently without a single exception, winter hibernation has begun.

If any activity remains on Middle Mountain, it is either my own or it is occurring with the pikas underground. However, sheep began staring incessantly toward Whiskey Mountain to the northeast several days ago, suggesting that once again an ancient voice was calling, and the annual migration to fall and winter pastures was at hand. By some unanimous consensus, all the sheep left the high country in a single dedicated migratory event lasting twenty-four hours or less. Having never observed the phenomenon before, I simply watched and wondered where everyone was going with such a sense of purpose. Radio collar transmissions now indicate only faint and distant signals far to the east and thousands of feet below in the direction of Whiskey Mountain. There is no seasonal ringer on my biological clock, and the sheep remind me that our companionship was one of mere circumstance and, in spite of my affections, entirely of my own making.

My intransigence on this mountain probably reflects a less highly de-veloped grasp of the obvious. Torn by separation from my many summer companions, I feel an unfamiliar loneliness aggravating an otherwise per-fect solitude. Clearly, it is time for me to break camp and migrate down the mountain with the sheep, but I somehow feel as though my work here is incomplete. All the experimental forage selenium study plots have been disassembled, and in expectation of continued work next summer, stored in a deep protective recess within the nearby boulders. Rainwater collection tarps have also been gathered up, folded, and stored as well. Only my little weather station remains standing, collecting more valuable and disturbing data in the form of snowfall and progressively plunging temperatures. As the summer weather pattern has changed, pH values have risen into less-acidic ranges but continue to hover below normal. Tropical and subtropical circulations of global atmosphere are now being replaced by air originating in the more pristine but nevertheless troubled skies of the far north. Before the tundra soils of Middle Mountain are locked once again in ice, perhaps the infiltration of less-acidic precipitation will have some buffering effect on the accumulative impact of the more acrid snows and rains of summer. Unfortunately, however, the soil is already begin-ning to freeze superficially, and so further moisture infiltration will soon be impossible.

I fumble around and finish my usual meager breakfast made even more uninspiring by wet, clumsy fingers brought on by the overnight return of winter in the form of a stinging, blowing snow. I trudge out across the white lifelessness of Middle Mountain's north-facing slope. Usual morning chores, like checking radio collar locations and recording weather data seem unnecessary. The sheep are conspicuous only in their absence, and a six-inch plug of frozen snow in the rain gauge tells me all I need to know. Today snow clouds churn all around in great billowing curtains of frozen icy fog that pepper my face and draw protective moisture from my nose and eyes. My peregrine reconnaissance across the mountain is partly the discharge of some familiar sense of responsibility and partly the need to flee some pervasive heaviness of mind and sprit that has been hounding me all morning. The sky continues to darken, and churning clouds of snow tumble over me like a white frozen surf. The wind is stiff and steady, and so in defiance of gravity, all movement of the snow lashes by horizontally like bundles of white switches. Although this is the most familiar part of the mountain to me, and a relatively safe distance from camp, the more obvious landmarks are starting to become unrecognizable in the surrounding pervasive whiteness. Soon the high country will be locked in the seasonal permanence of snow that can pack down to twenty or thirty feet and drift or blow over a cornice to one hundred. A single snowfall lasting less than a day will sometimes deposit four and five feet. Each day spent at this elevation is now a toss of the dice, and the odds are increasing that a heavy and permanent snowfall will blanket the mountaintop. Postholing off the mountain with a backpack in a foot or eighteen inches of snow is inconvenient but possible. However, without snowshoes, forty-eight inches of fresh snow that will neither melt nor blow away would leave me trapped with my almost depleted stores of food and fuel. The depleted remains of my better judgment tell me to load up and bail off this mountain, but a more powerful urgency pleads for me to stay just one more hour or maybe even one more day. For reasons I do not fully understand, the prospect of leaving Middle Mountain seems a dreadful notion. A dense snow cloud begins to enshroud the mountaintop. In Wyoming it is said that people have become disoriented in their own front yards during a whiteout and have been known to wander off and die. Large boulders one hundred meters up the mountain are now undifferentiated shapes and gray shadows. Winds pick up from around thirty miles per hour to forty. My body is losing heat. I squint through seething frozen mists and notice a particularly dark irregular geometric shape in the boulders ahead, suggesting a deep recess within the rocks that might provide me with a temporary shelter while the squall passes. At the base of one of the great pinnacles whose upper recesses are completely obscured by howling horizontal snows, a distinct and inviting dark shape offers a welcome alternative to the threatening whiteness pressing in all around. A gigantic flat boulder fifty feet across is held horizontal by other large supporting stones and resembles some ancient architectural lentil, appearing to hold the mountain of stacked megaliths above like the granite shoulders of Atlas. I stoop only slightly, ducking beneath the boulder and enter through a roughly trapezoidal opening ten feet across, and as my eyes adjust to the shadows I find a large space opens up within. The relatively level floor of the space is composed of fine washed sands and gravels. Without any suggestion of organic debris or refuse, the smooth pale floor has been interrupted only by the small tracks of one or two passing rodents. Vertical spaces between the great boulders allow shafts of diffused light to dart downward here and there, permitting a level of visual assurance that I am not sharing this space with unwanted company. Mistlike snow filters gently down from the loosely stacked rocks overhead, and although it's not a perfect refuge from the gusting winds, the stinging blasts are largely excluded. A fissure between two large stones above allows me to stand, but then I spot a small rectangular stone jutting out from the back wall, conveniently forming an inviting chair of smoothly contoured granite. Making myself comfortable, I pull a nutrition bar from my daypack and begin munching. Eventually my tense muscles loosen. While relaxing and ignoring all the reasons I should leave the mountain, my immediate surroundings come into focus. A cozy almost smug feeling overcomes me as the accommodating space begins to feel more and more appealing. I start entertaining thoughts of erecting my tent inside this perfect enclosure but remind myself of the inadvisability of seeking shelter within the confines of rock overhangs or rock shelters. It is logical that during thunderstorms, rain eventually forms millions of small rivulets over and through nested boulders, and when lightning strikes the otherwise poorly conductive granite, the enormous electrical charge disperses and scatters through the rocks for hundreds of feet in every direction, like a great liquid superconducting spiderweb.

Observing the ideal shape and size of the shelter, I wonder why no Sheep Eater people ever took advantage of this space. No soot stains the coarse surface of the granite ceiling, no flecks of black charcoal or burned bone mix with the otherwise pale yellow gravels of the floor. Although no sign of continuous Sheep Eater occupation seems to exist on the summit of Middle Mountain, I occasionally find the tailings and workings of their flint industry scattered here and there. This mountain supports a vast tangled labyrinth of enormous granite boulders, like piles of gigantic irregular watermelons and squashes. And were it not for this blizzard, and an unusually large dark shape of the opening contrasted in the snow-covered rocks, I might never have stumbled across this place. Indeed, in my various wanderings about the mountain, I must have passed within a short distance many times. Perhaps the early hunters, likewise, never chanced upon it.

Snow like fine white dust settles down through the dim light of the shelter. A bit numb of mind and body, I sit relaxing on the back wall facing the brilliant opening in the rocks as mesmerizing swirls of powdered snow dance across the fine gravels of the floor. My neck and head settle down into my fleece collar like an upright but sleepy turtle. In a comfortable torpor, a mindless state of relaxation, a twinkling glassy glint catches my eye among the sands of the floor. Below this faint sparkle of light, midway between my feet and the shelter entrance, a small, dark silhouette contrasts with an otherwise smooth and uninterrupted pale surface. I overcome a powerful inertia and hobble over to investigate. I bend over and pull some odd object out of the pale sand. My tired eyes widen as I realize that a small glassy obsidian knife lies in the cradle of my clumsy gloved hand. Dumbstruck, my mind begins first to stir and then to whir as I return to my granite chair, spellbound. My own footprints and this glassy little blade are the only suggestions that anyone has taken shelter here. Irony and coincidence stir my dulled mind into wakefulness. My eyes dart around my enclosure observing that not one element of these surroundings has been altered—or could be altered—in the smallest or most trivial way in at least thousands if not tens of thousands of years. Perhaps one hundred years ago, perhaps five thousand, but without question, someone else stumbled upon this obscure protective cloister of ancient stones and took refuge. Perhaps it was a place temporarily removed from howling mountain winds or, as in my own situation, removed from the blinding and stinging snows of an unanticipated winter come in a day. Someone seeing this same dark shape within the snow-covered stones could have ducked and entered this welcoming sanctuary and retreated into the comforting dimness. Without question, some other mountain wanderer sat on this same accommodating stone chair while looking around at these same massive boulders, same graveled floor, same ceiling. This person could have also sat quietly while a storm passed, pulled this sharp blade from a protective leather bag, and passed the time performing some small task. As if I had just taken a newly vacated seat on a bus, someone else's presence is made apparent. How similar is our occupation of this small space? How could our experience of it differ? Time is such a relative thing, and now it appears to be illusory or at least in some way irrelevant. As this precious tool slipped from some mountain wanderer's grasp and became lost, did a thousand years also slip away and become misplaced, or, perhaps remembering, will a dark silhouette appear at the door to retrieve this fine knife and this lost moment in time? The individual's proximity is tangible. I am no longer alone on this mountain, and a solitude that may have at last grown tiresome has been relieved in a most unexpected way.

Even though it is only the middle of September, winter is now hovering around the upper reaches of the northern Wyoming high country and will by October begin its inexorable descent into the warmer canyons and valleys below. Distant aspen groves are beginning to emit a bright golden glow thousands of feet beneath—irrefutable evidence that freezing temperatures are descending the mountains and gripping the timbered slopes in winter's brittle embrace. Bighorn sheep, dispersed throughout the alpine high country all summer, are now becoming concentrated in large herds at lower elevations. At last the Whiskey Mountain herd has returned to the upper reaches of its winter range and may be seen peppering the expansive southwest-facing slope many miles in the distance and at an elevation of around 10,500 feet. Whiskey Mountain is characterized by enormous expanses of rich, open grasslands that now provide an untapped wealth of summer forage. Although peaking at over eleven thousand feet, only the actual summit of Whiskey is distinctly alpine. Its lower elevations—geologically and botanically—are different from the classic alpine ecology of Middle Mountain. The geology of Middle Mountain is granitic with typical alpine flora, but Whiskey Mountain is composed of fault block, sedimentary shale, and limestone. Whereas granitic soils tend to be slightly acidic, limestone soils tend to be alkaline, or *basic*, supporting different plant communities and perhaps even buffering the effects of acid rain. Predictably, it appears that the vegetation on Whiskey Mountain enjoys a more successful uptake and consequent availability of selenium. Within weeks, nutritional deficiencies in lambs will begin to improve but unfortunately not in time to repair the irreversible damage that has already occurred in many. A few hopelessly weakened lambs will continue to die even after making the journey down to their rich fall pastures. But lambs can also become disabled as a result of a mechanical injury brought on by a fall or a near miss from a mountain lion or other large predator. The many visible scars and injuries indicate without a doubt, all Rocky Mountain bighorn sheep have a tough rigorous life.

As the sheep begin concentrating on the broad grassy slopes below, we will soon begin the next phase of the study, which involves moving my base camp to five hundred feet beneath the summit of Whiskey Mountain. There John and I will join forces and begin a census, determining summer lamb survival expressed as "lamb–ewe ratio" (a good annual ratio would be 35 to 45 surviving lambs per 100 ewes). In addition, we will also observe the number of surviving yearlings from the previous year's crop of lambs, and these yearling numbers may be further subdivided by gender as young rams are now easily distinguished from young ewes. Weather data will of course be gathered as well, with special emphasis on any changes occurring in the pH values in autumn precipitation.

I now realize that my continued presence on Middle Mountain is probably not justifiable by any feeble rationalization, and any reason for staying would be by now an indefensible pretext. Some prevailing and mysterious sense of obligation or responsibility has finally vanished and is replaced by a heaviness of spirit. Now when wandering aimlessly across the barren and lifeless summit of the mountain, I am just a dark brooding form amid an otherwise primordial and pristine wilderness landscape, now reduced to a more singular purity by the application of the white uncorrupting hand of winter. Visible for hundreds of miles in every direction, a pale and uniform white stratum hangs across the entire upper reaches of the Wyoming high country. The life beneath scurries in anticipation of the blanket of frozen down that will soon settle below, eventually securing the land in the icy blueness of a new winter season.

Even though by now all the water molecules in my body must have been replaced by the clear glacial meltwater that has sustained me for these months, they have not cleared my own turbid waters. The apparent perfection of this place has surrounded me for months. But in the end I am surprised and disappointed to find that I persist in simply being me. How could a person not be changed? How could this place not transform an ordinary human being into some other more refined creature? Are we such ephemeral and unworthy vessels that certain significant realities can only be experienced through their proximity—only so long as we remain immersed? The simple, irreconcilable, and probably childish question hanging over me is, Why must I return and yet all of this can remain? What is so inherent or peculiar in our being that eventually we must always be separated from this primordial wonder? The chipmunk's credentials must read with more substance and authority. I'm embarrassed by this self-indulgent mental crisis. Grief momentarily fills my eyes as a cold blue wind transforms warm water to icy droplets on my face. I'm disappointed and angry, but then suddenly I'm laughing. Bewildered but at least entertained, I take note of this irrational state with an almost detached curiosity, like watching the aberrant behavior of an otherwise normal creature I am relatively familiar with. How quickly solitude loses its charm when you find your own company intolerable. But perhaps the one truly irrational act was to accept this unusual employment, and all the rest was the simple manifestation of isolation, the accompanying effects of long-term solitude in an extraordinary place, and the inevitability that is bound up in our particular species' paradoxical but inevitable disconnection from the natural world.

Reality eventually settles over me in a mantle of sadness and resolve, as a numbing wind-burned face grimaces and strains with tent stakes that have grown, like me, secured in the partially frozen earth. Like a spoiled child, I find the prospect of returning to the tedium and pettiness of being me, of being any person, disappointing. It is only the persistent force of gravity that eventually lowers me slowly down the mountain. I am consoled only by the prospects and wonders of Whiskey Mountain, which for the next month or two will ease my transition into the human life and culture to which we are all, like Prometheus, inexorably bound.

16

GOOD WHISKEY

Leaving Middle Mountain meant having to recall how to drive and operate my pickup truck, which had been waiting patiently all summer at the trailhead. To some extent I have to relearn to speak the English language. The obvious absurdity of having food and hot coffee delivered to a table in an artificially heated room at the Cowboy Café in DuBois that evening caused me to laugh out loud, but I found it impossible to explain to the waitress why I was so amused. The sunset drive from DuBois to Lander is always serene and beautiful, but I noticed that the truck's stereo seemed to produce only an intolerable cacophony of noise.

On arrival in Lander, I found the little town buzzing with the activity of early-season hunters. Grocery store parking lots were crowded with trailers packed with horses, mules, four-wheelers, and camping gear as wranglers and outfitters stripped the shelves of hundreds of pounds of supplies. I spent three days at Mission Control, getting resupplied, rested, and ready for Whiskey Mountain.

The following year, my descent from Middle Mountain was a far less lonely experience. It was October. Winter had overtaken the twelve-thousand-foot level of the northern Rockies. Dave Keller had been scheduled to arrive around the first week of the month with ten pack goats to retrieve the bulk of our base camp from the summit of the mountain. Dave was a few days late, but I was in no hurry to leave. He arrived at my camp one morning just before sunrise. He had spent the previous day climbing the mountain and had camped right at the tree limit in an effort to keep goats from coming into contact with wild sheep. Domestic caprids can expose bighorn sheep to various deadly diseases, especially by nose-to-nose contact, so we try to coordinate things so that the goats spend as little time as possible in the wild sheep habitat.

After a cordial greeting, I finished stuffing my tent and helped Dave load gear that had already been prepared for his arrival. All my personal things went on one sturdy, trusty white goat named Blizzard—a goat I had come to know on other occasions. In two hours we had passed over the top of the mountain, slid down the two slushy glacial snowfields, and began weaving our way through the gnarly transitional tree line, negotiating a tangled maze of boulder-infested ravines, downed trees, and wet, marshy willow thickets surrounding rushing meltwater streams and springs. The complexity of the landscape and the necessity to boulder-hop prevents the formation of even the most rudimentary trail through this portion of the descent, so you just bushwhack your way a mile or so through this mess until things begin to look generally familiar. At last, the descending ridge that provides the passage off the mountain is revealed, and you are on your way. Until then, everyone—goat or person—finds a path, scrambling around with visibility less than a few yards. Finally, we arrived just above the old outfitter campsite—a sight that made my butt ache in memory—and Dave chose a good flat spot, pausing for a drink of water and an opportunity for the goats to reassemble. In a few minutes we were relaxed, surrounded by a small herd of reclining goats and catching up on current events, including the story about the two bears Dave camped with the night before. After a fifteen-minute break we stood up to begin the daylong descent down the mountain. Dave instinctively began counting noses and then casually remarked, "Um—someone's missing—there should be three white goats; I only see two." I recalled that the white goat carrying the only pair of green panniers was Blizzard, and there were no green panniers to be seen. "Blizzard," I reported. Dave agrees: "Yep, it's Blizzard—let's tie the goats and go back and get him, he may have gotten his pack hung up on a snag in all that mess back there."

We combed the mountainside for two hours like frantic bird dogs, but as we converged for the fourth or fifth time, Dave exclaimed, "He's just not here!" Blizzard appeared to have vanished. Dave then suggested that he may have gotten ahead of us in the maze and could be already on his way to the trailhead. "Goats know to do that if they get separated," then Dave added "and goats don't just get lost." He said that I should hike on down to the trailhead in case Blizzard was on his way, but he wanted to stay and thoroughly continue searching the mountainside just in case we may have missed him. He also reminded me that goats become quite vocal when they are left alone or in distress, and he was certain that if Blizzard was around he would probably start bawling. If Blizzard was at the trailhead, I would simply collect my things, put him in the stock trailer, and be on my way. Before I was completely out of sight Dave called to me saying, "Don't worry. He'll turn up!"

I hurried down the mountain without the burden of a heavy pack and glad that I had at least put my camera and journals in my daypack. However, as I descended the mountain, not only did I worry about Blizzard but I began itemizing all my expensive gear that I would need in only a couple of days when I began continuing my work on Whiskey Mountain. My good down sleeping bag, my expedition tent, my clothes, kitchen, and—uh oh—my tightly holstered but fully loaded Smith & Wesson .357 Magnum pistol. Damn!

By late afternoon, I arrived at the wilderness area trailhead and my fears were realized—no Blizzard—and not one goat track heading downhill that day. Mustering a little optimism, I waited at the trailhead until I could no longer see up the mountain—no Blizzard, no Dave. I had every confidence in Dave's abilities, but I felt sick as I realized, with darkness now enshrouding the wilderness and no gear of my own, there was nothing to do but drive away in the night and hope for the best.

The next day Dave called Kathy Pappas from Dubois to report that he had brought the goats out and was going back up the mountain and stay until he found Blizzard. Dave was understandably devoted to these goats and of course felt responsible. It is probably a human impossibility to work around pack goats without at least developing a sense of companionship if not an outright love for these gentle, hardworking, intelligent, and affectionate creatures. It is fascinating that like faithful dogs, goats simply choose to be with us and simply choose to do this difficult work. Goats are herd animals, and as such they abhor and fear being left alone. And, more disturbing, they are easy, delectable prey for bears and mountain lions, particularly when they are helplessly bound to a tree. Everyone was sick worrying about poor Blizzard.

Charlie Wilson went to help Dave in the search after trying to console me with the possibility of his business insurance covering any loss I might suffer if Blizzard was never found. Middle Mountain is immense and an absolute labyrinth of complex topography and thick forests where you could pass within a few meters of a yellow bulldozer in some places and not see it. And probably most disturbing, as Dave camped alone on the mountainside, he never heard Blizzard's cries for help, and a lonely goat in distress should be audible for a mile on a still night.

I was expected to take up residence immediately on Whiskey Mountain to begin the fall portion of the sheep study, which would eventually conclude with an accurate lamb census some time after the first of November. Back at Kathy's I began cobbling together every bit of extraneous gear I could lay my hands on—borrowing tents, parkas, sleeping bags, cook gear, even an antique Colt pistol Kathy had lying around in a drawer. We are not required to carry a weapon, but John always made it clear before the field season began that it was "strongly recommended." But before I could begin my work on Whiskey Mountain, I had to first notify the Fremont County sheriff in Lander that a pistol registered in my name had been "lost or stolen." Further, before I went up on the mountain, I wanted to also alert the Dubois police since the town was the nearest community to the study area. Conveniently, as I drove into Dubois, I spotted a police officer standing by his cruiser just down the main street. I pulled in behind him, got out, and we exchanged greetings. As I began explaining about the bighorn sheep study and describing the unfortunate affair with the lost goat, he seemed to maintain an air of sympathy until I finally had to drop the bomb. I had to explain that this particular goat was probably packing a loaded .357 Magnum handgun. Immediately I could see some element of incredulity wash across his face, and he could no longer contain an involuntary smile that quickly evolved into a distinct smirk. He picked up his handset from the front seat and radioed in the bad news: "Doug, you'll never guess—now we're on the lookout for a heavily armed goat." After he sarcastically inquired if I thought the goat could be dangerous as well, we laughed, shook hands, and he said he would keep his eyes open. Two hours later I was on the slopes of Whiskey Mountain trying to put recent events and five steep miles behind me.

Awakening that first morning to the inescapable crisp mountain air, I sat shivering on my familiar cliff face/kitchen area preparing my oatmeal and coffee as the warming sun began showing above the Wind River Basin to the east. Looking down the run of Torrey Creek I spotted a small single-engine plane headed straight for me. Charlie Wilson and John Mionczynski flew two thousand feet above the canyon floor but two hundred feet over my head as they expanded the search for Blizzard into the rough mountainous terrain of Whiskey Basin. Dave spent two more weeks searching on foot to no avail. But elk hunting season was getting under way and if Blizzard was still alive—by now an unlikely prospect— someone might find him. After a month had passed, however, everyone was heartsick and had given up any hope for sweet old Blizzard.

Then, in an almost unbelievable turn of events, Blizzard wandered into a backcountry elk camp in relatively good health but with big scabs on his back, indicating that he had been trapped somewhere but finally managed to work his way free of the saddle. With a month of good home care and feed, Blizzard was back to perfect health. We all wished we could hear him tell his incredible story.

In an ironic twist two years later, Dave accidentally stumbled onto the site of Blizzard's entrapment. Most of my gear remained scattered about completely shredded by bears, tent and sleeping bag in tatters, but my mountain parka was still in a stuff sack in perfect condition, and there was the Smith & Wesson, still holstered and loaded. I had replaced everything with insurance money, so Dave still wears the parka today, and Charlie got the titanium cook kit and the pistol.

Before beginning my work on Whiskey Mountain I met John at the Wyoming Game and Fish bunkhouse, lying near the northeastern foot of the mountain. After sharing all the interesting sheep-related experiences that the summer had provided, and with the aid of just a little too much port, we retire early, spending a quiet and restful night in warm beds. John and I rise early, eat a hearty breakfast, and climb into our respective vehicles an hour before sunrise. Six inches of fresh snow quietly blanket the world, and the cold steering wheel tells me the temperature must be at least in the teens. For the next hour we crawl slowly up the steep eastern face of Whiskey Mountain on a two-rut rocky trail made almost invisible by the fresh snowfall. As the trail becomes steeper, we crawl out of our vehicles and install chains over our snow tires, and once again are able to slide and grind up the vast open expanses of the mountain. After ascending several miles up the steep grade, we reach a less steeply inclined bench above

Torrey Canyon, Torrey Rim, just minutes before the sun reaches the eastern horizon. We stop and again climb out of our vehicles to perform
a quick reconnaissance, as sheep will often congregate on the open but
complex rambling grasslands above the rim. John walks uphill to look over
a little ridge while I walk downhill to see what lies over the wide rolling
slope of the mountain. As soon as I get out of site of John and the vehicles,
I stop and stare out across the pale blue vastness of the Wind River Basin to
the east while panting billows of warm mists in the biting stillness of cold
mountain air. Glancing to the north, I immediately see a curious dark object silhouetted on the horizon of the hillside two hundred yards ahead. I
recognize the shape of a large ram's head, with his body hidden below the
steep curvature of the mountainside. He stares intently, and with my binoculars I closely examine him and his massive curling horns. Then, with no
apparent provocation except for my proximity, the great ram bounds up the
mountainside at a dead run, charging straight toward me. With no protective cover of any kind, I watch in disbelief as the ram runs through a foot
of snow, kicking up frost like a 250-pound runaway snowplow. Standing
in a state of total helplessness, I instinctively whistle with all my strength,
not at the charging ram but for John. If I am going to get smashed, I want
to have a witness—I want professional documentation—and besides, if
the event has no significance in terms of expanding our understanding of
bighorn sheep behavior, John might at least find the event entertaining.
The obvious desperation in my tone sends John running. He appears over
the knoll above while the ram continues his charge—full tilt—straight at
me. I prepare for a bad morning. When the great ram approaches within
twenty paces, he breaks ninety degrees uphill and becomes airborne. In an
enormous four-footed stotlike leap, he leaves the snow-covered ground
with at least six feet of daylight under his hooves, he peaks, and then plummets back to earth landing hind legs first. With an exaggerated movement
he dramatizes his powerful descent by simultaneously slamming his front
hooves through the snow onto the hard ground with a powerful resonating *thud!* Instantly he catapults himself back into the air at a phenomenal
height above the snow, eventually returning to the ground with a similar
dramatic display: hind legs first and a simultaneous slam of the front legs
into the mountainside. He repeats this two more times and then he breaks
once again into a run, disappearing over the slope of the mountain in

seconds. I look up at John who by now wears an enormous grin and we both break out in laughter. "Well, that happened!" one of us quips. Giggling and shaking our heads, we retrace our steps to the vehicles acknowledging that we may well have witnessed some heretofore undocumented behavior. My heart rate remains elevated longer than a mere walk back to the truck would warrant.

There was no question that this behavior by the ram was an extremely aggressive gesture meant to convey in no uncertain terms the overwhelming power and mass of the creature and the magnitude of the will that was animating and driving such a force. John mentioned that although in his experience wild sheep are rarely aggressive toward humans, they are on occasion unpredictable, like many large wild animals, and he knew of at least one biologist who had been badly injured in an altercation with an angry ram. My suggestion is that the event may have been one of mistaken identity. I may have been mistaken for a predator, and there is some evidence to suggest that on occasion wild sheep may respond to the presence of a predator with fight rather than flight. Further, breeding season was at hand and several other large rams were in the immediate vicinity. My partial silhouette may have been mistaken for an adversary that only moments before was engaged in combat with this individual.

On one other occasion many years before, a ram made an aggressive gesture toward me, although in a much less dramatic way. As I walked alone along the edge of a steep cliff face overlooking an inaccessible area of the Little Popo Agie Canyon near a dramatic feature known as Wolf Point, I looked fifty yards ahead as a large mature ram was casually walking toward me. Bighorn sheep have the paradoxical predisposition to be the wildest and wariest creature ever encountered, and then on another occasion they can be fearless. This ram was of the latter disposition that day, and as I stopped and became motionless, he proceeded undaunted along the canyon rim until he was an intimidating twenty yards away. He stared at me briefly and then lowered his head and began rolling his great curled horns back and forth while slowly moving in my direction. Gnarly white bark and limber pines grew close to the cliff ledge, and I began looking for the nearest tree to climb. Then in a surprising turn, he apparently sensed my complete unwillingness to do battle; I was probably an unworthy adversary anyway, or perhaps he decided he would entertain me on another day if I continued to make myself available. Curiously, he withdrew what I had perceived to be a declaration of war and rather seemed to proclaim some sort of truce with the possibility of amnesty, and then he merely lay down a few feet from the vertical rock wall. As I stood with mouth agape, like a poorly rendered statue, he looked away stoically, stared out over the great opening of the canyon, burped rather loudly, and began leisurely chewing his cud. His resonating intonation registered with me as something like, "You will do well to make your retreat now, for thou shall not pass this way today." Stunned by his gentle nature that deemed me worthy of only a single ear canted back in my direction, I walked slowly away until I could disappear into the pines. Giving him a respectful and wide berth, I eventually returned to the rim and continued my quest for newly shed elk antlers. Sadly, the Little Popo Agie Canyon bighorn sheep herd plummeted in population during the 1970s and 1980s and is now extinct. Not one well-documented sighting has been made in over a decade. The Popo Agie Middle Fork herd has all but disappeared in recent years as well. As of January 2009, a conversation with a Sinks Canyon Park ranger revealed that only four or five individuals remain, although one new lamb has survived this year. By June 2009, it appears that only one lonely ram remains from a herd that only two decades earlier numbered over one hundred and fifty. Population declines are occurring in many wild sheep herds throughout the Rockies and the Sierra Nevada Mountains. Idaho sheep numbers are estimated to be down over fifty percent during these same years. No one knows why some wild sheep herds have, in these same years, fared relatively well.

Returning to our vehicles, John and I proceed along Torrey Rim until we encounter a small group of several mature rams lying in the snow close to the old broken-down fence marking the Fitzpatrick Wilderness boundary. The rams eventually stand and move toward the edge of the tree line that begins just past the collapsed fence. Here, John and I part company once again. Leaving my truck at the fence boundary, I will climb a few miles and install my new campsite near the top of Whiskey Mountain to begin a census of ewes and surviving lambs. John will spend the rest of the morning on the rim and eventually head back to Lander to conduct some business.

After hoisting a backpack, I begin climbing the two thousand vertical feet and the five-mile distance to the location that will serve as my home for the next four or five weeks. The first two-mile leg of the hike is made tedious by the steep, relentless incline that becomes even more apparent by the self-conscious confines of the thick forests. Then a spectacular view of Middle Mountain with its surrounding canyons and glaciers distracts the backpacker, making another mile of ascent less excruciating. Although lacking much of the brutality of the climb up Middle Mountain, the first few miles are tough. Once, I led a professional musician who writes scores for documentary films to our Whiskey Mountain campsite. Upon arrival five hours later with his fifty-pound pack, Sammy Tedder confessed, "Well, that was probably the single hardest thing I have ever done in my life."

Today, as October nears, I fall in behind five mature rams that must have a similar destination up the mountain. They seem to accept my company as I tag along fifty yards behind. Uncharacteristically for bighorn sheep, the rams readily wander through the thick forest, alternately stopping to forage and occasionally offering me a disinterested glance, displaying a disregard for any preexisting trail. It is widely believed that bighorn sheep prefer to avoid heavily forested areas and are consequently often limited in their access to otherwise suitable habitat. The Whiskey Mountain herd seems to readily traverse large expanses of relatively dense forests in their various migrations from one seasonal habitat to another and even, it seems, from one daily foraging area to another. It is not uncommon for sick or old rams to actually seek out the seclusion of the forested zones below the tree line and make their death beds there, whereas, in my experience, dead ewes are more often found concealed in rocks but well above the timberline. The shutter on my camera fires repeatedly from a distance of thirty meters as the rams and I share a pleasant morning ascending Whiskey Mountain, aided by the leverage of the rising sun. Emerging through the timberline above the ten-thousand-foot level, my path diverges from the rams, which continue their ascent. I begin traversing two more miles straight across the steep south-facing slope of the mountain that rises thousands of feet above the creek and canyon floor below. At last, with one leg now distinctly shorter than the other, I arrive at a site near a small glacial pothole, perhaps 500 feet below the actual 11,200-foot summit of the mountain. The pothole remains filled all summer with beautiful blue-green melting ice and snow and provides the only available water on the upper reaches of the mountain. The pothole is an interesting and active feature because this man and every other beast on the mountain must share water. In the dry autumn, mud is exposed and the low waters of the pothole reveal a history of unfortunate events with the recent and ancient bones of animals large and small. Other humans have taken advantage of the opportunities the water provides, as flint, polished stone, and even wooden artifacts were left by ancient human hunters. Scattered across the nearby slopes, scant evidence of human occupation remains, and just like the extraordinary animals their lives revolved around, the Sheep Eater indians were a rare people.

Reminiscent of old dilapidated split rail fences, the dim, weathered remains of ancient "drive lines" stagger through my campsite and down the side of the mountain. As seen from high above, a few bleached remains of slender polelike tree trunks resemble an intermittent dotted line and trace the remnants of old wooden fences or barriers that probably once led to a clever trapping enclosure that has long since faded into the past. Stone "blinds" that once concealed well-armed bowmen are common at strategic locations along drive lives or alongside an accommodating gap in a cliff face. After months of life in the habitat of the Rocky Mountain bighorn sheep, the remains of the enigmatic people who shared this same ecology gradually become visible everywhere.

By the time early ethnographers knew of the existence of this unusual culture, the Sheep Eaters had all but slipped into extinction. The earliest known brief contact dates to the 1830s, but few comprehensive interviews or observations were gathered, and the last official description of the Tukudika people—the Sheep Eaters—dates to the late 1870s. By this time, judging by all accounts, the culture was already in disarray and largely displaced or extinguished from its original areas of occupation. It is generally surmised that the disappearance of the gentle Sheep Eater people was brought about by a combination of small pox infections and an inability to defend themselves from marauding Sioux that began making excursions into the historic land of the Shoshones in the mid-1800s. Although the Sheep Eaters were known to belong to the diverse Shoshonean language group, they apparently shared few cultural traits with other contemporary Plains Indian traditions. It has been suggested that if true Stone Age people still existed and even persisted after the time of European contact, this shy and obscure culture could fall under that loose definition. But the so-called Stone Age description should not be confused with primitive, for without question, the Sheep Eaters seemed to be perfectly adapted to their ecology, their Stone Age technologies were highly evolved, and ample evidence exists that verifies the existence of an extraordinary religious tradition. The dog was their only domestic animal, as they never developed a fascination with the horse like other Indian people who were known to be more dependent on the wandering bison. Bison were seasonally migratory, and many native groups followed the herds as they moved from one range to the next. Sheep Eaters were never known to be truly migratory, as their annual movements were more likely in response to local seasonal changes; they were merely following the snows and perhaps the bighorn sheep as both moved up and down the mountain. Precious little is known about Sheep Eater culture except that the group's economy and survival was in some large part focused on the bighorn sheep and the rich but limited ecology of the high mountains. By all accounts however, they made the single most sought-after weapon ever produced by native people—the legendary and powerful sheep horn bow. Historical accounts describe this coveted bow as bringing between five and seven ponies when bartered, and bows were known to be traded far and wide. In spite of the prowess of their weapons, the Sheep Eaters were not identified with the aggressive cultural traditions of the many warrior societies of the day and were never known to engage in hostilities with whites or other Indian people. The visible remains of their flint and stone industry may be seen at any subalpine site offering a logistic advantage, and their fine projectile points turn up as isolated finds all across these mountains. Not only are the weathered remains of their drive-line fences common, but their shelters are also occasionally found still standing. The traditional wickiup was constructed like the better-known conical tepee but fashioned entirely from closely stacked wood poles without spaces, and they were probably built as a more permanent structure. The closely nested poles were then covered in grasses, mud, and plant matter rather than bison hides to make them weatherproof and possibly warmer. Today particular species of grasses grow near the remains of wickiups and probably represent the surviving ancestors of the grasses that were used to cover the original structures.

In almost thirty years of exploring the Wyoming backcountry, I have only found three wickiups. One was in near-perfect condition in the area of Atlantic Peak and South Pass; another one was within the area of the sheep study, largely collapsed and in poor condition. John located a well-preserved wickiup a few years ago in the sheep study area and upon entering found a leather bag still hanging from a pole and a small unbroken steatite stone bowl on the floor. The bowl and the bag may be seen at the DuBois Museum and Wind River Historical Center, and the site of the wickiup remains undisclosed. Tragically, now that Wyoming is experiencing wildfires with more regularity because of the changing climate, these precious sites are being destroyed with heartbreaking regularity.

Rock shelters were also enclosed with tightly stacked poles and plant matter, and where Sheep Eater people lived, rock carvings or petroglyphs can usually be found nearby, representing the most dramatic surviving elements of their mysterious culture. Petroglyphs that are associated with Sheep Eater sites are often recognized by forms and motifs, but the interpretation of these forms without bone or carbon dating, like rock art everywhere, is almost always conjectural and remains mysterious. The petroglyphs on and around Whiskey Mountain—and there are many—are extraordinary in their complexity and suggest a powerful spiritual significance, and their remotely anthropomorphic forms provoke a chilling sense of the preternatural.

17

OF WOLVERINES AND EAGLES

Tracks of marmots, pikas, bighorn sheep, elk, bears, and mountain lions are interchangeable and often in evidence around the glacial pothole. Unlike the upper extremities of Middle Mountain, it is always advisable to take a look around before climbing out of a tent on Whiskey Mountain, especially in the darker hours. Frequently in the night I am awakened by the shuffling or coughing of large animals as they rummage around in the thick grasses near my tent. A dear friend—that same unfortunate documentary film musician from Florida, Sammy Tedder—opened the door to his tent just before sunrise one brisk morning only to be greeted by an equally stunned but curious mountain lion a few yards away. It was once my naive opinion that like Middle Mountain the upper reaches of Whiskey Mountain were used primarily by bighorn sheep, but other large animals were more restricted to the dense forests below. After my first blanketing snowstorm, I awakened to a mountaintop covered in every manner of large animal track—like Grand Central Station but for wildlife. There were elk, deer, moose, black bears, lions, wolves, and the unmistakable wanderings of a grizzly with three-inch claws on the front paw and a rear track considerably larger than my own booted foot.

This campsite will be my home for the next few weeks, and I pitch my tent just out of site and below the glacial pothole—a discreet few hundred yards down the mountain. My kitchen is another one hundred yards below my tent site, situated on a cliff face formed by a small outcropping of flint that provides a safe nonvegetated and noncombustible cooking site.

Open fires in the upper elevations of the northern Rocky Mountains are impractical in the ceaseless winds, and except for times when the ground is completely covered with snow, a fool's devise, overwhelmingly predisposed toward disaster. In thirty years of backcountry camping winter and summer, I have never built a fire in the Rocky Mountains.

My experience as a national forest firefighter familiarized me with all the horrendous possibilities of a camp fire—the equivalent of holding a loaded gun to a loved-one's head and putting your finger on the trigger.

A convenient rock backdrop is also provided, offering some relief from the cold prevailing westerly winds, as well as nooks and crannies to store cooking gear. The rock outcrop also serves as a fine home to a fat and appreciative marmot I have developed a good working relationship with over the years. A particular golden-mantled ground squirrel, which I am certain recognizes me from a great distance, always appears waiting in the "kitchen" in anticipation of an inevitable bite of my bagel. Although the site does offer the possible disadvantage of a careless diner falling to a certain death, the kitchen faces due east with the earliest possible exposure to warming sunshine and a spectacular overview of Torrey Canyon with its meandering creek, glacial lakes, and the entire expanse of the Wind River Basin beyond. Further, the rock rubble that has accumulated below the cliff face is filled with the entertaining activity of pikas and chipmunks. Across the canyon to the south lies the tilted vastness of Arrow Mountain, which is geologically identical to Whiskey Mountain. The two mountains were once united as a single great geological entity. The mile-wide glacial behemoth that plowed down Torrey Canyon forever divided a single mountain into two. Tilted and exposed strata on both sides of the canyon, although miles apart, still line up perfectly, like some enormous slice has been cut from a great lopsided multilayered birthday cake. One unstable stratum crumbles perpetually in identical pale yellow landslides miles apart. Both mountains include the two great limestone formations, the Bighorn and Madison, which lie in perfection opposition in towering stratified vertical walls on either side of the canyon.

Toward the southwest, rise the opening of the great, dark granite jaws of Bomber Canyon with the cascading waters of Bomber Falls several miles up the canyon. Each morning when the sun begins to rise above the horizon of the basin, Crowheart Butte gradually becomes apparent as a distant volcanolike darkness, silhouetted on the landscape some twenty miles away. A close two-hundred vertical feet directly below, the thick subalpine spruce and fir begin with a poorly defined and ragged tree line ecotone of open parks and wet, grassy meadows alternately mixing with the suddenness of the tall forests. Below this abrupt forested edge, the canyon becomes increasingly steep while ancient and narrow serpentine trails wander upward from the valley, connecting many living things to radically different worlds. Elk may be seen occasionally wandering up or down through the edge of the timber as they browse and visit the springheads that slowly well up from the percolating water stored in the mountain above. At dusk a patient observer may on occasion view all manner of activity and traffic below involving bears, moose, elk, deer, coyotes, red foxes, badgers, the elusive mountain lion, wolves, and on at least two occasions now, wolverines.

In early July of 2007 I was making observations from the open expanse of Whiskey Mountain's westerly slope seated on the approximate center of the broad, high, and grassy saddle we call Whiskey Pass. From this position it is possible to visually scan the mountain in both directions for a mile or more. As I watched with notebook and camera only thirty meters from seven mature ewes that were casually grazing, the group suddenly began staring with interest down the slope to the north. Perhaps a half mile down the mountain we could see the small but conspicuous dark shape of an animal running at a steady lope straight up the wide-open expanse of the pass. As the strange shape moved closer, the sheep began to gather closely together, eventually standing motionless and watching the dark silhouette as it moved with steady and oblivious determination straight toward us. Its peculiar locomotion quickly identified the creature as some sort of a large mustelid, the taxonomic group that includes weasels, otters, fishers, martins, minks, badgers, and so on—often stinky and occasionally disagreeable creatures. At two hundred meters, its size and unmistakable markings revealed it to be none of the previously mentioned animals but rather their great and powerful relative, the wolverine. Entirely ignorant of proper wolverine protocol, I merely sat, joining the sheep in a cautious jaw-dropping rapture as it approached at an unwavering and steady cross-country pace—as if it had a specific destination in mind and a fearless disregard for anything that might lie in its path. Having boldly abandoned any suggestion that the wolverine should ever have to take cover, it proceeded toward us, up the great grassy expanse a half mile above the protective tree line and far from the nearest rocky cover. I expected the sheep to take flight at any moment and wondered if prudence dictated that I follow their example. The small herd instead began gathering closer together—shoulder to shoulder, nose to tail—one contiguous and inseparable mass of bighorn sheep the size of a pickup truck and probably weighing half as much. In an astonishing gesture, rather than displaying caution and surrendering the road to a large predator with a notorious and nasty reputation, they began to move slowly toward the beast. At last, the great bulging hulk of horns, hooves, and hair became impossible to ignore, and the wolverine began to alter its course slightly to avoid a direct confrontation. Dumbfounded, I watched as the sheep never broke ranks but with complete resolve and solidarity aggressively took out at a run, chasing the creature straight down the other side of the pass. For several minutes I watched the sheep pursue the wolverine down the slope until it was a dark speck disappearing over the sloping horizon of the mountainside. As luck would have it, I was able to document the entire encounter with my camera but unfortunately without my telephoto lens. Helge Swanson, an environmental scientist visiting from Florida, happened to be with me that day and appeared over a little ridge just in time to watch most of the encounter. Even the existence of wolverines in the Wind River Mountains has remained controversial as sightings have been poorly documented.

Bald and golden eagles pass by camp morning and evening on expeditions to and from high alpine pastures and the deep glacial lakes lying below in the canyons. During the nesting season, eagles regularly sail past in the thin mountain air, visibly panting with mouths agape, pumping powerful wings, and oftentimes carrying a heavy dead marmot or some monster cutthroat trout that would easily feed two people. In some areas of the Rocky Mountains and the Sierras golden eagles are suspected of being a significant limiting factor in wild sheep populations, and occasionally these aggressive birds are seen transporting a limp and lifeless lamb down the mountain. Although documented sightings of eagle kills are made with some regularity, in most cases it is unclear if dead lambs have been merely scavenged or if true predation is occurring. On several occasions John observed golden eagles as they swooped down and made powerful passes, scattering lambs and ewes across the mountainside, perhaps testing for newborn, sick, or injured individuals.

Golden eagles are fierce and powerful predators known to occasionally take the young of many other large mammals besides bighorn sheep, such as mule deer and antelope. Such sightings in the Middle Mountain area are

not uncommon, particularly in spring during lambing season when vulnerability is at its peak. One year around the first of August, John suggested that
I hike down from Middle Mountain to visit some canyons to the east and
far below to investigate eagle nests for signs of lamb remains. Red Creek
flows out of these mountains to the east, passing adjacent and just below a
five-hundred-foot-high but relatively small feature known as Table Mountain (not to be confused with the rather large Table Mountain rising just
southwest of Lander). The Table Mountain of Red Creek is probably a classic butte formation, a surviving remnant of the sediments that once covered
the entirety of the Wind River Mountains and all the surrounding red Triassic sandstones. Red Creek flowed onto reservation lands and immediately
through the ranch of Mr. and Mrs. Frank Cady. Mrs. Cady was Shoshone,
and Frank, as the reader may recall, was one of the previous owners of the
Greenough Ranch in Red Canyon. Frank appeared to have affection for
red rock, as the Greenough place and his Red Creek Ranch were both surrounded by the identical continuous red Triassic sandstone formations, although eighty miles apart. However, by comparison the Red Creek Ranch
was arguably the reddest place I've ever seen—canyon walls, soil, juniper
trees, water, laundry, vehicles, horses, dogs, cattle—everything. And when
the wind blows even the sky can turn brick red with dust as fine as talcum
powder. Frank was probably in his seventies then and known far and wide as
a true old-time Wyoming cowboy. Another Swan Cattle Company cowboy.

John had known Frank for many years and received permission for me
to hike onto the ranch. The canyon walls immediately south of the Red
Creek Ranch are formed by the north-facing limestone cliffs of Table
Mountain and have always been favored by two or three nesting pairs of
golden eagles. From Arrow Mountain, John can look directly down on
Table Mountain and keep a watchful eye for eagles nesting in the red-rock
canyons surrounding the Cady place.

Frank Cady was a tall, lanky man and the picture of a salty old cowboy.
His Shoshone wife appeared to be perhaps a few years younger and was
a stunningly beautiful older woman with long raven hair, smooth tawny
skin, and fine features. She was quiet and reserved compared to Frank, and
perhaps a little suspicious if not actually resentful of my activities. However,
she was at least cordial to this rather strange white man who wanted to go
poking around in their eagle nests.

A mile up the canyon from the Cady's ranch house, I began seeing the unmistakable splashing of eagle droppings below rocky ledges—like white paint splattered all down the rock walls below large billowing nests constructed from great heaping loads of sticks. By that date, young eagles had all fledged and were following the adults up and down the mountainsides and no longer visiting the nests. It appeared that of the three nests sites at least two were used that season. First I climbed a few hundred feet to the top of the butte and crawled out on overhanging ledges to glass down to the nests. I saw a few unidentifiable long bones from young mule deer, antelope, or lambs as well as the obvious remains of several rabbits. Curiously, the articulated bones of a large, fully adult mule deer's hindquarter were also included in one of the nests. However, I couldn't retrieve it without some technical rock climbing gear and a willingness to rappel fifty feet over a five-hundred-foot vertical cliff face. I had neither the gear nor the inclination. After working my way back down the mountain, I climbed up to the steep slopes directly below each nest where I collected dried leg bones from mule deer fawns and several cannon bones from bighorn lambs with identifying hooves still attached. By far the most abundant remains, however, were from rabbits and marmots, and so it appeared that these particular eagles had not represented a serious limiting factor in the survival of the lambs in our study area. A number of large eagle feathers had been molted and dropped near the nests, including a beautiful white juvenile tail feather with the usual striking black tip. Thinking it somehow appropriate, I presented the feather to Mrs. Cady on the way out in appreciation for letting me onto the place. She thanked me with a warm connection of the eyes, and I told Frank it was an honor to finally meet this Wyoming legend that I had been hearing about for decades. Explaining that I had been a former manager at the Red Canyon Ranch and had lived in the old Greenough house, we found that we had many things to share, and I quickly realized Frank was a living gold mine of information about the history and ecology of Wyoming.

After spending the next day gathering fresh supplies of food and fuel, I began my assent back up Middle Mountain. After several days away from my camp, I was anxious to return and resume my responsibilities. I imagined all sorts of interesting things occurring and felt resentful if any significant event may have happened in my absence.

After so many trips up Middle Mountain, the day of ascent has become something I look forward to and is not at all dreadful. It is a long, physically demanding day that is rich in sensory diversity—and the entertainment that is provided by this ecology is the ultimate diversion from any discomfort or inconvenience. And without fail, the traveler is at last stunned by an environmental wonder that can never be fully anticipated. Our capacity to retain a sense of the actual magnitude is hopelessly inadequate, and each time I ascend through one mountain ecology into another, there is some inevitable transformation and it seems a different creature emerges—one who has left his self-conscious indulgences below. A great mountain seems to always inspire some liberation from the petty tyranny of the self.

After wading across Torrey Creek, I began seeing horse tracks as I ascended the first steep leg of the climb, and it became obvious that horses had been led up and back down the mountain in my absence. Halfway up the rugged switchback trail, I spotted a bright unspent brass cartridge case from a .30-06 rifle that had obviously rained down from a saddle or pannier that was no doubt being violently rattled and shaken as horses lunged and scrambled to maintain their footing up the steep slope. Three-fourths of the way up the slope my suspicions were confirmed by the freshly detached lower leg and hoof of an adult ram, obviously fallen from a packhorse and lying among the riprap of loose rocks that were dislodged as several horses slid back down the mountain. Wild sheep hunting season begins in August, and now we knew that at least one ram had been taken from Middle Mountain. Although in principle, not in opposition to the process, I selfishly perceived that *my* mountain had been violated, *our* precious bighorn sheep herd had been violated, and although the annual ram harvest is well managed, I found the intrusion disturbing. My pace increased as I imagined some possible mayhem that may have occurred at the top of the mountain.

In recent times, hunting Wyoming's Rocky Mountain bighorn sheep has been carefully controlled, and only rams that have reached old age could be taken in strictly determined numbers from each herd. These determinations were made through a rigorous survey of the ram population conducted the previous winter. A few of the oldest rams can be culled by a designated number of licenses obtained through a local and nationwide lottery that by anyone's standards would be considered expensive. Legal rams are individual males that have lived about seven years and have achieved a horn growth approximating three quarters of a curl. A full-curl ram is deemed to be a legitimate trophy-size animal. Revenues are directed toward continued management and improvement of "the resource." The chance of being drawn in a lottery is remote, and once a name is drawn, the recipient is ineligible to reapply for five years, whether a ram was taken or not. Rams in this age class have met or exceeded their normal life expectancy and may have already been excluded from the breeding population by younger, more vigorous individuals. A Rocky Mountain bighorn ram is a rare trophy game animal and one that is always difficult to collect. It is not unusual for tags to go unfilled. With little innate fear of humans, adult rams are not at all challenging to hunt or kill, but their extraordinary ecology can make them extraordinarily difficult to find. Merely trying to approach a ram at twelve thousand feet can be the real challenge. However, as of late, regulations have been mysteriously relaxed, and in many hunt areas any age ram may be killed. If a sound management strategy is involved in the new regulations, it is difficult to fathom, with the possible exception of a new strategy that increases the number of hopeful applicants and therefore the amount of revenue received. Disappointed hunters are bad for business.

Leaving the timberline below, I climbed the last leg of the hike to the Middle Mountain campsite that lies just over the summit, a slow mile or so above. It was a relief to observe that the hunters exercised some good judgment by not trying to take the horses beyond the trees, and no tracks were visible on the fragile tundra. The sun had followed me all day up and over the mountain but at last became devoured by dark menacing clouds hanging among the many cliffs and peaks across the great surrounding canyon. My campsite was a welcoming sight, but first I had to retrieve my tent and other gear that was securely hidden in a safe recess within the surrounding boulders. Reconstructing my humble abode in mere minutes, I unconsciously began stowing my things by creating familiar piles in corners and in the net "gear loft" overhead. My comfortable compartment, like magic from a hat, appeared around me. With an appetite only for sleep, and an unwillingness to be tormented by gale-force winds, a few bites from a nutrition bar seemed to satisfy my imagination like a big steak and a baked potato. Enveloped by a warm down sleeping bag and a trustworthy tent that had endured hurricane-force winds on several occasions, I drifted comfortably into sleep, in spite of winds that were starting to shake the mountain like a train passing close by. Yes, the mountain shakes.

A strange phenomenon occurs in these high elevations that I presume other mountaineers have experienced, but I have never heard it described. When certain weather conditions are right, localized storms with great wind speed and intensity seem to roam, not across the mountains, but they each seem to actually meander around the mountain as if searching. I call them prowlers. I have only experienced them in the dark of night, so any accompanying cloud formation that may be occurring is not visible and remains a mystery. With the surrounding winds relatively mild, prowlers may be heard coming from great distances, like the roar of a slow-moving jumbo jet searching in vain for suitable landing sites in the rugged mountains. In a ten-mile radius, several may be heard at one time scouring the high country, scattered about at various distances, and they seem to wander in any direction like hounds searching for the scent of blood. But as one of these beasts begins to overtake the mountain, the roar increases until at last it becomes deafening. The ambient air remains strangely calm, so the storm can be perfectly identified in terms of its location, its trajectory, its approximate dimensions, and its awesome intensity. Other than the trembling earth and the howling roar, it projects no preliminary gusts to prepare you for the onslaught to come. I don't know whether these storms rotate in a wide vortex, blow in one general direction, or if winds are being directed in a downburst. The prowler hits like a great stone wall that falls from the sky and crashes over you. For perhaps a mere three minutes that feel eternal, your tent is pummeled and slammed by what is more like an enormous fist than a gust of wind. It hammers boulders, rocks, and tents with equal fury, and the sudden howling uproar finds you sitting upright, hands outstretched in a feeble effort to keep your tent from being flattened and torn to shreds. Instantly, however, the thin fabrics of the tent go slack and silent—like a sigh of relief—settling into motionlessness around the framework as the knife edge of the storm passes by. The howling beast then continues to rage across the mountain and shakes the ground until the sound begins to fade in the distance, joining in a chorus of other similar creatures that growl through the miles of surrounding wilderness. These creatures of the night are capricious and arbitrary but seem to somehow possess cruel objectives—they seem to each have their own individual motivation and project an air of viciousness that makes the heart of every creature on this mountain race.

On the night of my return to Middle Mountain, prowlers stalked. The devil is in the anticipation. Sleep is elusive when prowlers are about. Like prey to some great predator cruising for any opportunity, it is difficult to avoid thinking that it may even be possible to inadvertently attract the beast. Two storms attacked in the night, and one was a glancing blow just to the north.

In the morning, after updating weather data and tending to the forage selenium study plots, I climbed above camp to check on the locations of collared sheep. It was obvious that lambs and ewes had been on the move, with only one signal to indicate a single collared sheep might be in the area. By midmorning I was moving up the mountain to hunt for any others that could be in the area. There were no ewes or lambs within a one-mile radius of the campsite. Hoping to gain a better perspective, I gradually began working up into one of the largest pinnacles that lies half a mile above the area of the camp. This pinnacle is an enormous structure that forms the highest elevation on the northern summit of the mountain. Because of its immense size, it is steep but easy to approach, and the natural passageways wandering into its heights are broad and lush with soft green tundra vegetation. After wandering up a few hundred meters through a labyrinth of well-planted boulders, I arrived at a relatively open, flat, meadowlike expanse, protected by irregular walls of tightly stacked megaliths. Suddenly, some small white object flashed across the green tundra ahead and caught my eye. Wandering over to the object, I quickly recognized that soiled toilet paper had been deposited directly on the ground somewhere nearby, and was now blowing across the top of this pristine and uncorrupted mountain. Any charitable regard that I had reserved for the hunters who had briefly visited this mountain vanished. With this one symbolic monument, this perfect human metaphor to callus disregard and overwhelming ignorance, they had now, in every way, defined themselves as unworthy intruders. After trapping the paper under a large, loose rock so it could decompose, I continued working my way up into the labyrinth of the towering pinnacle.

The soft, spongy meandering pathways up into the distant reaches of the stone tower are spellbinding in their seemingly perfect design that might bring tears to the eyes of some frustrated landscape architect. Reaching the peak of the pinnacle, I glassed the upper reaches of Middle Mountain for miles in every direction, but no sheep were to be seen. After taking a few photographs of a visual panorama that even the finest and most highly refined German optics could not do justice to, I began working my way slowly back down through the inner recesses and pathways of the pinnacle. Just as I began descending onto the lower slopes of the great tower, something to my right caught my attention. A stone's throw away, a fine adult ram stood motionless atop an immense ovoid boulder and watched me. Immediately, I realized he was in the company of two other equally robust rams. The rams were magnificent, but their position on the stacks of gigantic boulders, with a backdrop of sheer dark granite walls and sparkling white hanging glaciers overlooking a mile wide abyss was a visual spectacle bordering on the impossible. I clumsily fumbled with my pack, trying to retrieve the camera before the moment was lost forever. Considering that hunters had been on the mountain, I thought the rams would become nervous and move away. My camera fired time and again, but to my dismay, I reached the end of a roll of film after only a few shots. Dropping down to my knees, I fought with my camera—rewinding, reloading, and securely closing the back. Certain that the possibilities would be lost in an instant, I was almost shocked as the rams remained on the boulders, milling about, hopping from rock to rock, but never wandering away. I fired away, shot after shot—thirty-six exposures—gone in an instant. Knowing that my good fortune would soon end, once again I moved to reload, dropping down a second time. To my surprise, the rams stayed a mere seventy-five meters away—alternately observing me but then occasionally stopping to graze on vegetation growing between tightly nested boulders. Finally, willing to risk the entire opportunity by moving even closer, I began slowly tacking back and forth in their direction, hopping from boulder to boulder, seventy-five meters, fifty meters—yet another thirty-six frames exposed in seconds. Again, I awkwardly bent down and rummaged through my pack, retrieving film and reloading, but still the rams held their ground as I positioned myself to construct the most outrageous compositions of wild sheep and landscapes that I could ever imagine. My shutter fired over and over as I moved within fifty feet of two adult rams that had been hunted only days before. Even though I was accustomed to close proximity with wild sheep, this was proving to be phenomenal. At last, five rolls of film of thirty-six exposures each were all expended, but yet the rams remained. After finally putting my empty camera away, I sat down to observe these incredible creatures. It soon became clear that these rams were not oblivious to my presence, they were unwilling to leave. Suddenly I became suspicious that there was more at work here than mere good fortune and an unlikely willingness by the rams to be accepting of a human presence. While trying not to disrupt them further, I worked closer into their midst with the nonthreatening techniques I used while trying to work with ewes and lambs. Then, finally, glancing down in a crevasse between two large boulders, the answer to this odd behavior became apparent. There lying on a green patch of tundra earth six feet below was the remaining carcass of a fourth ram that had been recently killed. To their credit, the hunters had taken almost everything— front- and hindquarters, all meat along the back and pelvis, and of course the head and entire hide. All that remained of what surely would have been the most spectacular ram in the group was the articulated but bare raw bones of the neck, spine, and pelvis—all stripped completely clean. Yet these rams were so attached to what was undoubtedly the dominant individual, that after days, they faithfully refused to leave the scant remains of their comrade, their brother ram. Respectfully, I moved back a short but comfortable distance and took a seat on a rock to observe.

It is difficult to speculate on the objective experience of any wild creature, and when drawing comparisons to what many perceive as unique attributes of the human species, casual observers and scientists alike become uncomfortable. As I watched these brave rams, it became impossible to avoid projecting my own sensibilities of affection, loyalty, devotion, sympathy, grief, and mourning, but, so powerful also, was the palpable projection of their experience. I realize that we can say nothing with authority about these attributes as they pertain to the motives of other creatures. But my suspicions are that our most stirring and important emotions are in fact evolutionary artifacts that reside somewhere among our most ancient of organic experiences, probably residing in the limbic region and far removed from the highly organized cerebral cortex. Even our most exquisite emotions and motivations are by no means the peculiar province of the human species. As I sat with these great and powerful animals, it was impossible to understand their objectives or feelings, but I did know, without question, we all share but one experience of this inherently unknowable universe. And of all our possible common bonds, wouldn't life itself represent the ultimate? As living creatures, we all share in an experience that connects us in the most fundamental ways, and these connections suggest in some sense that we are all members of the same complex family. And if a lifetime of intense observation has taught me only one thing, it's that there are simply no dumb animals.

The three rams eventually lay down nearby with sleepy eyes and overlooked a plunging mountainside steeped in warming afternoon sunlight. For some reason, I became embarrassed and ashamed, and I wandered back down the mountain with a heart that was now aching. Confused, I wondered, *For whom does my heart ache?*

18

BACK TO WHISKEY MOUNTAIN

Even before the installation of my Whiskey Mountain camp is complete, I can see large numbers of sheep in groups of ten and twenty individuals milling about the open slopes. Groups wander in and out of the glacial pothole above and alternately browse through the campsite with an acquired disregard for my benign presence. Many or most of these sheep are also summer residents on Middle Mountain, and by now most of them know me all too well.

Bighorn sheep are constantly on the move. The herding instinct in these wild sheep is more of a tendency than an instinctive obligation, and so it seems that the larger populations of sheep in the Whiskey Mountain area arbitrarily mingle, perhaps more in response to ideal forage availability than to an actual need to herd in the strictest sense. Smaller family groups appear to stick together, and, in fact, smaller groups I have become familiar with on Middle Mountain still remain closely aligned and appear to be only loosely associated with sheep from other summer ranges.

Humans tend to see only superficial similarities in other creatures. At first glance, all sheep look alike. But, each sheep, like every human, is unique and can in time become as recognizable as an old friend. From year to year I continue to easily identify many old acquaintances of the remote high country that without question also recognize me as a familiar face. On my first excursion up the Mountain in the spring, I am often greeted by sheep I have followed in previous summers. A greeting perhaps born of simple recognition, like, "Oh yeah, it's that guy." At times, I experience a distinct acknowledgment of my own individuality, if only as an expression of a trust founded upon a long-term and persistent failure to do them harm.

The broad, expansive southwest-facing slope of Whiskey Mountain consistently holds the greatest concentrations of bighorn sheep and not surprisingly provides the richest and most abundant forage on the mountain. Except for the occasional wandering wild sheep, these natural pastures remain devoid of other large herbivores all summer, saving their bounty and providing the sheep with abundance in fall when stores of fat are most needed in preparation for the leaner times that are sure to follow.

The western slope is broad and open but deceptive in the complexity of its irregular contours. From various positions, however, it is possible in a single glance to count lambs and ewes that are spread over most of a square mile. Sheep often enter the area to forage but simultaneously drift onto different parts of the mountain in search of other suitable pastures or water. As a result, sheep numbers can vary from only several at certain times to over one hundred at others.

A typical census technique would be to gain a vantage point that will reveal the greatest number of sheep possible and then sit motionless and begin scanning with binoculars. The observer might start counting from left to right across the slope, conclude, and then immediately begin a new count from right to left. Sheep are constantly milling about, and a standing sheep can obscure one that is lying down. Consequently, it is common to get a slightly different count with each sweep of the binoculars. But after several passes, the observer begins to get a more and more accurate count with only a variation of one or two. Finally, after what appears to be your best count, you begin counting again, using the same technique but only looking for the small lambs, which are easy to distinguish. After determining the number of lambs, it is possible with careful scrutiny to further separate the yearling ewes and rams that have survived from the previous year. These yearlings often remain with the adult ewes but have not contributed any lambs. At last you arrive at the approximate number of available mature ewes and the pool of surviving lambs expressed as a ratio. Logically, the greater the number of sheep in a single count, the more statistically significant the numbers become. In counting many smaller groups it is probable that some sheep will be counted that have left one group and joined another and inevitably accuracy will be diluted. However, after performing hundreds of counts, the statistical ratios begin to stack up in complete agreement.

Although not as catastrophic as previous years, my first year on Whiskey Mountain in 2000 was another in a series of unfortunate years for lamb survival with a ratio of only fifteen or eighteen lambs surviving per one hundred ewes. Thirty-five to forty-five surviving lambs per one hundred ewes would be more representative of a healthy year. In the two months I spent on Whiskey Mountain in 2000, I observed several unhealthy lambs throughout the fall that would continue to sicken and eventually die. The following year was a slight improvement with twenty or so survivors per one hundred ewes. Subsequent years have seen lamb-ewe ratios return to more normal numbers and interestingly correspond perfectly to years of record drought. Some of the wettest years on record, culminating in 1998, resulted in a catastrophic and unprecedented die-off of lambs— almost 100 percent mortality—whereas the recent record drought may have facilitated the return of lamb survival rates to near-normal levels. The graphs depicting lamb mortality from year to year rise and fall in nearly perfect correlation to the curve of the rainfall. The most obvious interpretation for this correlation between rainfall and mortality is that if bad things shower down on the land, there will be detriment to the creatures living there. Turn off the tap with a few years of record dry weather, and organisms predictably begin to recover. It is a most unfortunate irony that our precious rainfall may be the culprit. The reams of data accumulating by many scientists from different areas of inquiry and expertise from around the world are making this assertion all but irrefutable. Simply put: We may have reached that point in human history, and arguably in the history of the natural world, where even in our most pristine environments rainfall may cause living things to die.

The morning is gray and blustery on Whiskey Mountain after a fitful night of gusting winds and intermittent snow. I was awakened this morning by a great, full-bodied growling cough just inches from my head—a powerful sound that could only originate in a body cavity much larger than my own. Although rarely conscious of any danger from large animals, the prospect probably always prowls about subconsciously, and in a split second I found myself on all fours with my pistol in my hand. Cautiously unzipping my tent door a few inches, I observed an indifferent adult bighorn sheep grazing three feet away. A quick glance around revealed ten more sheep in a twenty-foot radius around the tent, which sent me flopping over onto my back. As the cold steel of the revolver pressed down on my chest, my rapid pulses lifted and lowered the gun in my hand—bump, bump, bump. Awakened into some sort of combat mode, I chuckled with relief that it was only a few gentle ladies casually dining outside my door. But I was made aware that many sheep may have moved in during the night, resulting from deeper accumulated snows at higher elevations.

This is one of those mornings where dark clouds, dampness, and swirling winds conspire to make breakfast an experience to get beyond as soon as possible. Somehow, a twenty-eight-degree snow is ten times colder than one at eighteen. The cold wet boulders draw the heat from my rear and legs as I sit, clumsily fiddling around with my cook stove. My rear and legs sting. The immobility required during food preparation makes the inescapable chill seem even more vicious. I need to keep moving to stay warm, but first I need fuel. Holding a cup of rapidly cooling coffee to my face with cold, damp gloves is a meager consolation. I eat my unappetizing oatmeal and stale bagel then clean up as fast as I can.

After checking my daypack for food, spare film, and full water bottles, I stride out and upward across steep grassy slopes and gladly leave the fleeting drudgeries of morning behind. Darts of driven snow paint the mountainside in a uniform mosaic of light and dark forms, all oriented in the direction of the prevailing wind. An occasional fat flake of snow drifts by on the breezes, but long-range visibility suggests the bulk of this snowfall is already on the ground. Further evidence in the form of brief patches of blue sky is occasionally revealed on the western horizon.

As I reach the first prominence above the campsite, less than a half mile up the mountain, I see dozens of sheep along the entire expanse of the great western slope. Even from a relatively poor vantage point, more than sixty sheep are visible. Working my way higher above the slope, I see vast numbers of sheep spread out along the lower elevations of the open mountainside, and the optimal vantage point may be from the edge of the trees less than a mile below. I decide to traverse around and down, below the wide expanse of grassland, to gain the most perfect view of the slope.

In an hour I have discreetly circumnavigated the large numbers of sheep that are spread out over half a mile of mountainside as I enter the white bark pine forest below. For fifteen or twenty minutes I weave through the edge of the low, gnarly windblown trees, trying to further improve my position for a count of what must be more than one hundred animals. Gusts of wind move green pine boughs about, liberating snow that ranges from fine floating particles to occasional heavy clumps falling to the ground in a heap. The coarse gravel soils, grasses, and alternating patches of sepia-colored pine needles are soft and damp, and so with the assistance of the breezes moving through the pines, my progress goes unnoticed in an otherwise pervasive quiet. All my attention is focused on my relative position to the greatest number of sheep, and so the forested world around me moves by like the flickering of an old black-and-white movie that has slipped slightly off the sprockets. Looking down only to negotiate around rocks and logs, I search for the best position to begin counting.

There is a sudden movement in my peripheral vision, a shimmering blur that flashes back and to my left. My focus is pulled in its direction. Time becomes frozen as a vague, seething black form is transposed from some foggy ephemeral vision to a wolf running, not at the pace of a big dog on a mission but rather as fast as a wolf can run, and bearing straight down on me as if its entire life was depending on this one encounter. At thirty yards, our eyes meet with an impact that is jolting—a visceral impact, which in recollection I am certain forced some strange vocalization from me that may have resembled a huff or a primitive bark. The startled wolf slides to a complete halt only twenty yards away. A big, robust, dark charcoal gray beast stands motionless, staring with blazing amber eyes straight into my depths in such a way that I feel abject fear and something else, almost like embarrassment. This animal seems to stand with the scale and mass not of a large dog but more like that of a Shetland pony—simply enormous. In one eternal instant our gaze bridges one universe to another, and then the wolf is gone. Only shadows of waving pine boughs and snow drifting silently down remain.

I've always been a fearless admirer and casual student of the gray wolf, and I have on many occasions enjoyed the animal's company and voice. But now, in an unfamiliar state of wonder and apprehension, my heart pounds so hard it hurts. Spontaneously, I sit straight down on the wet ground to recover my breath, my thoughts, and perhaps even time itself. Some perfect clarity seems to surround me as I realize that this extraordinary creature did not strike a simple note of fear in me, but rather I am virtually resonating from a major cord that must have its origins in our most distant and primeval past. Astonished, I discover this wolf has always dwelled somewhere within me, and no wonder this animal has always been the object of so much human controversy. Without question, in some dark hidden recess, the wolf still lurks in our bones.

After counting over 120 sheep, including about twenty-four young lambs and three old acquaintances with radio collars—Y-13 with lamb, Y-25 with lamb, and Y-9, who lost her sick lamb earlier in the summer—I work my way up the great west-facing slope of Whiskey Mountain. As snow begins to recede, the day warms nicely into a sparkling high country autumn afternoon. After finally arriving above the sheep once again, I work my way down into the herd in hopes of making close observations and perhaps gathering some freshly dropped fecal pellets. Plenty of fresh snow lingering in the shadows makes it possible to maintain fecal samples in refrigerated and pristine laboratory condition.

I amble down the mountain, wandering back and forth in an aimless manner, acting as if I am just some strange and clumsy herbivore that has no interest in bighorn sheep. My approach is probably more of an obligatory etiquette that these sheep still demand of me in spite of my familiarity and their habituation. As if concerned with anything and everything other than bighorn sheep, I bend over now and then and show great interest in imaginary things on the ground and occasionally turn my back to the group and stare with intensity in any other direction. In this way, over a period of an hour or so, I find myself sitting in the midst of thirty or forty lambs and ewes that are by now discreetly pretending to ignore me. I must, however, avoid staring, making eye contact, or showing too much interest in any one individual, or invariably the herd will assume I am up to something that could involve bighorn sheep and begin ever so slowly but steadily grazing away. A few ewes know me well and will allow me in their immediate proximity, but with the exception of an occasional wet nose applied to the tips of my outstretched fingers, they will not allow me to actually handle or stroke them. Now, however, I am ashamed to admit that even though it is scientifically bad form and probably altogether inappropriate, I would give them all a big hug if I could. It is ultimately gratifying when a small group of these definitively wild creatures compliments me by lying down nearby. Some of the most satisfying hours in my life have occurred while lying on a vast wilderness mountainside in the company of a group of contented bighorn sheep.

And sometimes it may become necessary to stand up, and without averting my eyes from a newly dropped pile of little fecal pellets, walk as politely as possible to the fecals, pull out a plastic bag, and collect the sample. Small and inconspicuous, fecal pellets are easily overlooked and become lost in the deep grasses on the slope. Walking straight into a group of wild sheep at this point in our relationship is only a minor breach of etiquette, but nevertheless they feel compelled to move away.

Bighorn rams are stunning and magnificent with their sculptured robust proportions and massive curling horns. Ewes on the other hand can be considered charming and even beautiful in their way but perhaps make a less-spectacular visual presentation than the rams. Adult ewes might even be lacking in a certain visual grace, possessing some subtle but nevertheless irrefutable element of the awkward. Perhaps they lack some of the sleekness of form that is characteristic of other resident herbivores like deer, antelope, or elk. Lambs are irresistible, undeniably cute, and when healthy they are always spunky, always springing around, bouncing from rock to rock and playfully butting heads with other lambs. Adult ewes, by comparison, are businesslike, deliberate, and metabolically conservative in their peregrinations and activities about the mountain. On occasion, an adult ewe will give chase to an annoying yearling or briefly butt heads with a rude ewe that has somehow violated her sense of space, but normally they remain quite composed, stoic, and even, one could say, dignified.

This afternoon, I watch fifty or sixty ewes and lambs as they graze in my direction, down and across the great slope from Whiskey Pass. They soon begin milling about in a curious manner that is unfamiliar to me, and then the entire group breaks out in a run, storming down the open expanse of the mountainside. All the ewes and lambs become airborne, more like springboks, impalas, and gazelles than bighorn sheep. With a shocking acrobatic display, the sheep go stotting and bounding high in the air, arching their back upward and dropping their head down like bucking horses but with seemingly impossible kicks straight out to the side. Eight feet in the air and twenty feet in a bound from takeoff to landing, it is a display of absolute, uncontrollable joy and exuberance—uncharacteristic of the wild sheep that I have observed for years. The show lasts for only a minute but covered a half mile of mountainside, ending with the group's churning about in playful ritualized chasing and head butting. Within seconds, however, the curious event has ended, and the ewes and lambs resume their placid and self-absorbed routine of grazing across the mountain.

After several weeks camped high on Whiskey Mountain, I began to feel confident in the accuracy of the census. Further, the high mountains were beginning to be overtaken by the inevitable white icy onslaught of true winter. My thermometer registered a nose-numbing seven degrees below zero this morning, and my season with the Rocky Mountain bighorn sheep has at last, regretfully, come to an end. If we each could choose the one perfect life that would satisfy us and fill us with light and joy for all eternity, I would surely be content to roam these high mountains forever—every day awash in pure mountain light, the companionship of so much teeming life, and the unspeakable perfection that defines this great mountain wilderness.

EPILOGUE

The gate near the Wyoming Game and Fish Department's bunkhouse that seasonally allows access to Torrey Rim on Whiskey Mountain closes on the first of December. The gate will exclude all vehicular traffic up Whiskey Mountain until May.

The recent years of record drought have ironically ended the die-off of bighorn sheep with lamb survival rates back to nearly normal levels. However, troubling news comes in different forms.

All the glaciers of the Wind River Mountains have been in a dramatic recession, and many smaller glaciers have already disappeared. Some glaciologists are predicting that within ten years all the glaciers in the Wind River Mountains will have vanished. The Middle Mountain portion of the bighorn sheep study had to be cancelled in 2007 by the first week of August because of a complete lack of available water on the mountain—either in the form of precipitation or meltwater. To everyone's shock and dismay, only one significant rainfall was recorded for the entire summer—*one!* This condition has persisted into the summer of 2008 and is expected to continue in 2009. Remember, this is a mountain that typically can expect some form of precipitation, rain or snow, almost every day during the summer season. By no means could this be considered to fall within the bounds of cyclic annual variations in weather. During the summer of 2007, John and I both independently recognized that much of the alpine habitat in the northern Winds had lost a critical defining characteristic of true alpine ecology. By mid-August, only six weeks after the spring thaw, all water had ceased to flow in the customary and familiar rivulets of clear water normally discharged across the entire top of these mountains. Temperatures in the eighties—unheard of at these elevations—occurred again and again throughout the summer. Permafrost had at last ceased to exist within the alpine soils of these mountains, and ground water reserves were no longer being replenished throughout the summer. Once the early snows of autumn have moistened the first inch or two of the soil, a cap of ice is formed that prevents any further moisture from penetrating and recharging the ground. The amount of winter snow accumulation has no effect. As winter snows melt in spring, this frozen cap of soil will be exposed to the thaw after the overlaying snows have melted and are discharged from the mountain as runoff. If summer rains fail to fall, all opportunity for a groundwater recharge is lost for the year, and permafrost will fail to be reestablished. It appears that Middle Mountain and much of the alpine ecology of the Wind River Mountains, at least for the geological moment, may have become a high desert.

Most of the agricultural irrigation for the entire Wind River Basin is provided by glacial runoff that normally contributes water during summer and fall, long after all previous winter snow has melted. An absence of glaciers in the Wind River Mountains is disturbing for many reasons, but it certainly may have a disastrous effect on ranching and farming in the valleys below. As glaciers melt more rapidly, the tributaries downstream swell all summer, giving the impression to ranchers below that there is more water than ever. In fact, there is, but that is because warming temperatures have pulled the plug on hundreds and perhaps thousands of years of stored water. We are making massive withdrawals on an account that is no longer receiving deposits. Our liquidity is vanishing.

Normally, by November the rugged two-rut trail up Whiskey Mountain has been blanketed in deep snows, but in 2007 John Mionczynski and I merely lock his hubs into four-wheel drive and crawl up the mountainside with only a few inches of snow hiding in the shadows of sagebrush, rocks, and the protected north-facing slopes. John and I visited Whiskey Mountain at different times in October and early November of 2007 to attempt a census and, strangely, found that sheep appeared in small groups of twenty or thirty individuals, but the aggregate Whiskey Mountain bighorn sheep herd was nowhere to be found. Our normal expectation would be to see in excess of one hundred lambs and ewes by the end of October. In separate three-day visits to the mountain, my best count only included thirty-seven ewes and seven lambs. On his first visit John encountered the same thirty-seven sheep, but then on his second he counted eighty-three. However, by this date the rut was beginning and the rams had at last joined the lambs and ewes. Our assumption was that so little snow had fallen in the high country that sheep were probably still dispersed over a hundred square miles of alpine habitat.

As we near the great open expanses of Torrey Rim, we see a large gathering of sheep peppering the steep, rolling grassy mountainside above us. John shuts off the engine while we each grab our binoculars and begin mumbling to ourselves as we conduct separate counts. After a minute or two John says, "What did you get?" I reply, "Eighty-three, but that includes quite a few rams." John says, "That's exactly what I counted the last time I was up here—eighty three." We follow the trail higher on the mountain, climb out of the truck, and then begin trying to count all the lambs. With a quick sweep of the binoculars across the scattered herd, John counts twenty-one lambs and I get nineteen. A recount confirms that John got it right the first time with twenty-one. Next we begin the more complex task of counting yearlings that are difficult to discriminate this late in the year and then immediately begin counting rams, young and old. After an hour or so spent wandering across the mountain slope on foot we finally agree—twenty-one lambs, forty-eight ewes, fourteen adult rams, and ten yearlings. We see only one collared ewe—W-17—but we know there should be three more, so obviously a small group is out of sight. We don't have the radio receiver, so it is impossible to determine in which direction they may be grazing. The total number of bighorn sheep in this count is ninety-three. Of course this count did not include the entire herd, and although this was without question a good year, the actual lamb–ewe ratio would be slightly less optimistic. Still, this is good news, but there is bad news as well. The reproductive hole in the herd that we had anticipated from the many catastrophic die-off years that failed to recruit new lamb-bearing ewes is now being expressed in a smaller overall population. Many of the old ewes that survived those years are now dying out. This summer, lying in a sunny meadow on Whiskey Mountain, I even recovered the yellow radio collar from old Y-24 that I had known and followed for many years. She was a good mom and although losing at least one lamb in 2001, contributed several healthy lambs to this herd.

Naturally, the population decline can also be observed in rams. Typically, this herd only supports fifteen or twenty adult rams that have lived three or more years. Pioneering wild sheep biologist Valerius Geist, studying the population dynamics of bighorn sheep throughout the United States and Canada, found that sex ratios in lambs average about 50:50 but that mortality tends to increase in males as they mature because of stress associated with the rut. Geist's many studies concluded that a majority of wild sheep herds might expect typical sex numbers to average eighty or ninety adult rams per one hundred ewes. The last decade has been a stressful time for the Whiskey Mountain herd, and yet, for unknown reasons, ram populations here have always averaged lower with only twenty or less per one hundred ewes. It is likely that two or three of the older rams from this herd have been taken by hunters this fall. One particular ram that I have followed for many years with a distinguishing horn configuration is now missing.

The afternoon is clear and sparkling as the winter sun glides low across the southern sky. The wind is relatively gentle for Whiskey Mountain at this elevation and may be moving between ten and fifteen miles per hour. We came well prepared for a winter day in the Wyoming high country, but unlike John, I optimistically chose to wear hiking boots rather than pacs. As we wander across the mountainside with bighorn sheep milling all about, we snap photos of the massive rams as they alternately wander through the various gatherings of ewes and lambs in hopes of finding a female signaling a willingness to be receptive to their attentions. We photograph the preoccupied rams only a few meters away as they obsessively but politely explore among the ewes, yearlings, and lambs. Always, an inevitable sense of gratitude overtakes me on the golden grassy slopes of this great mountain as we are accepted in some way into the presence of these magnificent animals. Again and again, I am astonished by this perfect place and the creatures that are so obviously woven into this magical fabric. After so many thousands of hours spent in this rare domain, it is as clear as mountain air that the experience of this exotic realm can never become routine or ordinary. Like an excited child I scurry from one impossible point of view to the next, unable to avert my eyes from this panorama, and so my feet fail to find their way through the many exposed rocks. I carelessly trip and stumble about as my eyes refuse to be diverted from one outrageous vision to the next.

At last it occurs to me that my toes are aching and my gloved fingers are stinging from the cold. My core temperature is comfortable, but all my extremities are beginning to hurt. Curiously, the motor drive on my camera seems to operate in slow motion as if it has been lubricated with cane syrup. John passes by briefly as we photograph three fine rams, and I notice icicles hanging from his mustache. The sun, although seasonally low in the sky, suggests that its golden glow on the mountainside must be bathing us in warmth, but John's laser thermometer reflects off a nearby rock and suggests that the temperature is fifteen degrees below zero. Finding it difficult to articulate words because of a numbing face, I warble to John as we finally climb back into the truck, "I'm having fun now." John lights up and replies, "Me too!" We start the truck, and as our hands gradually thaw, we begin scribbling in our respective field books and work up the numbers—forty-four lambs per one hundred ewes—not bad. Although this count does not represent the final census, this is without question a highly successful and productive year and probably the best I've seen since joining the project many years ago. Our joy is overshadowed by the corresponding and more significant corollary of perhaps the lowest rainfall total in recorded history.

The Whiskey Mountain Bighorn Sheep Study is alive, but it seems to have landed in a political environment where appropriations have been deemed inappropriate or at least not constituting any real priority, considering that bighorn sheep numbers are, at least for the moment, in an apparent recovery. The Wyoming Game and Fish Department has withdrawn much of its support based perhaps on our approach, which is now starting to look more like biochemistry and soil science than actual wildlife biology. But the agency still seems to be attentive to the findings. And further, as new developments and data seem to pour in by the minute from this country and others, the study has been at a loss to offer any possible management plan. And now the study has been turned upside down as record amounts of devastating acidic rainfall in past years are now suddenly reversed by record high temperatures and a mysterious lack of moisture in any form throughout the high country of the Wind River Mountains.

Pat Hnilicka has left the Wyoming Game and Fish Department and is now with the U.S. Fish and Wildlife Service studying a decline in sage grouse numbers. Habitat lost to the oil and gas industry as well as a particular vulnerability to West Nile virus has brought the sage grouse close to an endangered state. The University of Wyoming, however, has in recent years picked up the torch under the leadership of Stephen E. Williams, professor and former head of the university's Department of Plant, Soil and Insect Sciences and former dean of the graduate school. Steve seems to have a deep-seated understanding of the gravity and urgency regarding the frightening developments occurring in the alpine environments of Wyoming. Financial constraints are of course an issue at the university, but Steve and his department have been successful in recruiting bright young personnel to make observations on the complex chemistry that now appears to be creating havoc in these alpine environments.

Gary and Cathy Keene sold the Ancient Ways trading post on the Wind River Indian Reservation in January 2009. Gary is again working as a full-time scientist with the Wyoming Department of Environmental Quality. The two of us hope to investigate and explore a vertical cavern in the Winds this next summer to establish if it may have been an ancient natural animal trap above the timberline within the area of the sheep study.

This bighorn sheep study, and many corroborating studies around the world, are demonstrating beyond any reasonable doubt that increased precipitation with abnormal acidic characteristics, among many other ills, can result in a precipitous decline in availability and the subsequent uptake of selenium in alpine forage. John Mionczynski and Bruce Mincher have been invited to participate at the Fifth World Conference on Mountain Ungulates in Granada, Spain, in 2009 regarding their research with alpine fauna and the diseases that may result from variations in soil chemistry because of rainfall and climate change. There is little disagreement among those who have bothered to look at the data that the optimism being expressed in recovering bighorn sheep numbers and overall lamb survival rates could be dashed into the rocky slopes of disappointment if and when rain and snow returns to the mountains of Wyoming. This question of if and when is an ominous one, as the warming of the planet could ultimately dictate that precipitation, acidic or not, may never return to these mountains in great quantity.

However, in the spring of 2009, snow and rainfall amounts were extraordinary in that they approached accumulations that would be considered historically "normal." As expected, John's five-day reconnaissance on Middle Mountain in early July revealed several lambs with some distinct crippling ailment. This mystery must be solved.

An interesting corroborating research project published in 1994 by the Ecological Society of America in its journal *Ecology* regarding declining populations of black-tailed deer in Shasta County in northern California has gained our attention. Wildlife researcher Werner T. Flueck, working through the University of California at Davis, has made certain startling discoveries[2] that were published in his article "Effect of Trace Elements on Population Dynamics: Selenium Deficiency in Free-Ranging Black-Tailed Deer." The research revealed that black-tailed deer were suffering from a nutritional deficiency in selenium, which appeared to have seriously limited fawn survival rates for several years. Flueck's team implanted nondigestible boluses in a large group of female deer estimated to be of breeding age, several months prior to the spring birthing season. The boluses were designed to release 1.3 mcg of selenium per day as a supplement, and each deer was marked with a radio transmitter for future observation and then returned to the wild. Of 1,695 deer sampled, blood tests at the time of capture revealed that 80 percent were deficient in selenium, according to official livestock standards. Another 15 percent showed at least a marginal deficiency. The study group and their subsequent fawns were carefully monitored throughout the spring and summer and into fall. The test results on recaptured deer indicated that selenium supplementation had dramatic effects on fawn survival rates and blood levels of selenium. On average, selenium blood levels were 3.1 times higher in females when compared to levels measured prior to treatment. Flueck writes, "Productivity [fawn survival] due to Se supplementation was increased by 2.6 times . . . over unsupplemented deer [a staggering 250 percent increase] and resulted in an *additional* [my italics] 51 fawns per 100 females." Flueck further reminds us of the growing body of data that suggests "anthropogenic manipulation of ecosystems," in the form of acidic atmospheric precipitation, has now been widely demonstrated to reduce the bioavailability of selenium in free-ranging herbivores. References were also made to several authors who have "described a world-wide increase in the incidence of selenium responsive diseases in animals." In this same study, Flueck points to research substantiating our suspicions regarding the relationship of the acidification of soils by atmospheric pollution and a corresponding reduction in plant selenium concentrations. Flueck concludes his discussion by stating, "This implies that the impact of large-scale anthropogenic activities may alter

Se or other trace mineral cycles in remote areas, which would reduce the effectiveness of small, isolated areas [i.e., wilderness areas, etc.] for protection of biodiversity."

John continues to shepherd this bighorn sheep study in spite of limited or no financial compensation, and works closely with the University of Wyoming and all the other agencies and individuals who occasionally offer support. John is being challenged by an apparently incurable case of Lyme disease contracted from a bite several years ago on the Middle Mountain lambing grounds. After some thirty years he still lives in his one-room log cabin with no electricity near Atlantic City, and people far and wide continue to seek out this reclusive scientist when a need arises for his encyclopedic knowledge and understanding of Wyoming's vast ecology. He has been invited to return to Ethiopia in 2009.

Wyoming, like most areas of the country, continues to expand with oil development and population growth but perhaps not with the unconstrained aggression seen in some areas. Because of the oil and gas boom, formerly protected areas are being opened to new roads and drilling. Most disturbing perhaps in our immediate vicinity is the opening of formerly inaccessible areas of the Red Desert by the Bureau of Land Management to new drilling operations in spite of the objections and desperate cries of the concerned residents of Wyoming. The Red Desert is not only the highest desert in North America but a great fragile expanse characterized by a multitude of unique geological, ecological, paleontological, historical, and prehistoric features. The greater Yellowstone ecosystem, the Wind River Mountains, and the Red Desert are the richest and most environmentally diverse expanse of wilderness left in the lower forty-eight states—the jewel in the crown of American environmental conservation. Any large-scale industrial development in this remaining wonder of the natural world that contains meager petroleum reserves can only beg the question, What in fact do Americans find sacred?

Red Canyon rancher Henry Slingerland died a few years ago, but Nan is continuing to operate the portion of the ranch that was not sold to the Nature Conservancy. Nan is actively running the operation with a modest but gorgeous herd of registered red Angus cattle that are sold in the fall as organically grown beef. Further, she has received national attention for her efforts to help in the recovery of the nearly extinct breed of sheep known

Travis and Tom Lucas repairing corrals.

to the Navajo Indians as *churro*. Churro sheep were introduced to native people by the Spanish in the 1500s and produced the wool that made the original Navajo blankets so desirable. After ten years of breeding, Nan supports a flock of over two hundred, and each spring the rare wool is shorn and the valuable material is sold to be woven into the most durable and luxurious of blankets.

Admitting that it is impossible to stay away, I have been a full-time resident of Wyoming again for a number of years and ironically, live in one of the old ranch houses connected with the Slingerland ranch. Encouragingly, Nan has in her employ, not one but two, "real" working cowboys. It has been my privilege to get to know Tom and Travis Lucas. In his midthirties, Travis manages the operation for Nan, and his father, Tom, helps out when Travis needs another really good hand. Tom Lucas is no longer a kid, but he hasn't slowed a bit and can put in a grueling day working cattle, repairing corrals, and mending fences with the best of them. Frequently they drag this old hand along for brandings and working cattle.

Tom Lucas and the sheep horn bow.

Tom Lucas has also become recognized in the world of Western Art. He has not only become a skilled painter and artisan of traditional Indian tools, weapons, and garments, but by studying ancient artifacts that he has obtained, and those that he has been allowed to closely examine in museum collections, he has recovered technologies that have been lost over the centuries, including the art of making the revered sheep horn bows of the obscure Sheep Eater people. His exacting reproductions are included in museum collections around the west.

Tom's son, Travis, now in his thirties, like his father, is a classic do-it-all, legitimate cowboy. Besides running an entire ranching operation he also finds time to fashion beautiful knives made in the traditional Indian method using bighorn sheep horn and blades, which he painstakingly and beautifully knaps from local mountain flint. And when Travis gets a day off, he is not predisposed to go to a town, but instead saddles up a horse and quickly disappears out his back door up into the forests and canyons of the Wind River Mountains. Now I have new friends who like to hunt for shed antlers in the spring, ancient Sheep Eater sites in summer, and big fine bull elk in the fall.

If any question remains regarding the continued existence of real cowboys in this country, Tom and Travis Lucas represent the resounding answer: Yes, thank god, there are still cowboys in Wyoming!

SOME THOUGHTS ON OUR DILEMMA

This morning as I jogged down the old gravel drive that leads from the ranch south of Lander to the highway a mile and a half away, a movement to my left caught my eye. A coyote, like some ghostly apparition, paced with deliberate intent across a sagebrush slope one hundred yards away. With darting glances and quick intermittent turns of the head, it gauged the rate of my progress and calculated that its speed and trajectory would bring it across the road a safe distance ahead of me. The coyote continued on its path without any apparent interruption in its gait or any alteration to its objective, but obviously found the precise location of our intersecting courses disturbing, as it perfectly anticipated my inevitable arrival. The prospect of sharing that same space, even though at distinctly different times, made the animal uncomfortable, causing it to break into a run over that precise point. Immediately, it resumed its deliberate pacing stride and continued with the occasional cautious glance in my direction. It was a fine, handsome animal, robust, healthy, and with a full complement of winter fur well established. Momentarily marveling at this good-looking little wolf, I slowed my pace to a walk. Although it had already passed far to my right, my change of speed brought the coyote to a halt as our eyes locked. Stopping, I turned, and we examined each other with a mutual intensity—the coyote's born perhaps of a need to know the nature of my sudden interest, and mine, absolute admiration for a seemingly perfect creature—self-reliant, deliberate, contemplative, persistent. Its resolve and self-confidence could be interpreted as a well-earned arrogance honed by a thousand triumphant acts of cunning and aggression, a blend of sensitivity, heroism, artful guile, and, when necessary, the ability to kill without remorse.

Quickly, the coyote dismissed our interlude as at least unprofitable and continued on some mission that led it over the sagebrush hillside and out of sight. But I was left stunned by our similarities. Coyotes and humans—we are such similar creatures. Isn't it an irony that we find them so easy to despise? It is probably an uncomfortable familiarity that breeds such overwhelming contempt. Is their apparent dominion over their world an affront to our own sense of unquestioned authority over ours? Our nature probably precludes the possibility of sharing resources with another distinctly successful creature. Is it our human predisposition to simply kill the competition—either man or beast?

This brief encounter caused me to ponder not only our similarities but also our vast differences and the far-reaching influence our species is having on vital biological systems across the globe. These are the many complex systems that sustain and foster an otherwise healthy and symbiotic world. Only the most phenomenal creatures could prosecute their lives with such aggression that their activities adulterate otherwise pristine ecologies halfway around the globe. What possible bearing could an obscure wild sheep on the highest and most remote reaches of a continent have on our understanding of the world and on our participation in it? Do our findings suggest that at last there can be no pristine ecology left on our precious planet?

Life is an expression of the adaptive possibility inherent in all living things. Each organism in its way is always seeking to improve its economy by being better suited than another at surviving. Each employs a certain strategy to exploit resources in a manner that gives them an adaptive edge over other organisms as well as an edge over those of their own kind. Typically, these adaptive strategies are accomplished through greater and more refined degrees of specialization. Most organisms have chosen *specificity* as a means to successfully outcompete or exploit resources that are unavailable without their particular specialization. A certain sand piper with a 4.5-centimeter bill lives off one particular invertebrate that lives only between 4 and 5 centimeters below the surface of a specific zone at the water's edge. In this way the animal world is replete with the most outrageous mechanisms of physiology and accompanying behaviors. Specificity has its strengths, but it often involves an inherent dependence on a particular habitat and a particular resource that can leave a highly specialized creature, at last, highly vulnerable. The fossil record is a veritable junkyard of the inevitable obsolescence of the physiology of specificity.

However, a less-often used or applied strategy for the adaptation of creatures to various environments is a departure from the more commonly employed rigors of specificity. Occasionally a creature emerges that takes a differing path—one that evolutionarily speaking marches to a different drummer. These organisms choose to do many diverse things rather well. Known as adaptive *generalists*, they might be more properly identified as *promiscuously adaptive*, and may be seen scurrying around diverse habitats, opportunistically taking advantage of every available resource.

Various species of birds are often characterized by extraordinary individuality expressed as a particular striking color, a particular voice, and unique behaviors employed in a narrow range of habitat types, suggesting that birds generally could be evolutionarily vulnerable, often fragile, and intolerant of disturbances or perturbations to their particular ecology. But along comes the remarkable crow, which lives in the wildest and most remote reaches of the landscape, foraging on sedges and grasshoppers, and then simultaneously is seen availing itself of the discarded hamburger lying between speeding automobiles on the interstate highway, exploiting many diverse resources in many clever ways. And the crow is the last bird you will ever see killed on a highway.

Wild dogs, like the African wild dog, are highly specialized and consequently are being displaced and threatened with extinction worldwide. But then, in complete contradiction, along comes the little prairie wolf, the coyote—god's dog, the trickster—and in spite of over one hundred years of relentless persecution from firearms, traps, poison, bounties, and introduced diseases from around the world, everywhere they prosper. They disperse into every imaginable habitat, from the remotest reaches of the Rocky Mountain high country to the most polluted and urbanized areas of North America. They have proven that they can live well off of absolutely anything—animal or vegetable—from the southern tropics to the extremes of Death Valley to the frozen reaches of the far north to towering mountains of garbage spilling over from our most intensely metropolitan areas.

In general, rodents have chosen specialization in their various adaptations, and predictably there is no shortage of members from this group on the rolls of endangered animals. But occasionally a more universal approach has been chosen in their adaptations, and we have a creature that can live anywhere, however hot or cold, whether in a pristine ecology or in abject filth, surviving as either carnivore or vegetarian, such as the Norway rat, a beautifully and perfectly designed animal. *Warranted or not, it is interesting that success in nature often leads to vilification by humans.* And any creature that becomes seemingly too numerous or too conspicuous, irrespective of its superficial appearance or behavior, quickly becomes in our eyes *unattractive.* The word *vermin* is merely our pejorative synonym for any other successful creature. Who has stopped to admire the spectacular male starling in the last one hundred years?

Nowhere in nature is more diversity and specialization expressed in such profusion as in the insects. The extremes and varieties that have emerged over millions of years of selective adaptation is staggering. But some have chosen an evolutionary path of a more universal adaptive strategy. Scarcely an entomologist alive is without at least a secret admiration, if not an abiding love, for that phenomenal and ancient group of successful insects known collectively as the roaches. Magnificent in their adaptive varieties, they have literally scurried beneath the feet of millions of failed evolutionary experiments, persisting today even in the face of the full weight of Western civilization's chemical and technological assaults.

Then there is that most fragile and highly specialized group of mammals that is so rigidly defined by its orientation to a particular ecology. That group, in general, has always limited its range to the most exotic and peculiar habitats characterized by abundant food resources, but those resources are limited in distribution and typically flourish within the narrowest confines of temperature, weather, and soil chemistry in the savannas and forests of the equatorial tropics. Nowhere does life exist in such overwhelming diversity and yet remains so intolerant of environmental change as in the tropics where speciation runs rampant. And among these many creatures few are so fragile and vulnerable to environmental perturbation as the primates. When change comes to the tropical forests, primates are nearly always among the most susceptible, the most predisposed, toward biological catastrophe.

However, even among the primates, in the midst of so much evolutionary specialization, along comes that rare creature that perhaps in lieu of doing anything particularly well chooses a strategy of doing many things satisfactorily—the quintessential omnivore; it hunts, gathers, scavenges, pilfers, scurries about, makes do. These are all strategies that involve flexibility in adapting to an array of environmental parameters. This is a creature that can flourish entirely through its adaptability and ingenuity, one that can live in every extreme of weather and temperature from the arctic tundra to equatorial deserts and rain forests, on the highest mountains and the shores of the sea. This is a creature that seemingly knows no limits to population, one that is not bound by the normal laws regulating the carrying capacity of the land, and that can eat anything, live in abject squalor, filth, and disease but still, unlike all but those most generalized of generalists, persists. Of course, this most unspecified and unconstrained of all the generalists, the most ecologically and adaptively promiscuous of all creatures, is man. We are that supercoyote—self-reliant, deliberate, contemplative, persistent, and with an unmitigated resolve born of an all too well-substantiated arrogance. At some point in our remote past, a nervous and tentative grasping hand picked up a sharp stick, and humility was forever abandoned in an exchange that has been reverberating across the planet for a least three million years. And remember, at three or four million years from hominoid (protohuman) to modern human, we are the ultimate evolutionary flash in the pan. Many of our most familiar birds would have already been entirely recognizable twenty million years ago. We are the evolutionary barbarians who have only recently stormed paradise.

It is at last now universally recognized by anthropologists that all human attributes are merely quantitative in nature, and with the possible exception of the peculiar human foot, are all shared with many other creatures. Modern humans have spent at least thousands of years trying unsuccessfully to divorce themselves from any relationship to other beasts, but all these efforts have fallen like dominoes to the empirical method, DNA testing, and common sense. It appears that we cannot be entirely distinguished by our intelligence, society, agriculture, binocular vision, the opposable thumb, bipedal gait, economics, or consciousness. All these attributes we share quantitatively with many other living things. In fact, except for our odd little feet and a conspicuous ability to manipulate symbols and store overwhelming amounts of information, our most salient and defining characteristic may not even be a modicum of intelligence (that we toy with in our mountains of data), but rather an abiding and more defining arrogance. The human species seems to be possessed of an arrogance that perpetually serves to reorder or deny the gravity of our perpetual existential dilemma—a dilemma that is the inevitable outwash from our reservoir of analytical reason. Perhaps our upright posture enabled us to see too far down the road. Our inherent hubris is probably a vital evolutionary component of our cerebral architecture that allows us to press aggressively ahead with an optimism that flies in the face of all other reasonable evidence to the contrary.

A 1,400 cubic centimeter brain notwithstanding, our primary adaptive mechanism as a species has less to do with our physiology but rather resides more in human culture, particularly technology. Society and culture are not peculiar to human beings, but the elaboration and development that has occurred in our species is probably unprecedented in the evolutionary history of the earth.

Culture provides an adaptive interface between the hard, cold, and often brutal realities of life and an otherwise fragile creature. We, unlike other organisms, have in essence created an ecology of the mind that by virtue of ingenuity and material culture sustains us. But remove the elements of culture and the rudiments of technology from a human being, and in a matter of hours or even minutes you have an organism in grave peril. You merely have a clever oyster with no shell. Our culture—our species—is fraught with such paradox.

It is difficult to remember that the evolution of any organism is never a work in progress, but rather an organism is always at the pinnacle of its development at any given point in time. All creatures have achieved a relative measure of perfection in form and function but merely remain open to subsequent improvements in a system that operates largely on the basis of who lives and who dies. Our goal as living organisms is fundamentally turning minerals and chemical compounds into life—the most elemental function of economics. Often in the most circuitous ways, every organism, through its unique economy, is mining the planet for the fundamental elements of life.

Our particular adaptive choice—our culture—comes at the price of certain paradoxes. As homo sapiens became definitively human in terms of cerebral architecture and the ability to sustain the abstract and physical realities of material culture, one of the ultimate results of that culture could have been the elimination of the many deadly and dramatic forces that had been selecting for individuals with superior human traits. We would have, of course, applied our logic and used culture as an immediate means to circumvent the many powerful, even brutal, selective forces that may have made us who we are, derailing many of the normal mechanisms of natural selection that had so dramatically made us human. Some theorize that we may have even risen to our physical and intellectual pinnacle many thousands of years ago before culture began shielding individuals from the unpleasantness of natural selection. If culture and humanity began making its *own* selections many thousands of years ago, things have probably been all downhill since. How do we now compare on that poorly conceived progression between the wolf and the Pekingese? However, not all selective forces are external, and intelligence can be selected simply by female preference for apparently smarter males (all available evidence to the contrary).

Culture has evolved ever more complex technologies to preserve and propagate greater and greater amounts of information, but there is no correlation between the acquisition of information, the development of advanced technologies, and the genetic advancement of intelligence. It could be logically inferred that culture's effect on human intelligence has not advanced our cause in tens of thousands of years. The classic oversimplified metaphor taught in every Physical Anthropology 101 class studying population biology is type 1 diabetes—genetic, recessive, and formerly rare in human populations. Along comes therapeutic insulin, and in only a few generations a significant percentage of our population is now diabetic. The inevitable prognosis is that within several more generations all or most humans will be born diabetic or be carriers of the trait. If any trait or characteristic is allowed to merely *persist* in a population, whether good, bad, or indifferent, it will tend to eventually dominate. The fantastic projection of the futuristic human with the shriveled body and the gigantic head would be more accurately portrayed as a creature with an increasingly billowing physique, large mouth, and a head the size of a golfball.

Are there cultural forces that could advance the cause of human intelligence? The ultimate game of intellectual strategy is probably warfare—and like chess, the "art" of war is truly the ultimate determining battle of wits. It is hard to believe that the mindless brutality of war could in any way further the intelligence of a creature, but in all cases strategy is the engine that drives evolutionary development, and no more cerebral horsepower is called into play than when you know some other intelligent creature is coming to kill you in a variety of clever ways. The slightest edge in resourceful wit could determine which group persisted and which one perished. Most of humankind's greatest advances in technologies include the mechanics of the wheel, the trebuchet, the jet engine, the Saturn rocket, and advanced computer technology. They all had their genesis in culture's thoughtful prosecution of warfare—hot and cold. Civilization has always advanced most rapidly when catapulted by the technologies of war. Ample evidence suggests that warfare may well have contributed to the design physiology of the human brain. It is no coincidence that any group of otherwise gentle young men only have to come together on the ball field, an inner-city street, or the field of battle, and with a little hubba, hubba, hubba, dive thoughtlessly headlong and fight other equally gentle young men to the death. It is a troubling but irrefutable genetic predisposition we all possess.

Disturbingly, modern technological society has allowed us all to become nature's bubble children who artificially dwell in that vacuum of cerebral abstraction that we know simply as material culture. But of course our existence on the planet is not an abstraction. Human culture is not really the universe we live in. That we can so rigorously sustain the illusion that we are somehow removed from the forces that perpetuate and sustain life on this planet is a strong indictment of modern humanity's separation from nature and hints that simple human reason and common sense might also be largely illusory. Most people living in technological societies are completely unaware of how their bread is buttered—how our food animal has been killed—how the gasoline got to our tank, or how the electricity got to our lightbulb. We have no apparent connections to many of the complex cultural processes acting on our behalf. It could be that our division of labor also tends to separate our common sense from reality. Again, it could be that our species' arrogance, in all its many manifestations, is truly the most blinding, vicious, and destructive form of ignorance.

For better and worse we can only be who and what we are as an organism. We are capable of change, but we are unlikely to become a different creature. Culture can evolve rapidly but not outside the parameters that define us biologically. In the evolutionary history of the world, many plants or animals have probably achieved so much adaptive success that they have effectively competed themselves out of existence.

Humankind's history is a repetition of a classic developmental model, from paleo human to advanced contemporary civilizations. Without exception, all civilizations have developed, peaked, and declined as they successfully competed themselves into an exhaustion based on the limits of environmental resources. It is the nature of highly evolved and well-organized societies to extract resources through their advanced technologies with ever increasing efficiency, but naturally the availability of these vital resources is entirely finite. The inevitable historical model is always repeated. And it is never the "barbarians from the north," moral or cultural erosion, plague, or natural disaster that leads all societies inexorably down the path to oblivion; it is simply the expenditure and exhaustion of vital resources. The irony in every case is that destitution has never sneaked up on a civilization. Every society observes the wellspring going dry but typically finds it inconvenient or annoying to listen to the vocal few screaming bloody murder about all the dire consequences. Not once in human history have a people acted to effectively forestall the inevitable.

It is a curious phenomenon that as humans we can quite clearly see the speeding train of ecological disaster coming, but we find it culturally and perhaps even biologically impossible to get off the track. Surely paleo humans grew tired of hearing about the inevitable demise of the great beasts their ancient way of life depended on, for they were not blind and they were probably at least as intelligent as we. No doubt the residents of Tikal and Palinque grew weary of that vocal minority that warned of the consequences of the unconstrained denuding of the forests to make lime for mortar. And yet somehow it seems that the stone foundations of their cultural edifices were prioritized over the ecological underpinnings of their cultural and biological existence. How odd, these were highly intelligent people. Undoubtedly, every civilization has had its so-called environmentalists; they are simply the ones who choose a vantage point, look around, and shake their heads in disbelief.

Imperialism, wars of aggression, and genocide are never the result of differences in ideology, philosophy, politics, or religion. These are but the superficial emotional triggers and pretexts that we sometimes use for justification. The most cursory investigation into the history of human conflict will reveal that warfare is invariably rooted in the need and quest for basic resources (Vayda, *War in Ecological Perspective,* 1976).

From the depletion of the great megafaunal species of the late Pleistocene by paleo hunters to Easter Island and the great civilizations of Mesoamerica, Mesopotamia, Egypt, Greece, and the Roman and even British empires, each in turn exhausted their natural resources, turned rich soils and ancient forests into barren ground, then desperately extended themselves beyond their reach, and finally, with only a gradual whimper, never a bang, perished. All it takes is an annual drop of 1 percent in your grossest of national products or in your exchange of commodities, and in one or two hundred years your great-grandchildren are doing boiled dirt for lunch. In the words of biologist, Marcia Murdock, "Historically, human cultures, even remarkably civilized ones, have had drastic impacts on their own environment. As is happening even today, past cultures have over-exploited their economic resources, fouled the waters, and heaped refuse upon their own doorsteps. They have done this not only to their own detriment, but to the harm of all other life surrounding them."

It appears that evolution, physical and cultural, is not always a neat, gradual progression but is often characterized by sputters and leaps. Cultures develop a sort of critical mass, an accumulated potential for the development of new technological advancement and then, perhaps with some common triggering device, a new inflorescence of cultural innovation occurs.

Something extraordinary occurred around 500 BC as the unrelated cultures of Mesoamerica, North Africa, the Mediterranean, and Asia simultaneously saw an explosion of advanced cultures as expressed in great cities, monumental architecture, sculpture and painting, writing, and of course large standing armies all controlled by a strong central authority. However, each of these civilizations experienced a similar progression that included a formative, a classical, or a peak period of cultural awakening and then gradual or precipitous decline. These periods of strong cultural development and evolution would often flourish and wither over a period of hundreds of years and could be said to conform to a classic model of entropy, whereby vital resources are collected, consumed, and finally exhausted. In other words, they simply ran out of gas, literally and figuratively. The entropic model is also used to describe the inevitable progression of societies, but this may be a case where the environmental egg always comes before the inevitable demise of the cultural chicken.

Typically, over time, it seems that some culture always finds yet another unexploited environment that can be developed, and the next great new civilization can emerge. The gradual emergence of Europe, beginning more than one thousand years later, somewhere between AD 500 and 1000, marked the beginning of the next great inflorescence of so-called Western civilization. Great empires and great monarchies flourished for the best part of a thousand years, but all eventually succumbed to that pesky paradigm of environmental and cultural entropy. The British Isles, like Greece and the "fertile crescent" of Mesopotamia (Iran and Iraq), were all rich, diverse, and incredibly fertile ecologies. But the mighty wealth of carbon stored in the densely forested islands of Great Britain were—in the geological and environmental blink of an eye—reduced to a largely inhospitable monoculture of short rolling grasslands most suitable for the grazing of sheep but no longer for the perpetuation of great empires. The expansion of the British Empire was in large part driven by the need to fill its empty larders with the resources of those who had not yet felled their last tree. The European diaspora into the Americas effectively represented the last great opportunity for mankind's expansion into a new environment with untapped natural resources. Today the industrialized world finally stands in a historically unique and unprecedented position with its back against the geographical and environmental wall and with fresh paint up to the corners.

By definition the evolution of culture implies the development of technologies that are superior in their efficiency and effectiveness in assimilating energy and resources into the system. A phenomenal and unprecedented spurt in technology was the Industrial Revolution. In less than one hundred years, humanity has advanced from Stone Age cultures and those characterized by the wooden wheel and the horse to all the most outrageous trappings of our contemporary civilization of the twenty-first century. Information now changes so rapidly that new technologies are obsolete before they can be exploited.

Worldwide the human race is prospering or at least proliferating as never before, and technologies have in large part managed to keep pace with a demand for resources that is unprecedented in all of history and unsustainable by any reasonable means of reckoning. The suggestion that such growth and development can endure would be, well, for lack of a better word, silly.

Imagine the flow of refined fossil fuel through every fuel injector, carburetor, every gas pump, pipeline, and every power plant in the world being confined to one single bulging artery. Envision not a ditch or creek but a large river flowing from one great reservoir within the earth twenty-four hours a day, attempting to satisfy a demand that accelerates by the minute. The visualization would persuade you that such a volume is unsustainable in the most immediate sense. Entropy is at play, and the signs of exhaustion are clearly visible. In other words, we are simply running out of gas literally and figuratively. As the thermometer rises, our filth builds up around our feet and darkens our skies, poisoning even our most remote and most distant ecologies. It seems incomprehensible, but every schoolchild is aware of this inevitability, and yet only a rare few seem to be screaming bloody murder. And how odd, we appear to be such an intelligent civilization. We are simply losing everything that is vital to life and we are running out of time.

We are inexorably bound to ourselves as an organism. Like other remarkable creatures, we are beautiful and admirable in our way, a marvel of perfect physiology and extraordinary behavioral attributes that quite rightfully may be thought of as phenomenal talents, as exceptional gifts. We are merely that perfect coyote that will struggle to survive in the face of adversity. We are the ultimate omnivore, the ultimate adaptive resident of the planet earth, and we will act ultimately in our own self-interest or occasionally in the interest of those closely surrounding us. It is noble that human beings can displace their own self-interest in favor of those close to them, but to suggest that a human should act in the interest of all humanity may be unrealistic. Global altruism may be a luxury that few but the most privileged have the time or resources to entertain.

This is our human dilemma: A man lives on the edge of an ancient tropical rain forest in the remote reaches of an "underdeveloped" South American country. He works fourteen-hour days, seven days a week, and makes the equivalent of US$300 in a year. Beneath his thatched roof and within his wattle and daub walls his poor wife toils similarly to sustain four children who are malnourished, riddled with parasites, will never see a doctor or be immunized against common diseases, and who have no hope for an education.

At the edge of the forest stands a thousand-year-old mahogany tree. That tree, not as milled lumber, but as a fallen log, is worth $5,000 to this family. It is scientific fact that the atmospheric and climatological health of the planet is heavily dependent on its rain forests, composed of trees like this one. However, no impartial observer witnessing this heart wrenching scenario in real life could possibly deny that ultimately that tree must come down. Even if a special fund was established to save that tree and provide for that family, millions upon millions of similar families around the equatorial globe share a similar plight. In light of this particular desperate crisis, any thoughtful human would say, "Of course! These kids are starving. Hand me the damn saw, I'll cut the thing down!" This is our dilemma. To ignore this individual crisis would be cruel and indefensible on entirely moral and ethical grounds.

We are entitled as living organisms to ultimately act in our own self-interest, if not to prosper then at least to survive. That is a legitimate moral imperative. And so, although we may realize that our survival as a civilization if not a species requires a high level of conservation to perpetuate the system, survival knows nothing of the principles of carrying capacity, the preservation of species, or the mechanics of entropy. Sadly, one desperate life at a time, the trees will all come down.

It is not the greed of multinational corporations with their vicious bulldozers, chain saws, and oil rigs that consume resources but rather individuals like you and me creating these insatiable demands. The real problem is all our many nonnegotiable needs for fuel, transportation, our modest twelve-hundred-square-foot houses, and worse, the incessant demand for industrially grown food that requires the proliferation of strip mines, chemical companies, and the mind-boggling complexities of the energy and transportation networks. Each of us standing on the brink of our own individual crisis fuels these insatiable demands.

It is at least controversial, and certainly an unattractive notion, that human beings have always profited evolutionarily and culturally from conflict, but the fact remains that aggression is a component of our strategic arsenal of behavioral attributes. Warfare is simply what we tend to do when we need to make dramatic things happen regarding our survival as individuals, societies, and as a species. When humanity has a need for things to happen *now*, we always resort to the bigger hammer. Whether we are using a rock tied to the end of a stick or a Hellfire missile, when a perceived need arises, humanity will never hesitate to bring the hammer down. Ironically—significantly—we have reached the technological stage where the threat of our weapons is so dire that their mere availability can resolve a conflict. Ritualized combat is no stranger to many human cultures, but this recent development has more far-reaching implications. So now we have this unique all-or-nothing concept that has precipitated the concept of the cold war. At last humanity concedes that the absolute destruction of the planet is probably impractical—how clever.

This prospect of annihilation, without the horrific consequences, still has all the requisite cultural inspirations, motivations, and commitments that bring together enormous resources and forge otherwise unlikely alliances. As a result, through a monumental investment motivated by the threat of losing their civilization, societies can harvest the technological windfalls that accompany every good old-fashioned war but not reap the otherwise bitter harvest of waste, destruction, human suffering, and death. The horrors of the atomic age may well have facilitated a leap in cultural evolution by allowing—demanding—the displacement of the mindless brutality of warfare with human rationality, and on a global scale! The cold war of the second half of the twentieth century directly ushered in the greatest advances in technology and the most extraordinary surge in economic prosperity in the history of mankind. This particular war may have also coincidentally been the wisest investment and the most profitable enterprise in history. It fostered computer technologies, the information age, global communication and networking, medical advances, the fall of repressive empires, but unfortunately also created an unprecedented demand for dwindling global resources. We cannot eat cyberfood, we cannot burn virtual fuel, most of us cannot afford an MRI.

Now, without formal recognition, we are again under assault and with or without a declaration, we are at war. The global imperialism of our own success as a species is overrunning the world. The schizophrenic paradox of our culture and our own cerebral physiology simultaneously dictate that we will prevail at any cost. But we are perhaps, *perhaps*, rational enough to perceive that we will become the social and biological architects of our own destruction. Surely no rational mind can fail to see the simplicity of the model. Our world, our humanity, is at last at war with itself. To suggest that a congressional bill limiting greenhouse gas emissions by 20 percent before the year 2020 is a start, let alone any kind of solution, is a myopic, infantile approach and will not begin to pull back on the throttle and certainly will not begin to apply the brakes to our runaway train. A 20 percent drop in your Dow Jones Industrial Average is preferable to a 100 percent drop in your civilization.

When John F. Kennedy made his famous declaration that the United States would put a man on the moon in seven years, it was not an altruistic science experiment motivated by an intellectual quest, it was an act of war. These strategies were considered to bear the gravity of a life and death effort, that in their zeal, a zeal inspired by the prospect of complete destruction to our civilization, managed not to reach the moon in seven years but five.

As our humanity now brings all its destructive muscle to bear on the planet, it seems we are faced with an ultimate showdown with our real capabilities and possibilities as an organism. Are we in fact the intelligent beings that we suppose ourselves to be? Where now do the limits of human intelligence end, and will mere human arrogance continue to blindly guide our way? Are we truly a generalized species and thus organically and behaviorally flexible, or does our peculiar culture in the end condemn us to the hopeless intractability, the obsolescence of our own specificity? Or do we have the capability to spawn an advance in our cultural and even spiritual evolution? War is always a test to determine ultimately who has the will, stamina, intelligence, and the necessary resources to survive. Can we in fact do battle with the fundamental and contradictory nature of our own species and perhaps witness the ultimate triumph of our greater humanity?

Some would naively assume these impending problems can be solved through the conservation apparatus as we have come to know it, but they have clearly not paid attention to the state of affairs in the real world. Our dilemma, in spite of a mind-boggling complexity of contributing variables, is all about the simple and unambiguous numbers. Aldo Leopold got it right in the 1930s when he simply took the time to stand back and take a close look at the land and the creatures living on it. He quite correctly surmised that the land, the earth, had a certain capacity within a relatively narrow range of variables to support only a certain number of organisms in a more or less static balance between the resource requirements of those organisms and the land's ability to replenish vital resources without suffering degradation. Carrying capacity is simply about the numbers, how many creatures exist, and what resources are required to sustain them in a balanced state of perpetuity. And of course some of our resources are nonrenewable. We have in large part exceeded the carrying capacity of our earthly habitat, and we must now learn to live in different ways, for the earth's capacity to sustain us will, without question, fail. We are beginning to draw heavily on an account with few remaining assets. Disturbingly our fate is not to vanish in the blink of an eye like a multitude of passenger pigeons, but our very special adaptive gift will allow us to systematically cut the pie into ever smaller slices until we snatch at crumbs, stand in excrement, drink fouled water, and the earth is made raw from the millions of bare feet trampling every available inch of ground. This is not Orwellian futuristic conjecture, for there are older, highly advanced civilizations that even now know the feel of exhausted mud and filth between their toes in a logical succession that has already overtaken their formerly idyllic and abundant ecology.

Humans have a peculiar predisposition—the ability to put ordinary but vital priorities like home, family, and even self-preservation aside; become one dedicated, unified, inseparable organism; and confront a hostile adversary as a unit. This remarkable but potentially dark aspect of our nature could ironically hold possibilities for the next profound constructive development in human culture. As a scientist, I am skeptical if not outright cynical about any species' ability to make such a leap, given such a rigid history of specific behavior. But such an innovative shift could possibly occur with a completely unprecedented global consensus born of intelligent forethought. Imagine, at last, an entire species may be called upon to decide its ultimate destiny as a living entity through the conscious process of rational thought. Let us remind ourselves, however, that the most powerful and potentially influential country on the planet is, without question, the single greatest contributor to these problems. And yet, as evidenced by their democratically elected representatives, nearly half the population is unaware of the problems, or worse, even suggests (or has been told) that these problems may not be real—*half!* The global scientific community is horrified, and a more literate and better informed world is horrified by our blind arrogance. That our society has not led the charge in what will become the most important struggle in human history is not only frightening but shameful.

Human beings are phenomenal creatures to be sure, and like any other form of life they may be objectively observed as the unusual and admirable living things they are. However, I am but one of many romantic scientists—and I meet them everywhere—who view the beautiful and mysterious fabric of the natural world to be the primary essence of our own species' existence, and recognize clearly that we can only reside and persist as a unique but indivisible thread within an infinitely more complex web. Similarly, many find it difficult, even ridiculous, to consider the human species as being more important than any other. Like objectively observing any other living thing in nature, it is possible to delight in our most remarkable biological and social peculiarities, but we are clearly just another miraculous creature who has come into this extraordinary world and flourished.

We have even flourished to an extent unrivalled in all of evolutionary history. We have proliferated unabated and unconstrained like no other. And now, any truly impartial and detached observer would look down upon this planet and observe us like any other organism that overruns its own ecology and concede that we have simply become, in a word, *unattractive.* Perhaps we have proved ourselves at last to be unworthy and undesirable. If by our own nature we have sown the irrevocable seeds of our own destruction, either evolutionarily or socially, it is possible, comforting even, to see the world as a better place after we have passed. For clearly, like the falling of the proverbial tree in the woods, this miraculous universe does not need us to lend it significance. And surely, in time—millennia or longer—the earth will have the capacity to clean up our mess. If our passing is to be lamented, it is because we are an extraordinary creature who came so tantalizingly close to being something infinitely more interesting than the creature we have become. We came so close to being that wise and noble creature that we all can imagine—that rare individual we know, on occasion, can actually exist at the extremes of the normal range of human variability.

But then we may be only one developmental stage away from a more extraordinary creature. Paradoxically, we can recognize and even advocate the ideals of wisdom, nobility, altruism, integrity, and even the sacred, but we cannot yet sustain them. For now, the visionary reach of our intellect and imagination, ever so slightly, hauntingly, exceeds the grasp of our humanity.

Unquestionably we have made a mess, fouled the water, poisoned the air and soil, depleted resources, and we are carelessly causing the extinction of other living things on a scale unknown in the history of the natural world. But humanity, life, and the earth are magnificently resilient entities, and so perhaps harmony can, with time, be restored. It will be a revolution occurring sooner or later, and it will occur with or without us. But for the first time in the living history of the earth, an organism may *choose* an evolutionary path and adopt a new and yet untested strategy in that most unforgiving quest that always lies balanced somewhere between survival and oblivion—a bold new strategy, founded in the adaptive specificity of *human consciousness.*

ACKNOWLEDGMENTS

I am indebted to so many people for assistance, expertise, and encouragement, I fear I can never thank them all. The Whiskey Mountain Bighorn Sheep Study has been sustained by a small army of dedicated individuals who have participated directly or offered support behind the scenes. Participating researchers and technical advisors are many, and include: Dr. Bruce Mincher, Dr. David Naftz, Dr. Nancy Stanton, Pat Hnilicka, Dr. Steven E. Williams, Dr. Mark W. Williams, Dr. Everett Brown, Dr. Jack States, Dr. Martha Christensen, Andrew Allgierer, Art Shoutis, Gary Keene, and of course John Mionczynski. John's unwavering devotion to the Rocky Mountain bighorn sheep has been an inspiration to me and to us all. Kathy Pappas has been the calming force that has tamed a great perpetual storm of paper and her untiring efforts and generosity continue today. This author is humbled to have been associated with so many great minds and these passionate, remarkable individuals with lifetimes of accumulated expertise and wisdom.

The bighorn sheep study has been endowed with support by caring entities, both public and private. The University of Wyoming, U.S. Forest Service, Bureau of Land Management, and of course the great folks at the Wyoming Game and Fish Department, have all generously offered support and cooperation through the years. Other endowments include, The Foundation for North American Wild Sheep, The Nature Conservancy, the Lucius Burch Foundation, Dr. John David and Jane Love, Laney Hicks, Deborah MacKensie, Jennifer Binning, Dr. Martha Christensen, Tory Taylor, and Anne Johnson. Dick and Jane Vander Weyden and the Whiskey Mountain Wildlife Conservation Camp have always been there to offer assistance, logistical support, and, not uncommonly, a warm bed and hot meal. Charlie Wilson and Wind River Pack Goats have literally supported us up and down the mountain on more occasions than we could count.

A special thanks to Stephanie Kessler and The Wilderness Society for providing data regarding Wyoming air quality and to Dr. Bill Landing for providing high-resolution spectrometry analysis services through the Florida State University Department of Oceanography.

For helping me make coherent many years of field notes, journal entries, books, monographs, and academic papers by the hundreds, as well as my own subjective and often incoherent ramblings, I am indebted to John Mionczynski, Dr. Bruce Mincher, Dr. Helge Swanson, Dr. George Wolfe, Dr. Bernard Sloan, Nan Slingerland, and Leslye Hutto. Biologist Marcia B. Murdock, with the Wyoming Department of Environmental Quality, has been a constant force for literacy, scientific acumen, and friendship throughout this process. Thanks to Cathy Keene for sharing her rare archival family photographs and her phenomenal family histories that have been used throughout the text of this book. Dr. Jim Miller's patient assistance with the remaining photographs helped usher me and my thousands of slides, kicking and screaming, into the digital age. My editor, Lilly Golden, once again, has gone beyond the call of literary duty and with tireless effort, skill, and friendship, helped clean up my mess. For her monumental patience, support, and hard work, I will always be grateful to my wife, high-altitude companion, and best friend, Leslye Hutto. Any errors or misstatements in this book are unintentional, but entirely of my own making.

REFERENCES

Akenson, J. J., and Akenson, H.A. 1992. *Bighorn Sheep Movements and Summer Lamb Mortality in Central Idaho*. Proceedings of the 8th Biennial Symposium of the Northern Wild Sheep and Goat Council. 8:14-27.

Allen, W. A. 1913. *The Sheep Eaters*. Shakespeare Press, New York.

Bonney, O. H. and Bonney, L. 1970. *Battle Drums and Geysers: The Life and Journals of Lt. Gustavus Cheyney Doane, Soldier and Explorer of the Yellowstone and Snake River Regions*. The Swallow Press, Chicago.

Bunnell, S. D. and Johnson, D. R. 1974. *Physical Factors Affecting Pika Density and Dispersal*. Journal of Mammalogy, 55:866-869.

Butler, G. W. and Peterson, P. J. 1963. *Availability of Forage to Ruminants*. New Zealand Society of Animal Production. 23:13-27.

Clayton, J. L. Kennedy D. A. and Nagel T. 1991. *Soil Response to Acid Deposition, Wind River Mountains, Wyoming*. Soil Science Society of America Journal, 32:1427-1433.

COMERN (Collaborative Mercury Research Network) 2004. *Ecosystem and Watershed-level Dynamics of Mercury in Aquatic Food Webs of Coastal and Inland Lakes and Reservoirs in British Columbia*. Research Project 3.

Craighead, F. C. 1979. *Track of the Grizzly*. Sierra Club Books, San Francisco.

Donahue, D. L. 1999. *The Western Range Revisited: Removing Livestock From Public Lands to Conserve Native Biodiversity*. University of Oklahoma Press, Norman.

Donald, G. E., Langlands, J. P., Bowles, J. E., and Smith A. J. 1993. *Subclinical Selenium Deficiencies: Effects of Selenium, Iodine, and Thiocyanate Supplementation of Grazing Ewes on their Selenium and Iodine Status and Growth of their Lambs*. Australian Journal of Experimental Agriculture.

Environ, T&B Systems, 2008. *Upper Green River Winter Ozone Study*.

Fielder, P. C. 1986. *Implications of Selenium Levels in Washington Mountain Goats, Mule Deer and Rocky Mountain Elk.* Northwest Science. 60:15-20.

Fiesta–Bianchet, M. 1989. *Individual Differences, Parasites, and the Costs of Reproduction for Bighorn Ewes, (Ovis canadensis).* Journal of Animal Ecology. 69(3):547-554.

Fisher, K. 1982. *Acid Precipitation and the Concerns for Fish and Wildlife Resources.* International Association of Fish and Wildlife Agencies Proceedings. 72:19-35.

Flueck, W. T. and Smith–Flueck 1990. *Selenium Deficiency In Deer: the Effect of a Declining Selenium Cycle?* Transactions of the Congress of the International Union of Game Biologists. 19(2):292-301.

Flueck, W. T. 1991. *Whole Blood Selenium Levels and Glutathione Peroxidase Activity in Erythrocytes of Black-tailed Deer.* Journal of Wildlife Management, 55:26-31.

Flueck, W. T. 1994. *Effects of Trace Elements on Population Dynamics: Selenium Deficiency in Free Ranging Black-tailed Deer.* Ecology, 75(3):807-812.

Frost, D. V. 1987. *Why the Level of Selenium in the Food Chain Appears to be Decreasing. Selenium in Biology and Medicine.* AVI, New York.

Geist, V. 1971. *Mountain Sheep: A Study In Behavior and Evolution.* The University of Chicago Press, Chicago and London.

Gibson, J. H. 1986. *Acid Deposition: Long-Term Trends.* National Academy Press, Washington, D.C.

Hallsten, G. P., Skinner, Q. D., and Beetle, A. A. 1987. *Grasses of Wyoming, third addition,* Research Journal 202, Agricultural Experiment Station, University of Wyoming.

Hebard, G. R. 1995. *Washakie.* Bison Books, University of Nebraska Press, Lincoln and London.

Hitchcock, A. S. 1950. *Manual of the Grasses of the United States.* U.S. GPO, Washington, D.C.

Jenkins, K. J. and Hidiroglou, M. 1971. *Transmission of Selenium as Selenite and as Selenomethionine from Ewe to Lamb Via Milk using Selenium-75.* Canadian Journal of Animal Science, 51:389-403.

Knight, D. H. 1994. *Mountains and Plains: The Ecology of Wyoming Landscapes.* Yale University Press, New Haven and London.

Leopold, A. 1933. *Game Management.* Charles Scribner's Sons, New York.

Little, C. E. 1995. The *Dying of the Trees.* Penguin Books Ltd., New York, N.Y.

Lyon, T. L. and Buckman, H.O. 1938. *The Nature and Properties of Soils.* The Macmillan Company, New York, N.Y.

Mincher, B. J., Mionczynski, J., Hnilicka, P. 2007. *Soil REDOX Chemistry Limitation of Selenium Concentration in Carex Species, Sedges.* Journal Soil Science.

Mincher, B. J., Ball, R. D., Houghton, P. P., Mionczynski, J., Hnilicka, P. 2007. *Some Aspects of Geophagia in Wyoming Bighorn Sheep, (Ovis canadensis).* European Journal of Wildlife Resources.

Mionczynski, J. 1972. *A Cooperative Study of Transplanted Bighorn Sheep.* WGFD, USFS, and BLM. Wyoming Game and Fish Department Publication.

Mionczynski, J. 2002. *Sheep/Selenium Study 2002.* 18 pp.

Mionczynski, J. 1992. *The Pack Goat.* Pruett, Boulder, Colorado.

Murie, O. J. 1951. *The Elk of North America.* The Stackpole Company and The Wildlife Management Institute.

Mushak, P. 1985. *Potential Impact of Acid Precipitation on Arsenic and Selenium.* Environmental Health Perspectives, 63:105–113.

Naftz, D. L., Susong, D. D., Schuster, P. F., Cecil, L. D., Dettinger, M. D., Michel, R.L., Kendall, C. 2002. *Ice Core Evidence of Rapid Air Temperature Increases Since 1960 in Alpine Areas of the Wind River Range, Wyoming, United States.* Journal of Geophysical Research, Vol. 107, NO. 0, 10.1029/2001JD000621.

Naftz, D. L., Rice, J. A. and Ranville, J. R. 1991. *Glacial Ice Composition—A Potential Long-Term Record of the Chemistry of Atmospheric Deposition, Wind River Range, Wyoming,* Water Resour. Res., 27m 1231-1238.

Ornstein, R. 1991. *The Evolution of Consciousness.* Prentice Hall, New York, N.Y.

Orr, R. T. 1977. *The Little Known Pika.* Macmillan Publishing Co. Inc. New York and London.

Peterson, R. L. 1979. *North American Moose.* University of Toronto Press, Toronto, Canada.

Pointer, L. 1977. *In Search of Butch Cassidy.* University of Oklahoma Press, Norman.

Raloff, J. 1989. *Where Acids Reign: Do Dying Stands of Bavarian Timber Portend the Future of Polluted U.S. Forests?* Science News, July 22, P. 56.

Rifkin, J. 1989. *Entropy: Into the Greenhouse World.* Viking Penguin, Bantam, New York.

Robbins, C. T. 1983. *Wildlife Feeding and Nutrition.* Academic Press, New York.

Robbins, C. T. and Parish, S.M. 1985. *Selenium and Glutathione Peroxidase Activity In Mountain Goats.* Canadian Journal of Zoology, 63:1544-537.

Rosenfeld, I. and Beath, O.A. 1964. *Selenium: Geobotany, biochemistry, Toxicity, and Nutrition.* Academic Press, New York.

Samet, J. M. 2000. *The National Morbidity, Mortality and Air Pollution Study, Part 2: Morbidity and Mortality from Air Pollution in the United States.* Research Reports of the Health Effects Institute, 24:5-70.

Schullery, P. 1997. *Searching for Yellowstone: Ecology and Wonder in the Last Wilderness.* Houghton Mifflin Company, Boston, New York.

Schaller, G. B. 1967. *Stones of Silence: Journey into the Himalaya.* University of Chicago Press, Chicago.

Scott, R. W. 1995. *The Alpine Flora of the Rocky Mountains (Vol. 1) The Middle Rockies.* University of Utah Press, Salt Lake City.

States, J. S. 1966. *A Survey of the Microfungi in Seleniferous Soils of Grand Teton National Park, Wyoming.* M.S. Thesis, University of Wyoming. 50pp.

States, J. S. and States, D. 2004. *Wildflowers of Wyoming.* Mountain Press Publishing Co. Missoula, Montana.

Swanson, H. R. 2002. *Researching Alternative Environmental Paradigms: A Mythic Search for a Land Ethic in Human Agency.* A dissertation submitted to the department of Geology, Florida State University.

Swanson, R. H. 1999. *Naturalizing the Archetype.* A dissertation submitted to the Department of Philosophy, Florida State University.

Tinbergen, N. 1989. *The Study of Instinct.* Clarenden Press, Oxford, England.

Trenholm, V. C. 1964. *The Shoshonis: Sentinels of the Rockies.* University of Oklahoma Press, Norman.

Wang, H. F., Ambe, S., Takematsu, N. and Ambe, F. 1998. *Model Study of Acid Rain Effect on Absorption of Trace Elements on Soils Using a Multitracer.* The Institute of Physical and Chemical Research, Wako, Saitama, Japan.

Vogelmann, H. W. 1988. *A 21-Year Record of Tree Forest Decline on Camel's Hump, Vermont, USA.* European Journal of Forest Pathology, 18:24–29.

Warneck, P. 2000. *Chemistry of the Natural Atmosphere.* 2nd ed., Academic Press.

Wehausen, J. D. 1996. *Effects of Mountain Lion Predation on Bighorn Sheep in the Sierra Nevada and Granite Mountains of California.* Wildlife Society Bulletin. 24:471–479.

Vayda, A. 1976. *War In Ecological Perspective: Persistence, Change and Adaptive Processes in Three Oceanic Societies.* Plenum, New York.

Williams, M. W. and Tonnessen, K. A. 2000. *Critical Loads for Inorganic Nitrogen Deposition in the Colorado Front Range, USA.* Ecological Applications, 10(6):1648–1665.

Williams, M. W., Losleben, M. V. and Hamann, H.B. 2002. *Alpine Areas in the Colorado Front Range as Monitors of Climate Change and Ecosystem Response.* American Geographical Society, Geographical Review, Vol. 92, No. 2.

Wilson, E. O. 1975. *Sociobiology: The New Synthesis.* Harvard University Press, Cambridge, Massachusetts.

Zajonc, A. 1993. *Catching The Light: The Entwined History of Light and Mind.* Oxford University Press, New York, Oxford.

Zwinger, A. H. and Willard, B. E. 1972. *Land Above the Trees: a Guide to American Alpine Tundra.* Harper and Row Publishers, New York.